HONO
BOUND

Best wishes

HONOUR BOUND

ADVENTURES *of an* INDIAN LAWYER *in the* ENGLISH COURTS

Sarosh Zaiwalla

HarperCollins *Publishers* India

First published in hardback in India in 2019 by
HarperCollins *Publishers*
A-75, Sector 57, Noida, Uttar Pradesh 201301, India
www.harpercollins.co.in

This edition published in India in 2020 by HarperCollins *Publishers*

2 4 6 8 10 9 7 5 3 1

Copyright © Sarosh Zaiwalla 2019, 2020

P-ISBN: 978-93-9035-102-2
E-ISBN: 978-93-5357-354-6

The views and opinions expressed in this book are the author's own and the facts are as reported by him, and the publishers are not in any way liable for the same.

Sarosh Zaiwalla asserts the moral right
to be identified as the author of this work.

All rights reserved. No part of this publication may be reproduced, stored in a retrieval system, or transmitted, in any form or by any means, electronic, mechanical, photocopying, recording or otherwise, without the prior permission of the publishers.

Typeset in 11.5/15.2 Adobe Garamond Pro at
Manipal Digital Systems, Manipal

Printed and bound at
Thomson Press (India) Ltd

This book is produced from independently certified FSC™ paper
to ensure responsible forest management.

Dedicated to Bahá'u'lláh, the founder of the Bahá'í Faith, whose aim is for humanity to work towards the goal of One World and One Mankind, who offers a vision of a united, peaceful and prosperous world and of the nature and purpose of life.

Contents

Foreword

Oh, to be in England.
Now that Zaiwalla's there![1]

I am delighted that the enterprising Sarosh Zaiwalla has written his memoirs: they are frank and fearless, replete with Indianness, and with a sense of pride at being born a Parsi Zoroastrian.

We Parsis, I must confess, are a proud lot. We often regale ourselves with the legend of how in 698 CE, the first refugees from the province of Fars in ancient Persia landed on the west coast of Bharat (now India).[2] From fragments of documents recently discovered, it appears that the first settlers from ancient Persia were industrious and had foresight: having landed on the western coast of India they spent six to eight months learning the local language, and only then wrote a petition to the local ruler (Jadi Rana) in Sanskrit,

1 With apologies to Robert Browning, 'Home-Thoughts, from Abroad': *Oh, to be in England / Now that April's there …*

2 Sanjan, Gujarat.

seeking refuge. He was so impressed with their effort that he granted them permission to settle – of course, on conditions mentioned by Sarosh in the book.

Our forebears from Persia cultivated the art of diplomacy because of an unerring instinct for self-preservation. Their successors continued the fine art for generations, which is how one of our high priests got invited to the court of the great Mughal emperor Akbar, to explain to him the basic tenets of our religion. This is also how generations of Parsi Zoroastrians were treated – with honour and dignity – by the British who first conquered and then ruled over an undivided India for more than two centuries. The Parsis, as loyal Indians, have prospered in the Republic of India, though in fast-diminishing numbers. But enough about Parsis.

I have known Sarosh and the entire Zaiwalla family – his dear mother and father, as well as his three brothers and sister – for more years than I can recall. I have seen the youngest in the family grow up and prosper and reach great heights in the law – in a country that is not his own, but which he has adopted. He is truly one of God's self-made men. It is to his credit that he has excelled in the profession, making known his presence to the high and mighty, not just to the legal fraternity in the UK.

In this elegantly written, detailed account of legal adventures (and a few misadventures) of a non-English lawyer, the author admits – with befitting humility – that a small part of his success has been due to good fortune: 'meeting the right persons, at the right place, at the right time'. The right person, who gave him the right push at the very start of his career, was a profoundly pro-Indian nglishman, Cedric Barclay, international arbitrator, who (as Sarosh ctly states) 'is still considered to be one of the most eminent of tional maritime arbitrators'.

en I first met Cedric in early 1980 he had trenchant comments on what he considered one of the disquieting features of modern international commercial arbitration as practised. His remarks were pertinent:

> Arbitrators do not have to imitate the courts. Commercial justice can be dispensed without the turn of phrase and the logic, which is expected from the Court of Appeal. The AAA and the Commonwealth associations have survived without giving of reasons. The short and concise decisions, which we have given hitherto, were much superior to the essays in jurisprudence, which the ICC and others deem appropriate. Our function was to decide, not to teach. It is a fallacy that the publication of awards will teach others something. More often it leads to confusion and equivocation. Look at this bundle of 1,500 reasoned awards. How many have we learnt from?
>
> It is not the motivation which one abhors, but the endless expositions and padding which we find infiltrating our system. Brevity is the essence of wit; justice needs no adornment.[3]

The 'endless exposition' and 'padding' have increased over the years, but the late Cedric Barclay – bless his soul – would today have been in a minority of one: in all modern-day commercial arbitrations, domestic or international, either in the common law countries or in states that observe the civil law, recorded reasons for an arbitral award are mandatory.

I keep seeing on my television screen every day the boast: 'When big men talk, they talk to the BBC'. There are big men 'talking' on almost every page of this book – not boastfully, but relevantly and frankly – in the course of the many stories the author has to tell of cases in which he had appeared or been concerned with. One big man of my time was the great Quintin Hogg, later Lord Hailsham

---

3 *Arbitration International*, Vol. 5 Issue No.2 (1989), pp 102–136.

of St. Marylebone, Lord Chancellor of England (1979 to 1987). In his autobiography he had written about the very useful lesson on advocacy that he, then an inexperienced pupil at the Bar, learnt from Sir Wilfred Greene, Master of the Rolls, or the presiding judge of England's Court of Appeal. Greene had been a great classical scholar, a superb judge of law and had written many judgements. But, being a chancery barrister, no one at the time rated him at his true worth as an advocate. He disliked examining and cross-examining witnesses, and in his last years at the Bar, he virtually confined himself to advocacy in the appellate courts. One night, Hogg was sitting next to Greene at a dinner, when the Master of the Rolls suddenly asked him a question.

GREENE: Supposing you were instructed in a case where you had two points to argue, both of them bad, but one worse than the other, which would you argue first?
HOGG: I suppose I would argue the less bad of the two.
GREENE: Quite wrong. You must argue the worse and put your very best work into it. Eventually they will drive you into a corner, and you will have to admit defeat. You will then say, 'My Lords, there is another point I am instructed to argue. But I am not quite sure how to put it.' And you will then put the better of the two arguments, but not quite as well as it could or should be put.

After a little while one of the old gentlemen on the bench will interrupt you, and say, 'But surely, Mr Greene, you might put it in this way.' And he will put it exactly as you really ought to have put it in the first place. At that stage you will lay your papers on the desk before you. You will raise your eyes to the ceiling. And, in an awestruck voice, you will say, 'Oh, my Lord,

> I do believe ...' And then you will be at least half way to winning your case.[4]

Excellent advice. Sarosh's book is mostly about winning cases – but also, sometimes, about losing them. And they all make for pleasurable reading.

In the nineteenth century Benjamin Disraeli, England's prime minister, used to say, 'Read no history: nothing but biography, for that is life without theory.'

I suggest that this memoir needs to be read, not just to know something about Parsis but to know a great deal more about the exploits of a highly successful Indian lawyer in a foreign land.

Fali S. Nariman
New Delhi, India
15 April 2019

4 Quintin Hogg, *A Sparrow's Flight: The Memoirs of Lord Hailsham of St. Marylebone,* London: Collins, 1990

Foreword

Sarosh Zaiwalla is the most remarkable solicitor I have known during my long practice at the English Bar. Our association came late in our respective careers. I had often seen him on the opposite side, but eventually he decided to instruct me. It was an immediate success. He gave me an element of glamour in a hitherto slightly pedestrian history. I gave him solidity within the legal establishment.

I was immediately impressed by the breadth of his international client base, which is without equal. One only needs to flick through this splendid book to see how much richness and diversity there is in his extraordinary career. This phenomenon reached its height, perhaps, in the case where he instructed me on behalf of the Mongolian government to bring a case in the English Commercial Court against the Government of Kazakhstan, for payment of a very old debt. The case had nothing whatsoever to do with England, save for the concept, now somewhat dimmed, of the English courts as the upholders of international norms of justice. We failed at first instance to persuade the Commercial Court that this dispute could be litigated in England, but we appealed. The appeal was settled on good terms, because the Kazakhs did not want to appear to be dogs in the manger. This was typical of Sarosh and exemplifies his extraordinary qualities.

He was ever resourceful, ingenious and charming; so is this book. After his early days in the Parsi community in India, his breakthrough was to find a way into the English legal world. He was, as he says, the first Indian to start an English firm of solicitors in the City of London. This was a very unusual and remarkable success. He never looked back.

Between 1992 and 2000 there were a number of setbacks, which he recites in this book with great openness and honesty. As he explains, the challenge was to be accepted within the starchy English establishment without losing his essential qualities as a developing country's champion. Chapter 4 is, perhaps, worthy of especial attention.

I encountered him after he had reasserted himself. Our successes can be summarized in respect of two cases. The first was *Jivraj v Hashwani,* where we challenged, on discrimination grounds, a contractual clause that required disputes to be decided by arbitrators who had to be members of the Ishmael community. We had a good win in the Court of Appeal, which sent the world of arbitration into a flat spin. We lost in the Supreme Court, but I still think that the Court of Appeal was right in principle, however inconvenient this might have been.

The second case was *Bank Mellat v HM Treasury*, where we persuaded the Supreme Court, by five to four, that the UK government had acted illegally by singling out the Iranian bank for sanctions. By this time, it was important that Zaiwalla & Co. had an established reputation in England. It was a high point in my career, and the ultimate acceptance of Sarosh Zaiwalla as a fully functioning member of the English legal community, bringing together (as he does) the loyalties of many people from many countries, whose main joint interest is the preservation of English law in the diversity of the modern world.

Michael Brindle QC
London, United Kingdom
13 May 2019

Preface

I arrived in London in January 1975 intent on qualifying as an English solicitor, like my father before me. It was a different England to the one I know today. Diversity was barely beginning to plant its roots in English society, let alone in the law.

I recognized early that it was not necessary for me to be clubbable. Provided I dedicated myself to my clients and maintained a high level of competence and integrity, I need not seek to be popular. *'I am here not because I like you, but because I respect you'* was the best compliment I had received from the then president of the London Maritime Arbitration Association (LMAA). This was a typical English way of recognizing the arrival of my firm in the City of London.

While I hope my story still has many more chapters ahead of it, I can look back on those I have already completed with satisfaction and, on occasion, amazement. I hope that it will inspire others like me to come to the United Kingdom. My role has been partly that of a pathfinder, and I have laboured to help lay the track on which others can now run. I wish them every success.

As a young man, Indian politics called to me. Like many an adolescent idealist, I hoped one day to become the prime minister, and to lead my country to prosperity. Instead, I did something nobody from India, or indeed anywhere in Asia, had done before. I established a law firm in the City, the 'Square Mile' that was and still is the world's leading financial capital.

Do not think for a second that this was ever straightforward for me or for my firm. As this book details, there have been plenty of bumps along the way. It was challenging to take on the big, established English solicitors' firms, let alone to do so and win.

For all that, in many ways my ambitions have been surpassed. Through a combination of industry, diplomacy, persistence and imagination, doors opened for me. I carved out for myself a distinctive place on the English legal scene. In doing so, I believe I have shown what is possible with enough self-belief and professionalism.

Over the years I have become known to, and sometimes friendly with, ministers, diplomats, industrialists and even movie stars. Guided by the spirit of truth, I gained their trust, a commodity all too often in short supply in the commercial and political worlds in which I work.

As an outsider I sometimes faced prejudices, but these were never so bad that I could not overcome them. In a strange way, they helped me build my firm's client base in the international community outside the United Kingdom.

I came to England at the right time. The old attitudes of Empire were dropping away and the City of London was opening itself up to the world. With the increasing number of people and politicians from the East – India, China and Russia – coming to the West to do business, there was a need for active intermediaries, people like me who could understand and interpret cultural differences. In an often-crazy world, I was able to come up with inventive and workable solutions that might have been beyond those with a narrower point of view.

Behind everything I have done has been my commitment to support the UK institutions, for which I have immense respect. Not least amongst these is the English legal system and the fundamentally fair attitudes that underpin it. Wherever you come from, if you work hard, show integrity and apply yourself with skill, you will be respected in the English courts. The judges are honest and incorruptible, and long may this continue.

My firm and I have been allowed to make a substantial contribution to English law, with some 126 reported cases we have been involved in helping to develop shipping, commercial and arbitration law. Some of these cases have gone to the highest level, both the House of Lords and the Supreme Court of the United Kingdom. Zaiwalla & Co. – whose client base is mainly overseas – has also brought in many millions of pounds to the UK economy. I am proud to have played a small part in making London the world's leading legal centre too.

What I hope is that all this will show my readers, not least those starting their careers and whose roots lie outside the UK, that everything is possible with courage, perseverance and the occasional bit of luck. Fortune, as they say, favours the brave. The English love an underdog and give people a fair chance to demonstrate their ability and talent. They gave me that chance, and while it was never easy, I believe that my experience should ease the path of those who follow.

Space does not allow me to report many experiences and anecdotes, but I hope those I have shared will give readers a sense of the journey I have taken, the people I have worked with and the challenges I have overcome.

I dedicate this book to my daughter Freya and my son Varun. Their love and support are beyond value, and there is nothing in this world as precious to me as they are.

I would like to thank India itself, as without the support of its high commission in London I would never have had the opportunity to undertake the international arbitration work that made my firm successful.

I have taken great care to verify the accuracy of the facts with the persons or representatives of the countries and organizations mentioned. In particular, I would like to express my profound appreciation to Ambassador Liu Xiaoming of the People's Republic of China and the Right Honourable the Lord Burnett of Maldon, the Lord Chief Justice of England and Wales, for their valuable assistance in ensuring that the highest level of accuracy has been achieved in the chapters concerned.

There are many individuals whom I have worked with who were essential to this success. They are too numerous to list here but I am grateful to each and every one.

Particular thanks must go to Nari Hira, an important client of my firm and the owner of a well-known publishing house, who persuaded me to write this book. I also thank my personal assistant Emily Simons, without whose intelligence, patience and support the manuscript would not have come into existence in the short period it did, as well as Matthew Maxwell Scott for his editorial advice. I also thank Camilla Miller, Suchitra Iyer and Margarita Bogatiuc for their encouragement and support to write this book. I must also acknowledge my gratitude to the late Jangoo Gagrat for the understanding and support I received from him in my early years as a solicitor in London.

Finally, I pay tribute to and thank members of the English Bar and the judiciary for their integrity and sense of fairness. May this always remain.

Sarosh Zaiwalla
London, United Kingdom
19 September 2019

1

A Passage to England

As I sit on a bench outside my house on the green shores of Kingston Gorse, in West Sussex on the English Channel, my mind goes back to my early days in Bombay, the passage through time and a career in the United Kingdom. It has been a long, sometimes turbulent journey, starting with my arrival in Britain as a law student in my twenties to becoming the first non-European ever to establish a law firm in the one-square-mile financial district of the City of London. This was at a time when the need for diversity was unspoken and the legal profession was not a business but an honourable service.

Timing is everything, and I was fortunate to have arrived in London in the mid-1970s when attitudes were changing and international politics were shifting. These new conditions created opportunities for someone like me who was able to operate across boundaries and borders. The UK was coming to terms with a world much more complex than the old days of the British Empire. It had to negotiate new kinds of relationships with countries which, not so long ago, had been under its dominion. In the same way, businesspeople and politicians in the Middle East and Asia needed intermediaries who could create effective working relationships in London, which many believe to be the world's leading global city for finance and commerce.

To my great satisfaction, I was to find that as a London solicitor I could undertake that role. But, as a teenager in India, that was not how I envisioned my future. My dream then was to become the prime minister of my home country and transform India into a prosperous nation, where the poor would be well looked after. But fate has its own way of bringing about twists and turns in the road of life, and it can take you in a completely different direction. That is what happened to me.

My Parsi heritage

I was born after India's independence from British rule into a Parsi family in bustling Mumbai, the erstwhile Bombay, the fifth among five brothers and a younger sister. My father was then aged fifty, and as the youngest boy I learnt early on that whatever I wished to achieve would have to be primarily through my own endeavours. Nonetheless, my Parsi heritage was extremely important to me. It has shaped significantly my values, giving me a determination to succeed and yet be distinctive while adhering to the principles of natural justice, fair play and straightforwardness. Above all, I believe in the importance of keeping one's word – a virtue taught to me by my mother.

Parsis are a singular community with their roots in the Zoroastrian faith. They migrated to India following the defeat of the Sassanian Empire in the Battle of Nahavand in 641 CE and the consequent Islamization of Persia (now Iran). In memory of our origins, the first name of Parsis is almost always Persian. My eldest brother is

Bahman, and this was anglicized to Bomi. My second brother is Darius, which was anglicized to Dara. My third brother is Dinshaw, which became Dinsoo. The Persian name for the fourth brother, Khushrow, was changed to Khushroo; and my name, Sarosh, was Saroosh in Persian. The same applies to the women in my family. My mother's name, Nargesh, is Persian and my sister was named Zenobia, which originates from the extended ancient Persian Empire. Parsis also have surnames based on their occupation, with Batliwalla meaning someone who manufactures bottles or Daruwalla for someone in the alcohol business. The Indian test cricketers Nari Contractor, Farokh Engineer and Rusi Surti (which comes from Surat, a town in Gujarat) carry notable examples of Parsi surnames.

My family's deep origins lie in Persia but like so many peoples, the Parsis were compelled at a critical juncture in their story to emigrate in order to avoid being converted to Islam. Diehard Zoroastrians decided to migrate to India when the Islamic armies invaded Persia. History relates that when the first Parsis arrived by ship on the Indian shore, the local ruler sent them a cup of milk full to the brim to indicate that there was no space for them to settle. In reply, the Parsis sent back the cup of milk with sugar added to it to suggest that their presence would sweeten the welfare of the local community.

The local ruler was impressed and gave them permission to land – provided they took three oaths.

The first was not to proselytize. The consequence of this is that you have to be born into the Zoroastrian faith. It is not possible to convert into it. Hence, in India today a non-Parsi would not be admitted into an 'agiary' (or fire temple), the Parsi place of worship. The reason is simple: if people came to a fire temple and asked to become a Zoroastrian, acceptance of this would cause a breach of the undertaking given to the king.

The second vow the Parsis took was not to touch local women. With this came the custom that one could not marry outside the Parsi community. Even today, if a Parsi man marries a non-Parsi woman, then the children are born Parsi. But if a Parsi woman marries a non-Parsi, her children cannot be Parsis.

The third oath was to mix 'like sugar into milk'. Therefore, the Parsis restricted themselves to business and never entered politics. This shaped Parsi life in India for centuries. Keeping one's word is of paramount importance to Parsis and a key part of the ancient Zoroastrian religion.

This commitment to the world of business became particularly significant following the establishment of British trading posts at Surat and Bombay, both of which had large numbers of Parsis. Bombay, meaning the 'good bay' in Portuguese, had been leased originally to Portugal in the Mughal era. In 1662, it was gifted to Charles II of England as dowry for his betrothal to Catherine of Braganza, daughter of King John IV of Portugal. Charles II licensed it to the English East India Company in 1668 and it was the absorption of these areas under the British rule – together with the introduction of religious tolerance – which marked a turning point for the local Parsi community. The East India Company then transferred its western India headquarters from Surat to Bombay in 1687.

By virtue of their business acumen, the Parsis in and around Bombay were responsive to British influence – more so, it could be said, than the local Hindus and Muslims. An affinity seems to have developed between the British administrators and Parsi traders, and the latter gradually adopted the former's customs, dressing, education of girls and the abolition of child marriage. This resulted in relations between the Parsis and the British becoming strong. In Regent's Park, London there still exists a fountain with a plaque saying it was donated by a Parsi, Sir Cowasjee Jehangir, in gratitude for favours that the British bestowed on the Parsis in India.

Bombay's subsequent expansion in the eighteenth century was largely due to the enterprise and industry of Parsis, and by the nineteenth century they were a conspicuously wealthy section of society, with notable successes in heavy industries, particularly those connected with railways and shipbuilding. A British recorder of the city noted that under a 'just government' they 'speedily rose to be one of the most popular mercantile bodies in Asia'. Today, Mumbai continues to thrive. It has the highest number of US dollar-equivalent billionaires in the whole country. It is India's commercial capital and, importantly, one of its cinematic capitals too, popularly known as Bollywood.

Evidence of the success of Parsi entrepreneurs is still manifest today with notable business dynasties, including the Tatas, being among the biggest employers. The Indian justice system also features high-profile and widely respected Parsi legal giants such as Fali Nariman and Soli Sorabjee, ages ninety and eighty-nine respectively, both of whom are still practising law.

More generally, the Parsi community continues to be cultured, understated and well-respected throughout the world. It is particularly striking that the first three Asian members of the British House of Commons were all Parsis. In addition, they covered the full political spectrum. Dadabhai Naoroji (formerly professor of Gujarati at University College, London) was elected for Finsbury Central constituency from 1892 to 1895 to represent the Liberal Party. Sir Mancherjee Bhownaggree (a lawyer educated at the University of Bombay) stood for the Conservative Party in 1895 for Bethnal Green North East constituency and was a Member of Parliament from 1895 to 1906. Shapurji Saklatvala (who had attended my alma mater, St. Xavier's in Bombay) was the successful parliamentary candidate for the Communist Party in Battersea

North from 1924 to 1929. Such width of allegiances says something significant about the versatility of the Parsi culture and its ability to adapt to different environments.

Family roots in India, and the first brush with law

Interwoven with my religion as a Parsi is my rootedness in India. My surname, Zaiwalla, literally translates to a person from Zai, a small coastal village 130 kilometres north of Mumbai, near the railway station of Gholvad. It is within the borders of the state of Maharashtra, of which Mumbai is the capital. This makes my father a Parsi Maharashtrian – Maharashra and Gujarat are later formations, established after the independence of India. Earlier they were part of the State of Bombay. After the agitation by Gujaratis (Mahagujarat Movement) and Marathis (Samyukta Maharashtra Samiti), the Bombay province was divided into Gujarat and Maharashtra in 1960 – which is important to note because most Parsis are Gujaratis. This includes my mother, who was a Gujarati Parsi from Kolak, a village near Udvada, where the main Parsi fire temple is situated and where the flame that burns continuously, Atash Behram, is derived from the holy fire brought by that first boat from Persia. (My maternal grandmother later moved to Ankleshwar, which is now an important town in Gujarat.)

As in the case of many in India, there is little recorded family history. But I was told that my father's family had a dignified, perhaps aristocratic, background and that my paternal grandfather was one of the big feudal landlords in Thane district surrounding Dahanu and Gholvad.

My father, Ratanshaw, also known as 'Ratu', was one of many children in a wealthy family. Sadly, only two boys and two girls survived beyond childhood. While his older brother went into farming to look after his father's estate, Ratu was sent to an English school in Baroda, now a part of Gujarat, one of the 565 princely states ruled by maharajas, nawabs and such like. Baroda had its own laws, its own armed forces and, more importantly, was ruled by an enlightened maharaja who used his resources to develop an education system with modern schools and colleges (many of which were better than in neighbouring British-run provinces).

My grandfather, Bomanji, felt Ratanshaw would benefit from an education in Baroda. The fact that he wanted him educated in English indicated that he valued his son being taught in the language of the British rulers of the country. At that time, in the early years of the twentieth century, the idea that the British would leave India seemed inconceivable. So it was almost a natural progression for Ratanshaw, once his schooling in Baroda finished, to head for England to become a solicitor.

Law was a highly regarded profession, and, like many Indians of his generation, my grandfather felt it would be a mark of great distinction if his son became a lawyer trained in London. Ratanshaw could have become a solicitor in India, but no Indian qualification could match an English one. Bomanji was sure that once his son returned home with an English law degree he could set up his own firm and have what Indians called a 'roaring practice', meaning he would earn large sums of money. For him it was the best of both worlds – a son educated in the land of the conquerors of his country and returned to the land of his birth, practising the law the conqueror had imposed on the conquered land. As a rich landlord, my grandfather had no difficulty sponsoring his son's education in England.

Ratanshaw arrived in England in his early twenties in the aftermath of the First World War, having travelled almost certainly on a P&O liner (short for the Peninsular and Oriental Steam Navigation Company, founded in 1837) from Bombay to Southampton and then by train to London. I retain an original certificate which testifies that he obtained a law degree from the University of London in 1924. He was then articled for two years with a firm called H. Dead & Co., whose principal partner was a Mr Gilbert, a Yorkshireman who died in 1952. After qualifying as a solicitor, my father worked for a very short period in a firm called Warwick and Warren at 14 Queen Victoria Street (whose premises were bombed during the Second World War).

After this relatively brief but formative sampling of London life, my father returned to India and settled in Bombay, starting a one-man law firm called Zaiwalla and Company Solicitors. With his English legal qualification and experience of law, he was determined to be a person who, apart from his skin colour, was no different from the English. So, he affected a soft-spoken English accent to distinguish himself from his countrymen, referred to by the British as 'natives'. Those British clubs and institutions which did not permit entry to Indians displayed the sign: 'Natives not allowed'. Ratanshaw, freshly returned from England, had no desire to be perceived as a native.

Zaiwalla and Company Solicitors in Bombay could not have been smaller – one partner, a managing clerk, a court clerk and a typist. The only other employees in the firm were peons, workers who prepared tea and coffee, fetched and delivered files and, with no home of their own, slept on the office floor at night.

The office itself was located downtown in Readymoney Mansion, owned by the rich Parsi Sir Cowasjee Jehangir (whose surname was also Readymoney, following the Parsi custom of having surnames that reflected in some way their occupation). Readymoney Mansion was next to Akbarally, one of the city's most important department stores, and just around the corner from Flora Fountain, the commercial hub of Mumbai, similar to the City of London's Square Mile.

Ratanshaw was aware that a man of distinction in the Square Mile always wore a bowler hat. So, even in Bombay, he never left for work without a felt hat. He also carried a stick for a while and always wore white trousers and a cream jacket. His Englishness was particularly marked when he travelled. On train journeys, while his fellow Indian passengers gossiped freely and loudly, often sharing food and drinks, he would read a newspaper and, besides a courtesy greeting, rarely exchange any words. He had returned from England with an understanding that the English were reserved, unlike the more excitable Indians; this meant that in a country of cacophony and chatter, Ratanshaw was a man of few words, especially with strangers.

One reassurance for Ratanshaw, however, must have been that he only had to walk around Bombay to appreciate the enormously influential role that the Parsi community had played in making the city the commercial capital of British India. For example, a ten-minute walk from his office took Ratanshaw to the statue of Sir Pherozeshah Mehta. Like Ratanshaw, Mehta had studied law in England, qualifying as a barrister. On his return to India he drafted the Municipal Act of 1872, for which he was popularly accepted as the 'father of municipal government in Bombay'. He held various posts, was knighted by the British, became the vice chancellor of the University of Bombay and helped found the Central Bank of India, for long one of the country's most important private banks. The Central Bank of India also counted among its founders another Parsi called Pochkhanawala.

A further ten-minute walk would bring Ratanshaw to the Taj Mahal Hotel, built by Jamsetji Tata, the man who founded India's first iron and steel company – thereby disproving the British assertion that no Indian could ever produce steel. This put the House of Tatas in a different league compared to other Indian businesses. The story goes that Tata was refused entry to Greens, a

British hotel in Bombay, which displayed a sign forbidding entry to 'Dogs and Indians'. His response was to construct his own, far more opulent, hotel next door to Greens. This was a savvy move. Good hotels were few and far between in India, and this was the first to have facilities that matched those in Western countries. Tata was to prove a visionary, for the Taj is now not only a world-class hotel but the flagship of a chain of properties in the hospitality sector that can claim to be among the best on the planet.

Imperial rules

Adopting the style of the English made good sense, in terms of business, in the pre-Second World War period. In the 1920s and 1930s, the British rule in India seemed as permanent as Indian heat. There were many English solicitors in Bombay, including the two well-known firms Crawford Bailey and Little & Co., which continue to be active today with their original names. There was also Orr Digman in Calcutta (now Kolkata) and Delhi as well as King and Partridge in Madras (now Chennai). But there were not many like my father, an Indian who had qualified in England and was English in every respect apart from his skin colour. Being such an Indian was also profitable. It brought Ratanshaw lucrative work, and he established such a reputation that Indian maharajas would often turn to him. His clients included the Maharani of Baroda and Aga Khan III, the grandfather of the present Aga Khan.

Nonetheless, no matter how much my father adopted the style of the English though, he was not one of them. The British in India firmly classified themselves as 'Europeans' and the institutions they had established carried the name 'European', not 'British'. Hence, the British political association was called the European Association and there was a European Chamber of Commerce. Clubs like the Bombay Gymkhana or the Breach Candy Swimming Bath had signs at the entrance saying 'Europeans only'. Indeed, it was only in 1964 that the Breach Candy Club opened its doors to Indians.

My father never told us, his children, what it felt like for an educated Indian to work under a foreign regime. Maybe he had conflicting emotions. What he did tell me one evening when, as a teenager, I came back home a bit late was, 'I do not mind you coming home late, but if you go to England to study there and you come home after 8 p.m., the landlady will say you are not a gentleman.' He also often reminded us of the requirement in England of the three D's: dash, dress and address.

As in every colonial situation, there were tensions and conflicts which arose out of the British occupation of India. But the contrasts in culture and ways of life were not merely between the British and the local population. Colonialists develop their own manners, conventions and expectations, and over time these deviate from those in their home country. Thus it was that the British culture in India, as the Indians experienced it, was quite distinct from the culture in Britain itself.

These differences arose, almost inevitably, out of the challenges of imperial rule. In India, a relatively small contingent of 4,000–5,000 British white civil servants was presiding over, at that time, 400 million natives. This required them, as the ruling class, to adopt a code of apartness from the indigenous community, expressed, for example, in displays of pomposity and magnificence whose purpose was to keep the Indian populace at bay.

This had implications for those Indians who then stepped up, post-Independence, into the vacancies in government and administration left by the British and who, by following the model left by their predecessors, became known as 'Brown Sahibs'. In other words, they were filled with self-importance and would not easily mix with ordinary folk. And perhaps more than that, they had no care for the poor, imitating the example of the British in colonial times.

A good example of this tendency came from the legal profession. The judges of high courts and the Supreme Court in post-Independence India would not easily mix with the general public (or with other lawyers). In England, this has not been the case and judges, by and large, are approachable. As a wise mind once said, 'Greatness of a great mind lies in its humility.'

Marriage and children

Despite his English ways, my father was residually still enough of an Indian to enter into an arranged marriage with someone who had no doubt been introduced by a matchmaker. The bride they found was still in her teens with the very romantic name Nargesh, similar to the well-known Bollywood film star called Nargis who played the title role in the iconic drama *Mother India*.

The age gap between my parents was around fourteen years. However, unlike many Parsi couples, they were not related to each other. (It is not uncommon among Parsis for first cousins to marry. Thus, one's mother-in-law can also be one's aunt.) It could not be said to have been a totally successful marriage. The couple had strongly contrasting personalities. My father was always quiet and my mother, who might well have proved a successful politician, was the manager of the house and often critical of her husband. So, it was a stressful situation at home for us, the children.

I had come into my father's life at a wrong time. He was not only relatively old by this stage but also a heavy smoker and not keeping good health. He refused to change after India's freedom. Instead, although a nationalist, he clung to his English ways and was ostracized by his colleagues. This was probably one of the reasons why his practice dwindled after Independence. India was going through profound changes. It was partitioned, with Pakistan carved out as a separate Muslim state. Partition was marked by horrific killings and a massive migration, with Hindus and Sikhs fleeing to India and Muslims in the opposite direction to the new state. Bombay saw Sindhis, both Hindus and Sikhs, flood in from their homeland in Sindh, which had become part of Pakistan. Educated, shrewd, with many of them skilful businessmen, they gradually took control of enterprise in the city, dislodging the Parsis. So, it was not surprising that an anglicized Parsi lawyer's practice declined. He also lost business because, as India became a full-fledged democracy with universal suffrage, the influence of the maharajas waned, who had often been his most lucrative clients.

Practising law was not my father's sole business concern. My grandfather had passed away before my father returned from London. Upon his arrival he became embroiled in major litigation with his brother, Ardeshir, over the inheritance of the family estate. A substantial part of the properties – which included land, riverbanks, hills, grasslands, forests, mango farms and agricultural land – was awarded to him. Having secured this, it became a matter of principle for him to manage it. He would go every weekend to Dahanu and then visit the estate in Kainad some five miles away, where he had invested in a fruit garden. This may have been a source of distraction for him, thereby affecting his practice. My mother often told me, 'If your grandfather had not left us the estate, our family would have been better off.'

What made it worse, and added to the financial strain in later years, were the continuous court battles between my father and his brother over other parts of the ancestral estate. My father's dispute with his brother went all the way up to the Supreme Court, and one such dispute (involving accounts of a charitable family trust to feed poor Parsis) was closed only after Ratanshaw and Ardeshir died. I should emphasize, though, that as part of the Zaiwalla family's ethics, despite the two brothers not being on talking terms for most of their lives, their families attended each other's events. The two brothers also never spoke ill of each other.

Towards the latter part of my father's life, his income from the practice had reduced so sharply that the bread on the family table came from a flour mill in central Bombay, which he had acquired during the mid-years of his professional life. The mill, which still exists, provided a decent income, and it helped that my mother kept a tight rein on expenses. She was very cost-conscious.

The result was that while I heard stories of the family in their heyday, I did not enjoy a luxurious upbringing. My older brothers had grown up when my father had a good practice. But all the family wealth had dissipated by the time I was growing up. We were never without money, but we were not as affluent as many believed us to be.

Even when Ratanshaw had been a successful solicitor we had lived relatively modestly. We had a large apartment on Hughes Road close to the sea at Chowpatty, not far from where the governor of the province had his palatial mansion, known as Raj Bhavan. The area was considered smart and owning a house in this area meant being part of the city's elite. But this was something of a make-believe. From the outside, we looked comfortable and well-off, but this was not true. We had domestic help, which was not uncommon, and a cook, but we were not rich in the sense understood in modern India.

My school education

While the departure of the British had an impoverishing effect on my father's practice, nothing could shake his belief that Britain still embodied all that was good in the world. This meant that his children were all educated in English-medium schools. One of the best in the city was St. Xavier's High School, run by Jesuits. It was near the popular Metro cinema and a short walk from Crawford Market (renamed Mahatma Jyotiba Phule Mandai), Bombay's largest bazaar at the time. My brothers had already studied there, so it was natural that I should as well; there was never any question that I would not imbibe a Jesuit education.

My father did not drive, so we did not have a car. The three-mile journey from Hughes Road to school had to be covered by bus. St. Xavier's had its own vehicles to ferry its students; I have a vivid memory of travelling to school in the famous red school buses with the number 2 blazoned on its side. I used to bring lunch from home, which I ate in the school hall along with other boys, many of whom took the bus with me.

The school proudly displayed its Catholic faith and all the classrooms had a crucifix. Like all the students, I bowed my head in front of the crucifix and prayed to Jesus four times a day – before lessons began at 9.30 a.m., when classes resumed after the lunch break and finally before the school day ended at four-thirty in the afternoon. The morning prayer began with the words, 'Eternal God, Creator of all, I firmly believe Thou art now …', and ended with, 'We give you thanks, almighty God, and ask for forgiveness'. The prayers did have an impact. I liked the atmosphere of Christian prayer so much that during the short recesses at around 11 a.m. I would go to the chapel and pray. By the age of ten, I also went to the agiary at Hughes Road every morning before school. Around this time, I gave up eating flesh or fowl and became a vegetarian partially. We did not feel that by praying to a Christian god we were violating any command of our Parsi religion. This may seem extraordinary, but such religious coexistence was quite common in India. The Jesuits were not seeking to convert me, and my parents did not fear I would forsake my own religion.

The Jesuits saw their education as superior to that provided by others. They claimed, 'Give me the boy of seven, and I will give you the man of seventeen.' I am living proof of that and, looking back, I praise the Jesuits for making me who I am. St. Xavier's taught me the importance of humility and to deal with the richest and the poorest on an equal basis.

Even so, I was not a good student. At home my mother, the quasi-politician who wanted to keep everyone happy, pushed me to study hard. My father was a liberal. His response was always, 'Son, do what you want.' My mother, who never learnt to read or write English with any proficiency, was strict. Like many Indian mothers, she would force me to study. But that simply put me off my work. Instead, I used to go to the Bharatiya Vidya Bhavan, a leading cultural centre which was a stone's throw from my bedroom, to attend the many events held there.

I was also into playing cricket. There was a compound adjacent to the our building where young lads used to play. I became an ardent stamp collector too, though this got me into trouble. Two old men would sit outside the school selling stamps, and I used to spend a lot of time with them. On one occasion, after a recess, I came back late for class and was caned for it by Father Keating, a Spaniard who was the principal of our junior school.

These distractions meant that in the eighth standard I did so badly in my final term exams that I had to repeat the year. For some reason, I just could not get interested in my textbooks. The one consolation was that academic failure was more than made up for by my extracurricular activities, where I was way ahead of most of my schoolmates.

The only subject which really engaged me – apart from cricket – was politics. I was so interested that in the mornings, even at the age of eight or nine, I would rush to read the newspaper as soon as

I awoke. I had developed such an interest in the subject that by the time I left St. Xavier's I could claim to have had first-hand experience of several notable political events. I would attend political meetings alone because I was determined to become the prime minister of India, even though I was only a child.

The result was that, barely into my teens, I had attended historic events such as when Chakravarti Rajagopalachari, the first governor general of free India and a prominent politician, set up the Swatantra Party, a free-market party opposed to the socialism being preached by the Indian National Congress. Also, when Nikolai Bulganin and Nikita Khrushchev visited India in 1955, I was on the beach at Chowpatty (down the road from our house) to watch the Soviet leaders. As a mere eight-year-old at the time, I recall being part of the huge crowd watching Jawaharlal Nehru greet the Russians.

What makes this even more extraordinary was that I had gone there by myself, something that middle-class children of my age were not allowed to do. Even in Britain a boy of eight going on his own to a political rally would have been very unusual. In Bombay of the 1950s it was unthinkable. The fear among educated, well-to-do residents was that street gangs preyed on children and, unless they were escorted, these gangs would abduct them, maim them and then use them to beg piteously for money. But my family had no such fear. Being the youngest in the family had its advantages too. I was left alone.

Such political excursions also made me think of what the world should be. I was always a bit of a revolutionary. I don't know where I got it from – maybe from reading the papers. I would often insist that the help sit with me at the dinner table against my mother's wishes. Eventually, my mother got used to it. From an early age I wanted to change the world and make it more egalitarian.

There was one other thing that differentiated me from my peers. From my teens, I was earning money and knew all about the value of work. At fifteen, during the six-week summer break, I started working for Lala Tours, a tour company run by a Parsi called H.K. Lala. We also had three weeks off from school for Diwali, and during this period Lala would organize trips all over India – from Kashmir in the north to Kanyakumari in the south – and I went along as a helper. It was great fun. We were paid reasonably well, and I became a tour manager at seventeen. This was a great personal experience, which taught me how to deal with situations both good and bad and solve problems that arose.

Also, from the age of fourteen, I started managing the garden estate at Zai, which produced the chikoo fruit. My father was in his sixties by then but he had a strong desire to manage the fruit garden. Since he couldn't travel frequently, I went there instead of him every Thursday during term time, which the pupils at St. Xavier's had off to compensate for going to school on Saturdays.

I would wake up at six in the morning and go to Bombay Central and take the train to Gholvad. There I would find a seat in a tonga (horse carriage) to Bordi, where my father, when times were good, had built quite a luxurious house facing the sea. Then I rented a cycle to go to Zai. On some days, I would bicycle in the blistering heat to the large chikoo garden in Kainad, some five miles from Dahanu railway station. I managed to sell the wood from the forest that the family owned, and from the proceeds of the sale my father allowed me to buy a motorcycle for myself. Managing the estate fetched me reasonably good money and, most importantly, gave me confidence. We used to get very little allowance, and the fact that I could earn money was a considerable boost. At school, because I was not good at studies, I had absolutely no confidence. But, through working and earning, my self-esteem rose, and it made me believe in myself.

To university

My work experience made me want to become a chartered accountant, something of a departure from my family tradition. My brothers had pursued law, the eldest two going on to become senior counsels in Bombay (equivalent to a Queen's Counsel in the United Kingdom). My third brother took over my father's law firm, while the fourth, having qualified as a lawyer, managed the family estate along with his law practice. The only one of my siblings who did not study law was my sister Zenobia. She became a doctor and eventually settled in the UK, becoming a consultant at Oxford's Radcliffe Hospital.

But my aim was to get a bachelor's in commerce, a standard first step in India to becoming a chartered accountant. Bombay had many colleges which offered this degree, and I chose Hassaram Rijhumal College of Commerce and Economics, popularly known as H.R., within walking distance of two of the city's great landmarks – Marine Drive, which ran along the sea and is probably Mumbai's most famous road, and Churchgate, the city's busiest commuter railway station.

The college had only been set up a few years ago and this was a testament to the power of the Sindhis and how well they had adapted to life in Bombay. Some years before Partition, the Sindhis had established a commerce college in Sindh (now in Pakistan), believed to be the first such college in this part of the world. Displaced from their home, they gave vent to the idea in Bombay. The Sindhi ability to improvise is indubitable.

The college inspired me. At St. Xavier's I might have struggled to pass exams, but at H.R., helped by my growing knowledge of politics, I emerged as a student activist whom both the college and the university administrators came to fear. We had closely followed the revolutionary student movements that had swept the West in the late '60s – the sit-ins at American colleges and universities, the protests against the Vietnam War and the uprising in France in May 1968, which in due course forced President De Gaulle out of office. In Bengal, which had always been the hub of protest movements and where the communist influence was strong, an Indian form of protest had developed called 'gherao', *a* Bengali word meaning 'to surround'. Protestors would blockade offices, factories or schools and colleges and not allow the staff to leave until their demands were met.

Nothing on that scale ever happened, but I did manage to force H.R. College to close for one day. One of the grievances was that there was no students' union – hard as it may be to believe now, the university authorities would not permit it. So, along with some other students, I drew up an agenda setting out why we should have a union and organized a demonstration to support it. But the authorities would not budge. In response to their intransigence we went on a one-day strike. They eventually conceded our demands, but in retaliation for having led this revolt I was denied approval by the college to sit for the examinations conducted by Bombay University. It required the intervention of my second-eldest brother, Dara, along with Hotchand Advani, chairman of the college's board of trustees, for the principal to let me to take my exams.

I was not deterred and events at H.R. were merely a prelude to more political activity at Government Law College where, after getting my bachelor's degree, I enrolled to study law. The decision to abandon accountancy for law was a dramatic change in direction, although it could be said I was at last, after several false turns, finally following in the footsteps of my father and brothers. Government Law College, a few minutes' walk from H.R., was the obvious choice, as it was then the best law college in Bombay. And having tasted student activism, I was determined to carry on making life difficult for college administrators.

Government Law College was also where I had most fun. Tatya Tope, the principal, was quite a dictator. I insisted on holding student elections and succeeded in my aim. In my second year, I became the general secretary of the students' union, a position which had previously been inactive with the office-bearers appointed by the principal. I was by now involved in all sorts of social activities. Indeed, I have a particular memory of India's general elections in 1971. As general secretary of the union, I invited political parties to address us and explain what they stood for. I got a senior national leader of every major party to come and speak to us. The first of these was Piloo Mody, a Member of Parliament who was known for his sense of humour. George Fernandes, a South Bombay MP, also spared the time to address us. Many years later when I met Fernandes, who was by then the defence minister of India, at the British high commissioner's home in Delhi, he remembered our meeting in 1971.

My foray into student politics soon gained me notoriety. One of Bombay's evening newspapers began to call me a communist. I was not and could never be one, not least because I was a firm believer in God. But I was certainly politically active and wanted to change India, to make it a modern country which uplifted and looked after its poor citizens. In this context, I was introduced to Prime Minister Indira Gandhi as part of a *chhatra shakti* (student power) conference in Nagpur, Maharashtra. Gandhi invited our group to meet her, she chatted with us and we had a photograph taken.

But much as I enjoyed the political activity, I did not ignore my work at Lala's tours and the wonderful opportunities this provided. In 1972, I embarked on an unexpected adventure. Lala had started organizing trips to Europe. India was getting prosperous, so Indians were discovering foreign travel, not as immigrants but tourists, and I went along on my first overseas journey. We travelled with twenty-six Indians, mainly Parsis, and I was the assistant to the tour manager Homi Lala, managing the sightseeing and guiding. I had to do the running around and make sure everything was in order.

This tour was a game changer. It provided a first glimpse of London, and as soon as I had obtained my law degree I decided to head back and, like my father, qualify as a solicitor there.

However, it was no longer easy for an Indian to get a student visa. Gone were the days when Indians could travel to Britain without a permit. There was growing concern about what was called 'coloured immigration'. Enoch Powell, then a Conservative MP, had forecast in a famous speech that there would be bloodshed if certain immigrants were not stopped and persuaded to return to their homeland.

So, I could only get a visa if I was sponsored by someone in Britain. My elder brother Dinsoo rang his friend Bhagwan Hiranandani, a partner in a London law firm, Stocken & Co., and arranged for my sponsorship. This was a mere formality. The sponsor would provide an affidavit saying he would be supporting me financially during my stay in London. There was no guarantee I would get a visa. I had to go to the offices of the British deputy high commissioner, a fine white-stone building in Flora Fountain, just around the corner from my father's firm, to undergo a thorough medical examination and then meet a visa official for an interview to verify that I was a genuine student.

After this there was yet another hurdle to overcome. India still had tremendous foreign exchange restrictions. Its citizens going abroad were allowed just £3.50 in foreign currency, and in order to travel, the Reserve Bank of India had to approve what was called a 'P Form' before an airline could issue a ticket.

However, this is where working for Lala came in handy. I had some money and with the help of the black market in Bombay exchanged rupees for pounds and arrived in London with £60 in my pocket. In today's currency, it would be £600, which equated to about a month's average wage then. I knew I would need a lot more, but the confidence that I had got from working for Mr Lala and the students' movement made me feel I was ready for the world.

2

Challenging the Locals

I arrived in London on 18 January 1975. I had booked the cheapest ticket on Air India, which meant a tedious journey with stops at Dubai and then Cairo before terminating in Amsterdam. From there I boarded a British Airways connecting flight to London.

Unfortunately, while I had made the connection my suitcases failed to do so, which meant that after negotiating with airport officials at Heathrow to secure a promise that I would be reunited with my misplaced bags in due course, I walked out of the terminal with nothing other than my hand luggage. It underlined the fact that I was starting from scratch. Wrapping my thin jacket tightly around me, I boarded BA's airline shuttle to central London.

Everything about London was magical. Travelling along the M4 motorway, even the houses with their pitched roofs and television aerials sticking out fascinated me. A sloping roof was almost unheard of in Bombay, where nearly all houses had flat roofs that the residents would use for parties or sleeping on hot summer nights. Then there were the cars. On India's roads I was used to seeing only three models, including the old Morris Oxford –

renamed the 'Ambassador' and much favoured by Indian politicians and government officials. In London, by contrast, every car seemed to be of a different make.

The coach dropped me at the BA terminal on Gloucester Road (today the site of a Sainsbury's supermarket). Here I faced an immediate challenge as I had no idea how to find the Indian Young Men's Christian Association's (YMCA) hostel, where I was booked to stay. Thankfully, a kind English lady who was on the shuttle with me helped. She gave me a detailed underground map that set out my route from Gloucester Road to Warren Street, from where the Indian YMCA on Fitzroy Square was just a short walk away.

The YMCA was a popular and fairly comfortable place for Indian students, but when I woke the next morning I felt desperately homesick. The sky was grey and there was no sign of the sun. On my previous visit to London in 1972, it had been peak summer, and I had been much taken by the city having daylight until at least 9 p.m., in contrast to Bombay where the sun usually sets at 6 p.m. But it was January, damp, uniformly dull and dark by about 4 p.m. At home, apart from the monsoon season, I had been used to sun every day. In London, sometimes I didn't see it for days.

This made me feel very low. The cold and persistent London drizzle made me even more wistful as I was used to the warm monsoon rains. I also missed the hustle-bustle of Bombay – hawkers shouting out their wares at all hours, pedestrians chattering, cars honking. London seemed deathly quiet in comparison.

I was also friendless. At the YMCA I had just one acquaintance from back home, Marazban Patrawala (later to join Indian politics before his premature passing away). I had also been introduced to Bhagwan Hiranandani, the solicitor who, on paper at least, sponsored my stay in Britain. But most of my fellow YMCA residents were busy with their work or studies, so I was left alone that first week. I was bored, miserable and pining for home.

There was also the issue of money. The £60 I had brought with me was unlikely to last long, so I needed a job. Here, fortunately, Bhagwan was able to come to my rescue. I went to see him in his offices on Fleet Street to thank him for signing my sponsorship papers. He was very friendly, and I must have impressed him at our first meeting because he immediately offered me a job at the firm (which dealt primarily in shipping matters), for £14 a week.

Qualification and marriage

At Stocken's I worked industriously, frequently doing overtime on weekends and taking on the task of organizing and reactivating old files to which nobody else was paying attention. Life was hard, and I had little cash. But within a few weeks of my arrival in London, I had found a place to stay. Tatya Tope, the principal of the law college I attended and an adversary during my student union days, proved an unexpected friend. By then the vice chancellor of Bombay University, he intervened with Sir Hugh Springer, the Barbadian secretary general of the Association of Commonwealth Universities, and asked if I could stay at the International Students House on Great Portland Street. To my delight, the answer was affirmative, and I was given a room at York Terrace East, facing Regent's Park. Subsidized by a charitable trust connected to the British Foreign Office, it was cheaper than the Indian YMCA, and there I made many friends. It was my most enjoyable time as a student in the UK.

In between surviving on my meagre income and interacting with some of the best students from across the world, I was studying hard. To qualify as a solicitor in the UK, it is necessary to pass two Law Society (the governing body for solicitors in the UK) exams, blandly named Part One and Part Two. I had already passed the first part in my Bombay solicitors' exams. I got through Part Two in December 1975, less than a year after my arrival, a rare foreigner in those days in the sea of English faces in the vast examination hall at Alexandra Palace.

I had one final hurdle to overcome to qualify to practise law. I needed two years of post-qualification job training with an English solicitors' firm. This had already been arranged with Stocken's, but the bureaucratic British immigration laws meant I could no longer stay in the country on my student visa. Neither would I be given a work permit while I was already in the UK – I had to apply from overseas. So, I went back to India towards the end of December 1975 and remained there for a little over three months waiting for the work permit to come through. Stocken's duly organized this and on 6 April 1976 I flew back to London.

My brief stay in Bombay, however, was not spent idly – I became married. I had first met Renoo in the summer of 1973 while on a tour to Nainital, a hill station in northern India. She was also from Bombay and a commerce graduate from H.R. College. That is where our obvious similarities ended. She was not a Parsi but a Jain and with interests completely different to mine.

Candidly, there was no talk of love between us. The marriage was at her suggestion and primarily motivated by her wish to move to the UK. This was something she could only do so as my wife. I said yes, after she had agreed that she would go back in six months and we would divorce if we were not compatible. This was unusual, but I have found, on many occasions, that acting in good faith has been the right thing to do and has brought me to where I am today.

My mother was appalled by my idea of marrying Renoo as she was from a different religion. So we had to marry against her wishes, even if my father had a more liberal approach to such things. The wedding took place in a registry office with just a handful of guests. It was not a wedding to remember, and my main recollection of it is being very nervous.

Renoo's mother, a wonderful lady, gave us reception at a venue near Chowpatty, with forty-odd guests. Throughout the party, I kept asking myself what I was doing; I just wanted it to be over so I could run away. Today, I look back on it with no regrets because this union brought my two lovely children Freya and Varun, who are the joy of my life. Moreover, although our marriage did not start with a big romance, it did mean that I remained in the UK for the rest of my career. Had I been single, it is more than likely that I would have followed in my father's footsteps and returned to India after qualification as an English solicitor and, no doubt, entered politics as was my original plan. Had this happened, I would not have had the rich and exciting experiences which I have enjoyed in the United Kingdom. God works in a mysterious way.

So, as it was, Renoo and I flew to London, this time non-stop on a Qantas flight. My friend Hasmukh Gardi let us stay for a few weeks in his home in Edgware. For some time after this we moved from place to place, renting cheap accommodation because we didn't have much money. Fortunately, Renoo found a job as an accounts clerk and this helped.

Meanwhile, I was engrossed in my legal training. In the 1970s, this wasn't structured as it is now but was very much based on learning through experience. Hence, my first responsibility at the start of the day was to make tea for my principal, who oversaw my training. I literally carried his bags, learning on the job as I went along.

Towards the end of my training period, I was given the chance to work on my own on some small shipping cases, with the very first being a bagged cargo damage claim by the Government of India against the owner of a ship called *Hwa Gek*. I was working with counsel Johnny Veeder from 4 Essex Court Barristers' Chambers (who was made a Queen's Counsel in 1986), and the sole arbitrator was Dr Ralph Kingsley. It was around that time that my long-term ambitions started to shift from politics to the law. I had still been harbouring my ambitions to change India but soon after I started training, I had two encounters with people who would play a significant part in my life.

Cedric Barclay

Cedric Barclay is still considered to be one of the most eminent international maritime arbitrators. Cedric was among the founders of London Maritime Arbitrators Association (LMAA). I had met him early on during my time working at Stocken's, and quite quickly he suggested I should start my own firm once I had qualified. He warned me that if I was to join any of the English firms, at the end of the first year the senior partner would take me to lunch and say, 'Good job, old boy,' and that would be that, nothing would follow. This would happen every year and I would never progress while all my competitors moved up the ladder.

Cedric thought I was better than that and offered to help me set up a practice under my own name. Within weeks of starting my own firm, he personally took me to visit some Greek ship owners at their offices in London. This resulted in my first-ever Greek client, Minos Colocotronis, a famous ship owner.

It was a significant connection and Cedric and I remained friends thereafter – I have fond memories of Renoo and I being invited by Cedric and his wife Cora to spend a Sunday picnicking at a park in Wentworth. Cedric had a wicked sense of humour and was quick to take out a bottle of whisky and offer it to the parties during an arbitration hearing. Knowing I didn't drink, as he went around filling the glasses, he would still place his hand on my shoulder and warn me, 'In England we only start thinking correctly once we have had a drink.'

Once when I was representing Dubai's Global Shipping Company, which had a claim against the US-based Arabian Development Corporation concerning the transport of cargo to Dubai for the construction of the Jumeriah Beach Resort, the opponent's solicitor,

Anthony Glaister from Fox & Gibbons, an English law firm in Dubai, applied to Cedric, who was the sole arbitrator, to shift the venue of the arbitration from London to New Orleans. I objected and attended the hearing of the application. Before any party could say anything, Cedric gave us a piece of paper on which he had put figures which suggested quite how financially beneficial it would be if we were all to go to New Orleans. The venue was duly shifted there without any further arguments.

On the British Airways flight to New Orleans, I found myself in the first-class cabin with the opposing legal team, along with their counsel. Halfway through the flight their QC, Derry Irvine, fortified by the alcohol he employed to combat his fear of flying, introduced himself and his junior, a young Tony Blair, later to become the UK prime minister who appointed Irvine Lord Chancellor as Lord Irvine of Lairg.

It was to be a two-week arbitration, and once we had arrived at our hotel there was a message waiting for us that Cedric had organized the venue for the hearing at a well-known hotel in Bourbon Street in the French Quarter. At the start of the hearing the following day, Cedric informed both parties that he would expect them to meet at the hotel bar for drinks every day at 6 p.m.

Global Shipping's counsel team included Stewart Boyd QC, co-author of a book on international arbitration,[5] as well as Christopher Clarke QC and Peregrine Simon QC, both of whom would later become Lord Justices. Rather strikingly, the respondent's principal witness, a Mr Spindleberg, gave his evidence with a revolver belt around his waist. As Boyd started his cross-examination, I instructed him to apply to the arbitrator that the witness should remove his revolver during cross-examination, lest he got excited and started

5 Lord Mustill and Stewart C. Boyd, *Commercial Arbitration*: 2001 Companion, LexisNexis, December 2000

shooting. The application was made, and the tribunal made an order that the witness should leave the arbitration court and return to continue his evidence after entrusting his revolver to the hotel authorities for safekeeping.

(As a postscript to this case, I received a message from Anthony Glaister some years later asking me if I had kept a photograph of Tony Blair tripping on my briefcase and falling flat on his back in the course of checking in at our hotel in New Orleans. Sadly, I had not.)

Cedric always kept an eye on my progress. One afternoon, while I was in the middle of a client meeting, he called me, out of the blue, to give me some advice. He told me that I should never give up despite the many adversities I would face as an outsider running a maritime law firm in London. He encouraged me to remain strong and told me I was on the right track. To be honest, I was impatient to return to my client, and I regret to say I was a little short with Cedric. Nonetheless, he called me again just two minutes later, saying he had forgotten an extra point. 'Take holidays with your family every year without fail,' he said.

It was the last time we spoke. That very evening was the annual dinner of the LMAA. As the food was being served, I received a handwritten note from the Hon. Michael Summerskill (another well-known maritime arbitrator and author of a maritime law book) saying that Cedric had just passed away. After the dinner I rushed to Cedric's home in Kensington to pay my respects to Cora, who told me he had died peacefully. I felt his call to me earlier that day showed he had a premonition the end was near.

I had lost an important mentor.

The Hinduja brothers

The second encounter which was to prove invaluable was with the Hinduja brothers, at an event in the summer of 1977. In those days

I loved to network, using the skills I had picked up on Lala's Tours, introducing myself to all and sundry. On those trips I would be with sixty to eighty people for two to three weeks and had to deal with them at their best and their worst. So, when I met Srichand and Gopichand Hinduja they took an instant shine to me and asked me to meet them again.

I was fortunate that in the mid-1970s the Indian society in Britain was changing. Whereas in the past Indians like my father would come to Britain and then return home, by now many were emigrating. Soon after Independence, workers from villages in Punjab settled in parts of the West Midlands as well as Southall in West London, which quickly came to be known as 'Little India'. The second wave of immigration in the late 1960s and early 1970s saw people of Indian origin coming to the UK from Africa, having in many cases being driven out, most notably by Idi Amin in Uganda. Initially made to feel unwelcome in the UK, they gradually bedded in and brought about a cultural change to their adopted country. They were followed by a third cascade of Indians, and it was from this influx that I was to benefit. These people were not villagers or refugees but entrepreneurs, businessmen with money who were setting up shop in Europe.

In the autumn of 1977, the Hindujas asked me to meet them in their small office on the eighth floor of New Zealand House in Haymarket. They wanted me to be their in-house legal adviser. Despite their insistence, I turned them down. For one thing, I had not even qualified as a solicitor yet; I was still a trainee. Even so, as a young man in need of money and with a wife to support, perhaps it seemed odd to turn down the offer of secure employment, even if in those days the Hindujas were a comparatively small outfit with only seven or eight staff. But our family rule was that we would never be employed by others and would always work for ourselves. This probably stemmed from the fact that my grandfather was a feudal landlord, and even though my family had since lost most of their money, it was only in the narrow financial sense that I ever felt insecure. I had confidence. I had a sense of independence. Even if a major commercial business house had invited me to work for them, I would have turned them down. I knew Cedric Barclay was right and I was determined to set up my own firm once I qualified. No Indian had ever started a law practice in the City, and I knew that working for the Hindujas would not help me realize my dream.

Having said that, I still managed to have my cake and eat it, doing a deal with the Hindujas which meant they became clients of Stocken's. Towards the end of 1977, I also worked for the brothers every evening for £5 an hour. This would include accompanying the Hinduja brothers and their elderly confidant Krishna Golikeri to their apartment and having dinner with them every night before making it home at 10pm after a long journey on the London Underground.

Those were important formative years of my life and my education at St. Xavier's School stood me in good stead. Although educated in English, I had also learnt Hindi as a second language. I became a vital linguistic bridge between the Hindujas and their adopted country. They spoke Sindhi, which was their mother tongue, as well as Persian, which they had picked up from living in Iran, and Hindi. However, at that time they could not speak fluent English, the language in which all their deals were negotiated, so I became their interpreter.

Today, the Hindujas are best known as highly successful businessmen, but what struck me in those early days was that, above all else, they were kind. I also realized they were very smart. Noticing the tide turning against the Shah of Iran, they had moved to London. They did not arrive empty-handed. They came with a large amount of US dollars, in the millions. Srichand Hinduja, who was four years older than his brother Gopi, was the man in charge of the business.

He could also speak Gujarati and would use it to ask me what things meant and give instructions, which I would then translate. I would also translate and explain legal documents and draft letters for them to sign and send. Like me, they were newcomers to Britain. Over time they came to trust me, and we became close.

From the start, they liked my straight talking – a typical Parsi trait – and willingness to work hard and come up with my own ideas, which they found interesting. Together, we frequently travelled between London and Geneva, and in one year alone I made more than twenty-five trips between the two cities. The Hindujas launched their first banking operation in a joint venture with Credit Suisse First Boston. They called it Amas, a name Srichand came up with at a café in Geneva where he, Gopi, Golikeri and I were having tea. Amas is now the Hinduja Bank in Geneva.

Although they have a reputation for being secretive, they were open with their own team and I was proud to be a part of it. We got along very well, and Gopi and I remain good friends. This is not to suggest that we were equals. But they treated me with respect, and it has endured through the years.

Starting on my own

Within seven days of qualifying as a solicitor in 1978 I launched my own practice, starting Gagrat & Company with Hasmukh Gardi. He was a conveyancing solicitor who had the two years' post-qualification experience required to start a new firm. Gagrat was the name of a well-known Parsi firm in Bombay and Jangoo Gagrat joined us as a partner. I was hoping to attract business from Parsis in London. This did not materialize, and we soon went our own ways.

While the Hindujas were my main source of work, my first client was an English lady. Just before I had started my firm, I was walking along Russell Road in Kensington and as I was in the un-English habit of talking to strangers, I fell into conversation with a woman who was washing her car. Her name was Joanne Wilson, and she was a retired schoolteacher. When I told her that I was training to be a lawyer and was planning to start my own firm, she said she owned a building at 51 Russell Road and was having problems with the tenants. So, the first money I earned as a solicitor was from evicting them. Hers was a quintessential display of English support for an underdog. Joanne later appointed me executor of her will, and many years afterwards her nephew also instructed me to draw up his will and appointed me as the executor.

Not long after I started my firm, things began to improve at home. Renoo and I were now settled into married life, our different personalities reconciled. In 1979 we bought our first home in Raynes Park, South West London. It was a two-bedroomed flat and could not have been more basic. The second bedroom was a small box room, and there was no dining space, just an open-plan kitchen area. The flat cost £18,000, for which I had saved a 10 per cent deposit and borrowed the rest from a building society. The hassle involved seemed worthwhile the moment I got the keys to the flat. Seven years on from my very first visit to London, I now owned a small part of it. It was a happy moment.

Meanwhile, I was doing the kind of high-quality work that start-up firms were rarely able to handle. Through the Hindujas I was meeting legal luminaries from all around the world, including Swiss and Swedish lawyers. I was introduced to the Sethia and Parecha brothers, both of whom had flourishing maritime businesses in London. There were inevitably shipping disputes, and this is where I came in.

There were three Sethia brothers: Raj, Ranjit and Nirmal. Ranjit had a shipping company while the flamboyant Raj was a commodities exporter, doing business with Nigeria and other African countries. Raj had a private plane and used to throw lavish parties to which I was invited, including one for the visiting Indian cricket team when they came to play a Test series against England in 1982. I earned decent fees from the Sethia brothers and also got work from other freight companies such as Alaam Shipping, owned by the Parechas.

It was often a personal challenge for me to gain acceptance in the maritime arbitration circle. Such arbitrations were considered to be an elite type of legal work. London historically had been the centre of the maritime world and remained so until the coming of the internet. The Baltic Exchange in the City was where a major part of shipping business was agreed.

Maritime arbitrators were not used to seeing a non-English solicitor appearing before them. While the majority were accepting of the new face who was not part of their inner circle, there was a small minority that were hostile towards me. One of them was John Potter, a senior maritime arbitrator who disliked me so much that he publicly announced that he could not bear to deal with me. In fact, when he was appointed by a vessel owner as their arbitrator and I was representing the respondent charterer, he resigned from the case. This happened in several other cases and word got out. In another arbitration where I was not involved, one of the parties, who was Greek, wanted him to resign as an arbitrator, and so appointed me as his solicitor. He resigned against the protest of the other party. Soon thereafter he stopped resigning in cases where I was the legal representative of one of the parties. His resistance to me had failed.

One such example was the case of an ocean-going vessel called the *Kostas Melas*. I had been instructed by Sethia Liners, which had chartered the ship for a trip from Albany, USA to Alexandria, Egypt with a cargo of maize. My client had exercised the 'right of deduction', or set-off for their claims from the hire. The owners applied to the arbitrators for an award to be made on an urgent basis. The arbitrators, one of whom was John Potter, fixed the arbitration hearing on a short notice of two or three days. I appeared before the arbitration tribunal and within fifteen minutes the arbitrators made an interim award of $100,000 without giving me the opportunity to put forward my client's case. I challenged the award in court on the grounds that the arbitrators had misconducted the proceedings.

My client's application came up before Mr Justice Goff (one of the finest English judges) in a hearing that went on for four days. He reserved judgement. Strangely, at this hearing John Potter was present in the courtroom along with Michael Mabbs, another maritime arbitrator. To my client's surprise, the arbitration tribunal then fixed the final hearing some two weeks hence, before Mr Justice Goff had given his judgement.

I then filed a second application in court alleging further misconduct by the arbitration tribunal. In the maritime legal community, particularly in barristers' chambers, word had gone around that I had taken on a powerful tribunal. I had myself drafted the second application for misconduct against it. The opponent's solicitor, Ince & Co., somehow managed to get the hearing listed in the same week of my filing the application. I could not find any counsel to take on my firm's brief. All the maritime law barristers' chambers whom I had contacted told me their barristers were reluctant to take on this case, the general view being that it was not proper on my part to allege misconduct against an eminent maritime arbitration tribunal or to make a second misconduct application within days of the first one.

I did not know what to do, so I called John Hobhouse QC, whom I had known during my training days at Stocken's. In those days, when I used to attend conference at his chambers, 7 King's Bench Walk, with my principal, I would take notes and send him a handwritten report with my comments on his advice.

To my surprise, Hobhouse responded and showed himself to be an amazingly kind man.

When I told him that the application before the court was for 10.30 a.m. the next day, he told me he had heard about what was going on and said, 'Deliver the papers to me. I will appear for you.' It took me a few hours to get them ready, with him phoning several times enquiring when the files would arrive. When I delivered them to his chambers at 7 p.m., I could see he was angry at their late delivery, and he simply told me to leave the files on the desk and see him at 9.45 a.m. outside the courtroom at the law courts. The next day I duly presented myself and other than his reciprocal 'good morning' there was not a word exchanged between us. He went on working.

The hearing before Mr Justice Goff was listed for half a day, but it went on till 5 p.m. At the end of the day, he said, 'Judgement at 10.30 a.m. tomorrow, if I must.' At 6 p.m. the same evening, I received a telex from the chairman of the arbitration tribunal informing the parties that the tribunal had resigned. John Hobhouse had worked overnight, mastered all the facts and given the finest performance I have ever seen from a Queen's Counsel.

When Mr Justice Goff gave his judgement[6] on the first misconduct application, he gave a homily to the international arbitration community, which I believe remains relevant even today. He said as follows:

> No tribunal can necessarily conclude his work with two satisfied customers. But it can be done; and experience has shown that for this purpose it is sometimes desirable to give [a] party a little more leeway than he may strictly be entitled to. The price of such an action is often small; but the prize is large. With all respect, it is a point which arbitrators might well do to keep in mind.

---

6 Kostas Melas, SL Sethia Liners Ltd v. Naviagro Maritime Corporation [1981] 1 Lloyds Rep 18

Venture to Iran

Perhaps my most exciting brief in the early years was when the Hindujas asked me to go to Iran after the Shah had been deposed and Ayatollah Khomeini had come to power. The Hindujas were owed money by a company called Government Trading Corporation, concerning demurrage (liquidated damages to be paid to a ship for delay caused in the charging or loading of cargo) on a shipping vessel called *Rio Elle*. I was sent to recover it, taking the first Iran Air flight from London to Tehran after the revolution.

Arriving in the country, I was interviewed by representatives of the Committees of Islamic Revolution, better known as Komite. At every traffic light in Tehran, whenever the revolution's guards stopped our car or I heard gunshots, my stomach lurched. The Komite even came to my modest hotel room to see me, waving guns and asking me why I was in their country. Such are the challenges when trying to build an international law business – you need to be bold.

Developing work with India

In April 1982, I fulfilled my dream of being the first Indian to start an English firm of solicitors in the City of London. This was helped by an overdraft facility of £10,000 from NatWest Bank. However, there was a small but highly significant point that I had to consider before setting out on this project. Many of my Indian friends had anglicized their names, with Rakesh becoming Ralph and so on. This was in order to fit in with British society. It might have been thought that my name could be difficult to identify with for some potential clients.

Nonetheless, I decided against adopting an English name. I was determined I would remain Sarosh and not become, say, Sam.

I remained comfortable with my Indianness and believed that English people respected a person more if they maintained their individuality. It was in that spirit that within weeks of Zaiwalla & Co. coming into being, we moved to 95A Chancery Lane, and I wrote to the sitting Chief Justice of India, Y.V. Chandrachud, inviting him formally to open my firm's new offices. Fortunately, he was going to be in the UK on an official visit and he accepted my invitation.

Just prior to Chandrachud's visit, the Indian high commission in London appointed us as solicitors for the Government of India. Seyid Muhammad, the Indian high commissioner, was an English barrister who had joined Indian politics. When he heard that an Indian had started a solicitor's firm not far from the high commission, he invited me for tea and appointed my firm as their solicitors. For the next twelve years, I catered to their every legal requirement, with particular responsibility for maritime arbitrations.

There were plenty of these. In the mid-1960s, India was facing a famine, and US President Lyndon Johnson agreed to donate a large quantity of wheat to India under a scheme to help developing countries feed their population. India did not have to pay for the wheat but did have to charter ships to pick up the cargo from US ports. India would charter 200–300 ships a year and almost every shipment would have a dispute over late payment of freight, damaged cargo, demurrage claims, including collisions and allegations of boats being sent to unsafe ports or vessels not being fit for service. The charter parties for these vessels were all subject to English arbitration. That was where I came in.

Seyid Muhammad was extremely helpful. Having appointed Zaiwalla & Co., he took upon himself the task of personally ensuring that the job was delivered properly. He would call me to his office at the Indian high commission in Aldwych almost every afternoon to discuss the shipping cases. Seyid Muhammad became a mentor and generously introduced me to a number of new clients. Among these was Rukmini Devi Arundale, who had revived the classical Indian dance Bharatanatyam in India. Such was her status and influence that Morarji Desai, when prime minister of India, wanted to nominate her as president.

Not all of Seyid Muhammad's plans worked. In 1983, after the Indian cricket team won the World Cup, he decided to bring together some rich Indian businessmen with a view to forming a trust to assist young cricketers from India to receive training in England. I was invited to take notes at this meeting, which was attended by around twenty Asian millionaires. It was decided to create a charity foundation called India Sports and Physical Foundation. All those present at this meeting committed to donate £20,000 each. A year later, only one had actually paid up – Agha Hasan Abedi, the Chairman of the Bank of Credit and Commerce International, which later went into liquidation. Such are the ironies of life.

Encouraged by Seyid Muhammad, I visited India more often. I started going to Delhi and talking to people to try and develop business for my firm. I would travel economy, stay in cheap hotels and start contacting people as soon as I arrived. It was a very basic process. I would simply go through the phone book, calling various business houses involved in shipping and international trade and say, 'I am from London and would like to meet you.' Almost invariably they would invite me to come and have a cup of tea, and from these meetings work began to flow.

I also started to build up a portfolio with the Indian government, given that at the time most international legal work in the country involved the government. But I used the same approach as for businesses. Indian phone directories at that time included even the home numbers of important government officials, so I used to just phone them up. Again, business flowed in and I enjoyed working for the government, regarding it as an honour even if the reality was that you didn't earn much (and were generally owed money). India had enormous foreign exchange problems and I often had to fund my travel expenses to obtain evidence for government cases. Meanwhile, the high commission was paying £15 an hour, a pittance, which only went up to £35 in the early 1990s.

Sadly, my relations with the Indian government later soured when I was one of the three arbitrators sitting in an international arbitration, where I joined the decision of the distinguished chairman Lord Mackenzie–Stuart and the award went against a government department.

But I have happy memories of working for my homeland in that initial period. I used to deal mainly with a section called TransChart in the shipping ministry, which was in charge of chartering ships for government corporations and departments. I discovered that in those early days almost all Indian civil servants were honest and committed to their work. They were straightforward with not a whiff of corruption. I was never asked for any backhanders, nobody asked me to pay them a bribe to get business. More recently, it is believed the situation regarding corruption has become somewhat different, with bribes commonplace and work with the Indian State Trading Corporation depending on making payments. I will have nothing to do with this, not least because the UK Bribery Act would mean I would end up in jail.

While my political ambitions remained, my work meant I had to be satisfied with developing political connections rather than gaining high office. These were often at the highest level of the government. Soon after I started my own firm, I forged links with Rajiv Gandhi. He was the chairman of the special organizing committee (SOC) of the 9th Asian Games, held in Delhi in 1982. His mother, Indira Gandhi, was prime minister and she was clearly grooming him to succeed her. Two years later, there was a suit filed in the English court for $5 million compensation against the SOC.

A marketing contract had been entered into with METCO, a Dubai company owned by an Indian. The Indian government cancelled the contract and METCO sued in the London court. Rajiv instructed me through Ajay Shankar, the SOC secretary, whose wife Meera later became Rajiv's private secretary when he was prime minister. She also later became India's ambassador to the United States.

The case came before Mr Justice Mustill. The question was whether English courts had jurisdiction over the disputed contract. I instructed as counsel Richard Aikens, who later became a Lord Justice of Appeal. We convinced the judge that the English court did not have jurisdiction and the case was thrown out. Rajiv was happy and wrote me a letter of congratulations. He then personally recommended new clients to us whenever any of his family or friends had a problem. This included Sumatiben Morarjee of Scindia Shipping, an unusually strong woman who told me stories about her personal interaction with Mohandas Karamchand Gandhi, known as the father of the Indian nation, whom she knew well and who had on occasions stayed at her home on Juhu Beach, Bombay. Years later Rajiv's wife Sonia also instructed my firm to prevent an Italian film producer making a movie about her.

In the early 1980s I had still not met Rajiv but I was soon to do so. In 1988, when he was prime minister – this was after his mother's assassination in 1984 – he invited me to his birthday party and on arrival at Delhi airport I was received by a government official and taken to his home. There, he welcomed me and told me he was pleased with my work.

Meanwhile, the president of India was leaving the country to attend the funeral of President Zia-ul-Haq, Pakistan's military dictator who had died in an aircraft crash. Rajiv personally gave instructions to arrange for me to be taken to Delhi's VIP airport with Saroj Khaparde, who was then India's junior health minister. Rajiv was on his way there too, as it was protocol that when the president, who is the head of state, travels internationally, the prime minister sees him off. In fact, the whole cabinet came and stood in queue. I found myself at one end of it, next to the army and air force chiefs. Rajiv came over and introduced me to President Venkataraman.

By this time Zaiwalla & Co. had acquired many shipping clients from the United Arab Emirates, Greece and Venezuela. *Legal Business*, then a leading law publication in London, published a three-page profile of me, crediting me for building a high-class, multi-racial firm in London. We now had more than twenty-five staff members including lawyers, and my personal circumstances were improving fast. I had become a father, with a daughter Freya and a son Varun. We had moved in 1983 from our small, semi-detached house in New Malden to a large, detached property in Raymond Road, an upmarket area in Wimbledon, opposite a house the German tennis player Boris Becker used to rent during the championships. This was to be our family home until my divorce much later.

Working for the Indian government meant payment used to take some two or three years to arrive, but I was still comfortably off for the first time since settling in London a decade before. The ten-year period between 1982 and 1992 was the most enjoyable in both my personal and professional life. Watching the children grow up and spending time with them at home and during the holidays as a family was a delightful experience. The memories we made as a family will be cherished forever.

Things were looking up. My first car, a banged-up old Ford which cost me £75, had been replaced by a spanking yellow Mercedes for me and a brand-new Peugeot for Renoo. I had established connections with some of the highest echelons of the Indian political world and was seizing every opportunity to do the same in the United Kingdom. The status of the Indian community in Britain was changing fast and I was keen to be at the centre of this metamorphosis. I wanted to help make Britain a more open society, but with evolutionary changes that would not threaten institutions and culture. I never felt British society as a whole was racist, but it was class conscious. So, I wanted the British to know that Indians should no longer be treated as a poor, immigrant, ignored community but one which had the right to be at the high table, including at 10 Downing Street.

3

The Shining Years

Starting Zaiwalla & Co. was exciting and its first ten years were a great success. In a decade, between the years 1982 and 1992, I built a solid core of clients, notably in the maritime sector but also stretching out, every now and again, into new and sometimes exotic fields.

For a young man still holding an Indian passport to establish a law firm in Chancery Lane was something many would have said was impossible at that time. Diversity was still rare, but I generally faced no difficulties from the English legal and judicial fraternity, although there were racial tensions with some members of the legal fraternity during the early days.

The English love an underdog, especially one who is prepared to stand up and fight with courage and integrity. That was why I had decided to open my law firm under my own name. I felt that I would be better respected by the English – for whom racism was largely not endemic – for this simple gesture of identification with my own culture. Although there were occasionally exceptions, some of which I have mentioned later on in the book, the majority of the

British white population believes in fairness and has been willing to accept diversity.

Quite aside from issues of diversity, however, the English legal scene was very different in the 1980s and 1990s from its position now as we approach the 2020s. The ability to obtain justice and have their day in court was then freely available to all British citizens with the support of legal aid. Today, legal aid is virtually non-existent. The result is, only large companies and rich individuals are now able to afford to go to law on serious matters of dispute.

Solicitors' firms, even the larger ones, were then of modest size and so were barristers' chambers. For example, two of my favourite junior counsel in those years were Richard Aikens and Peregrine Simon, both of whom went on to hold senior positions in English courts. They shared a small office, and case conferences with solicitors were ordinarily held there in modest surroundings.

This was also a culture of maintaining courtesy and fairness at all costs. On one occasion, I had to complain to Clyde & Co., which was, and still is, a leading maritime law firm. They were the opponent in a maritime arbitration case that I was handling. The solicitor for the case was a young man who I felt was rude to me during a telephone conversation. Looking back, the rudeness might not have been anything more than a raised tone and possibly a sharp comment to put me down. Still, I did not like this, so I wrote a letter of complaint to Mr Whittaker, then a senior partner of Clyde & Co.

A week or two later, I had a call from Whittaker requesting a meeting at my office. I agreed. He arrived with another person whom I had not met before. He turned out to be the solicitor who was the subject of my complaint. Whittaker told me that he considered it necessary for them both to attend so both could apologize for what had happened. He added that he had brought along his junior to show that in London, discourtesy of any type towards an opponent solicitor was not tolerated. I have always remembered this, and it became a benchmark for my own behaviour.

In terms of office equipment too there were almost incredible differences from today, given the speed with which technology has advanced. There were no computers or mobile phones and no modern photocopying machines. Secretaries took dictation in shorthand and typed the letter in draft. The solicitor would then check and correct any errors, after which it would be re-typed on notepaper for signature. The only mode of fast written communication, both local and international, was by means of telex. Copies of documents for the court and the other side had to be typed or copied on cyclostyle, a very crude form of copier. One good consequence of this, however, was that in litigation and arbitration cases before the court of tribunal, both parties were compelled to limit the size of the document bundles before the court. This also ensured that counsels' fees were more reasonable.

A key trigger for change came in 1986 when what was called the 'Big Bang' reformed the financial services sector and transformed the City. Prime Minister Margaret Thatcher believed in deregulation and opening up the United Kingdom to foreign companies. Suddenly, they could enter the market without the need to apply for a licence.

Within a short time, US law firms opened offices in London. Their style was very different. Litigation and arbitration became a battle between the parties. 'Win at all costs' was their motto. How they presented themselves was also very important to them, and so they had opulent offices. Unsurprisingly, they had to earn large fees to pay for this opulence.

Memorable shipping cases

As mentioned, in these early years my firm had largely a maritime law practice and most of the cases were before a maritime arbitration tribunal or the Commercial Court. The Commercial Court had at any given time not more than two or three judges. The clerk in charge was David Bird, who managed every aspect of the court, including listings, with just one assistant.

One of the first shipping cases my firm was instructed to handle concerned a dispute over the vessel *Shirrabank* between its British owner, the Bank Line, and Global Shipping Company of Dubai, a client whose managing director was Mike Minwalla. A Parsi like me, Mike was a kind individual. Following the *Shirrabank* case, I started to receive a lot of work from Global, which was part of the Dubai-based Al Shirawi group. A key case was in the mid-1980s, when they placed an order to build three vessels but then went into financial troubles because the shipping market collapsed. I was given the task of negotiating out of the contract with the three ship owners in three different jurisdictions of Scotland, Japan and Singapore. I went with the client to all three countries and Global was successful in getting out of the contract after paying modest compensation to the vessel owners. Two of these vessels were handed back to the ship owners before the expiry of the charter party by paying to the vessel owner a modest sum of damages and in one case taking a successful legal defence in the arbitration.

The *Shirrabank* case also resulted in my meeting Ron Burley, a senior clerk at 1 Brick Court (now known as Brick Court Chambers). We got on very well and, knowing I had just started, he told me at our first meeting that if I needed advice on any matter or had problems with any barrister's chambers, I should come to him and he would sort it out. In the years that followed, I would often turn to him for help and he would say in his loud voice, 'Leave it with me,' and the problem would resolve.

The first counsel he put forward to me was in the case of *Shirrabank* and that was Roger Buckley. Buckley had a brilliant mind but what impressed me most was that in spite of the brevity of his submissions to the court, they got a positive outcome.

Burley and I were to build a strong working relationship.

I also enjoyed good relations with David Grief, senior clerk at 4 Essex Court, now Essex Court Chambers. Such relationships provided the basis of a successful professional practice.

The Anthoula case

In the early years, along with Global there were two other shipping companies that were our principal clients – SL Sethia Liners and Alaam Maritime. They kept my firm busy with some very interesting and challenging cases.

The first was an arbitration concerning the vessel *Anthoula*, which Sethia had chartered. The defendants were represented by Jeremy Thomas, a competent solicitor who was with Stocken & Co. during my training there.

In the afternoon of the first day of the hearing, Ranjit Sethia was giving evidence. That evening, I received a call from Dr Ralph Kingsley, chairman of the tribunal, whom I knew well. At that time, it was not unknown for arbitrators to speak to a party's solicitors because it was considered that it would not affect the judgement of the arbitrator. Such was the reputation of London maritime arbitration, where arbitrators were mainly shipbrokers at the Baltic Exchange or retired senior maritime solicitors.

Kingsley told me – I was sure in an attempt to be helpful – that Ranjit Sethia's evidence was hopeless and he would not be believed, so I should consider settling the case. Following the call, I phoned Roger Buckley and relayed to him the exact words of the conversation.

Buckley advised me immediately that Kingsley could not continue, and I had a duty to inform the client and to ask Kingsley to step down. I followed his advice in both respects and the next morning, Kingsley sent a long message to his co-arbitrators and both parties saying I had made an allegation of partiality on his part and therefore he had resigned.

Following this, however, he became very hostile with me – Cedric Barclay described him as my 'enemy' – and spoke about this incident to the maritime legal community. However, I knew I had done nothing wrong and kept quiet. A senior maritime arbitrator, John Selwyn, then replaced Kingsley and in the end my client succeeded. This was a very satisfactory win. It was a well-fought arbitration by both sides and Buckley was brilliant.

A few years later, I received a letter from Dr Kingsley inviting me for lunch at the Baltic Exchange. It was a different Kingsley and what he said was very moving. He had just lost his wife to cancer and his only daughter had cancer too, which had made him reflective. He said he wanted to apologize for having wronged me. I immediately accepted his apology and said that I had forgotten the whole thing. Kingsley and I became close over the years; he remarried, and I was pleased when he accepted an invitation to my firm's Christmas party.

The Everest case

The second fascinating case I handled for the Sethias concerned the vessel *Everest*. It was purchased by Ranjit Sethia's company for $600,000 and sailed from Casablanca, a port city in Morocco, carrying a phosphate cargo to Bangladesh. The vessel was insured for some $2 million and sank soon after leaving port, within the port limit. The insurers refused to pay the claim, so Sethia started proceedings against the underwriters through the solicitors' firm, Hill Taylor Dickinson.

The Sethia brothers did not come to me initially because they considered that they required one of the better-known firms to handle this case. However, some three months before the trial date, Ranjit Sethia called me and said he wanted me to take it over. I called his solicitors, who told me that this was an old ship and in their view the claim had few merits. They had instructed as counsel Jonathan Mance, who later became a judge in the Supreme Court. Mance repeated his advice to me.

The first step I took was to change counsel and instruct Anthony Diamond QC. This upset Mance and his clerk phoned me to suggest I should allow him to remain junior for the trial for a nominal fee. I agreed. Realizing that the key evidence required to succeed was not available, I personally made investigations with the previous owner of the vessel, a European who lived in Nigeria. I found what I needed, which was hard evidence that the vessel was seaworthy at the time of purchase. The previous owner agreed to travel to London to give evidence. The trial came up before Lord Justice Leggatt and closed just before the lunch break after two weeks of hearing. He said, 'Judgement 2.30 p.m., if I must.' He said he wanted senior partner at Ince & Co. to be present in court, which indicated that he was going to give a strongly worded judgement against the underwriters. Their solicitors, Ince & Co., saw the writing on the wall. As a result, the judgement was never given because during the lunch recess, the underwriters accepted liability and agreed to pay our client's costs.

The Nefos 2 case

Another challenging arbitration involved a vessel called *Nefos 2*. My firm was acting for an Indian government-owned corporation, which had chartered this vessel for discharge of cargo at Navlakhi, a minor port in Gujarat, India. The issue was whether or not discharging the cargo was safe for this vessel. Under the charter-party contract, the Government of India, the charterer, had an obligation to nominate a safe port for the discharge of cargo.

Nefos 2 carried a cargo of food grains to Navlakhi and the vessel owners complained that the vessel had touched the bottom of the sea while anchored. This caused considerable damage and so they made a substantial claim. I instructed Nicholas Phillips QC, who went on to become the first president of the UK Supreme Court. The arbitration tribunal was chaired by a highly regarded judge, Lord Wilberforce.

I did the research and found evidence that it was customary and safe for vessels anchored at Navlakhi to touch the sea floor because it was sandy and posed no risk to the vessel's safety. Nicholas Phillips QC still advised that we were going to lose the arbitration. I arranged for the Indian government's chief nautical advisor, a Mr Gill, to travel to London to give evidence on whether a vessel like the *Nefos 2* could have safely discharged the cargo at Navlakhi. My client was successful.

Many years later, after Nicholas had retired from the Supreme Court, I happened to meet him at an event organized by the International Students' House. I reminded him that his last case at the Bar before he became a judge was the one concerning the *Nefos 2*. To my amusement he said, 'We should never have won.' Nicholas's initial advice was that my client, the Government of India, did not have merits in their defence. We both smiled. He was one of the finest counsels I instructed. I would often disagree with him on the issues related to my firm's cases, but to Phillips's credit I found that he had the humility to consider what I proposed and produced new and sound legal arguments.

Indian Oil arbitration

Another interesting case which came to my firm was an arbitration award by three eminent QCs, Adrian Hamilton, Martin Moore-Bick and Gordon Pollock. By a contract, the Indian Oil Corporation

(IOC), an oil giant owned by the Indian government and a new client of my firm, had sold to Coastal Bermuda 1.5 million tons of Bombay high grade oil.[7] The contract required Coastal to nominate the carrying vessels and establish a period of lay time within which each vessel was to be loaded. For five of the voyages, the IOC failed to complete loading within the decided lay period. The contract price was fixed by reference to published market figures for five days before the bill of lading in date. Because the market was rising, the agreed price formula produced a higher figure than it would have done if the IOC had made shipments in time.

Coastal therefore had a claim for damages. The arbitrators made an award against the IOC for some $18 million. For this arbitration, the parties had agreed not to appeal, which was permissible and binding under the Arbitration Act 1979. This meant there was no remedy available to challenge the award in court.

Unusually, one of the arbitrators, Gordon Pollock QC, had added a postscript to the award effectively saying that the IOC's legal team was not competent. The postscript read as follows:

> I wish to record my regret that the sellers had not at some stage broadened the scope of their case …
>
> The documents gave rise to a strong indication that the buyers had intended to create clear impression in the minds of the seller that if a satisfactory settlement of the demurrage claim were made, nothing further would be heard of the 'enormous losses' said to have been suffered by the buyers …
>
> In the result I believe that the sellers had far stronger case than they allowed themselves to advance, one of which might well have succeeded had that been formulated differently.

---

7 Indian Oil Corporation v. Coastal (Bermuda) Ltd [1990] 2 Lloyd's Rep. 407

Right up to the arbitration award, the IOC was represented by the City's big maritime firm, Ince & Co. After the award was published, the IOC's legal team consulted two eminent QCs. Both said there was no remedy available under English law.

The IOC came to me in a desperate state. The head of its legal department, Mr Ramachandran, said, 'If we lost there was no problem, but this comment of Mr Pollock in the award will have our heads chopped off in India.' He urged me to do something.

The question was what, if any, remedy a party has when it loses an arbitration because of the incompetence of its legal team, which included both English counsel and solicitors.

I instructed a new QC from another leading maritime law chambers, 4 Essex Court (now Essex Court Chambers), suggesting a novel approach. He gave me a short, two-page written opinion saying my suggested approach was 'illusory'. So I drafted the application on my own without counsel's assistance, challenging the award on the grounds of English public policy. The essence of the argument I put forward was that the award, on the face of it, raised doubt about its legality, in that it was not based on a true legal analysis of the evidence. Therefore, it would be against English public policy to give leave in future to enforce the award as a judgement of the English court.

The matter came up before Mr Justice Evans and I instructed my old friend Michael Beloff QC. We succeeded.[8] The English court accepted our novel submissions, and Mr Justice Evans in his judgement accepted Lord Atkins's comment in a different context in the case of *Ras Behari Lal v The King – Emperor*[9] that 'finality is a good thing, but justice is better'.

---

8 Indian Oil Corporation v. Coastal (Bermuda) Ltd [1990] 2 Lloyds Rep. 407

9 Ras Behari Lal v. The King – Emperor [1933] 50 T.L.R.1

The case was another example of the importance of combining legal strategy with courage to bring success.

The Roachbank case

Although a lot of my work was linked one way or another to India, I was always open to take on work from elsewhere. But it was a surprise to be nominated by Compañía Anónima Venezolana de Navegación (CAVN), a Venezuelan state-owned shipping company, in the early 1980s, to act as their arbitrator in a case involving a ship called *Roachbank*.

Owned by the Bank Line, *Roachbank* was at the centre of a dispute linked to the liability for a delay caused by the ship's captain picking up Vietnamese refugees mid-ocean and then docking at a Taiwanese port.

I decided that I did not have sufficient experience to be an arbitrator and proposed to CAVN that they appoint my firm as solicitors, to which they agreed. I then appointed Sir Alan Mocatta, a retired judge, as an arbitrator in my place. The *Roachbank* case went up to the Court of Appeal but CAVN lost.[10] Despite this, CAVN was impressed by my firm and instructed us with many of its cases. Unfortunately, CAVN does not now exist as the Venezuelan government no longer owns shipping companies.

The Greek connection

My firm was well known in Piraeus, the centre of Greek shipping just outside Athens. George Lemos, a Greek ship owner who instructed my firm from time to time, was an Oxford graduate and son of Andreas Lemos, considered to be the father of modern Greek shipping. Andreas Lemos had worked in partnership with John

---

10 C.A.Venezolana de Navegacion v. Bank Line Ltd (the 'Roachbank') [1988] 2 Lloyd's Rep 337

Carras to build up the shipping industry in Greece. George's dispute with the Carras family concerned the splitting of the assets from the partnership after Andreas Lemos and John Carras had passed away. This claim was ultimately settled – which involved division of the ships belonging to the Lemos–Carras partnership – between the families.

Another client was Panagiotis Lemos. On recommendation of his protection and indemnity (P&I) club, Panagiotis had instructed Clifford Chance as his solicitors for a dispute concerning a vessel of his which had been delayed in discharging its cargo at the port of Calcutta. The delay had occurred at the entrance of the port, in an area called Sandheads. Clifford Chance advised Panagiotis Lemos that his company had no chance of success. Thereupon my firm was instructed by Panagiotis. I was successful in proving before the arbitration tribunal that the delay caused to the vessel at Sandheads was due to the ship's fault, not the owner's, and was thus successful in the arbitration. Panagiotis then wrote a letter to his P&I club in which he said:

> It is important to note that the original firm of solicitors we engaged, a very famous firm in London, had advised our principals that they had no case, as a result of which the P&I club withdrew their support.
>
> Our principals, however, were convinced that they were right, they engaged Zaiwalla & Co. who dealt with this case very carefully and thoroughly and, finally, they were fully successful in Arbitration and our Principals are now in the process of collecting from the Charterers.

The Louvaris case

Although maritime work was at the core of my activity in the mid-1980s, it was by no means my only source of clients in Greece.

One day, to my astonishment, I was contacted by one Professor Androulakis, known to be a top criminal counsel in Greece. He said he had come to me because of my reputation for both independence and integrity. His client was a certain Mr Louvaris, against whom there were allegations of criminal conduct in the Greek court. Notable political names were involved. There were allegations that the then Greek prime minister, Andreas Papandreou, had received a multi-million-dollar kickback in a deal concerning the purchase of Mirage planes for the Hellenic Air Force.

The Bank of Crete, owned by the Greek government, had started proceedings in the English court against several defendants, including Louvaris. They were seeking an order from the court compelling Louvaris to authorize his Swiss bank to give details of the monies in his account to the Bank of Crete. Professor Androulakis told me that because of the names involved in this dispute, he was not comfortable instructing a big firm and he had selected Zaiwalla & Co. instead.

In the High Court, Mr Justice Mummery ordered Louvaris to sign a letter of authority to his Swiss bank, United Overseas Bank. I advised my client to appeal. In the appeal, Louvaris was successful, with the *Financial Times* covering the case in its law report as 'Swiss Bank Instructions Set Aside'.[11]

Big bucks

One of the early multi-million-dollar court cases which my firm handled was in 1984 and had nothing whatsoever to do with the maritime world. It was for the Steel Authority of India,[12] against

11 Bank of Crete v. Koskotas and Others [1991] 2 Lloyds 587

12 Steel Authority of India Ltd v. Hind Metals Inc v Sail International Ltd and Steel Authority of India Ltd [1984] 1 Lloyd's Rep. 405

which an award had been made by an arbitration tribunal chaired by Elihu Lauterpacht QC, a respected Cambridge law professor. In this case, the seller Steel Authority of India sold to the buyers Hind Metals Zinc, a US company, 15,300 tons of steel sheets in coils. The steel was never shipped, and the buyers made a claim for damages against the seller.

The Steel Authority of India, a government-owned company, was represented in the arbitration case by a New Delhi law firm. The eminent counsel they had instructed was Ashoke Sen, a barrister who had held the position of minister of law and justice in the cabinet of three Indian prime ministers. The award was for over $10 million against the Indian client. Sen was very upset because it was clear that at the hearing there was a personality conflict – he and the chairman of the arbitration tribunal, Lauterpacht QC. They simply did not get along. I instructed Stewart Boyd QC and we succeeded before Mr Justice Hobhouse.[13] In his judgement, the judge ticked off Lauterpacht with the following words:

> However, the function of any tribunal is to separate the wheat from the chaff and to endeavour to arrive at a fair and just conclusion notwithstanding the lack of assistance they may be getting from one or more of the party's representatives.

God before the English Court

In the mid-1980s, the Indian high commission asked me to take over from their existing solicitors the case of retrieving Nataraja idol

---

13 Steel Authority of India vs. Hind Metals Inc [1984] 1 Lloyds Rep. 405

which had been smuggled out of India some years ago.[14] Amongst Hindus in India, Nataraja represents Siva, the almighty God.

The Nataraja idol was several hundred years old. To prevent its desecration during Islamic rule in India it was buried in the ground where it had remained for many years. In 1976, a man named Ramamoorthi, who lived in a hut near the site of a ruined Hindu temple at Pathur in the Indian state of Tamil Nadu, was excavating foundations for his new cowshed when his spade stuck a metal object. The object struck was the idol. Ramamoorthi realized that he had discovered something of value and he sold it to a dealer in religious objects. This Pathur Nataraja was in turn sold several times, eventually arriving in London via Nepal.

In June 1982, a Canadian company called Bumper Development Corporation purchased the idol, in good faith, from an auction house in London. Bumper then sent it to the British Museum for appraisal and conservation. While the Nataraja was at the British Museum it was seized by the London Metropolitan Police, in compliance with the British government's policy of returning stolen religious artefacts to their owners. Bumper brought a suit against them, seeking the return of the Nataraja. The commissioner of police then invited the Indian government to pursue the proceedings as an intervener. At the trial, the initial interveners in the court were the Indian government and the state of Tamil Nadu.

Proving the title to the idol was not easy. More difficult was the task of proving that what Bumper had purchased at auction was stolen. It therefore seemed a hopeless task for the Indian government to persuade the judge that the Nataraja idol should be returned to India.

My knowledge of Indian law came in handy. I was aware that in India a temple was a juristic personality. Further research during

14 Bumper Development Corporation Ltd v. Commissioner of Police of the Metropolis [1991] 1 WLR 1362

the trial revealed that the temple itself was a representative of the idol and therefore it must follow that the idol itself should be recognized as a juristic personality who could tell the court that he wants to return to his home in India. However, there was one big hurdle to overcome. For the idol under Indian law to be a juristic personality, it had to be consecrated. In other words, it should have been subjected to extensive religious ceremony before it attained the station of God.

After the trial began, an application was made to join the temple as well as the Nataraja itself as the third and fourth claimants. Nataraja asserted before the court that as a consecrated idol, which had assumed its status as God, he wanted to go back to his home to the temple in India. After fifty-five days of hard-fought trial, the judge granted the temple and Nataraja's wish that he had a right to go back home. Mr Justice Kennedy in his judgement said, *'The plaintiff at its maximum is God Almighty and at its minimum a mere stone.'* This was a historic judgement in many respects and my firm has since been contacted by both the Egyptian and the Greek governments as to whether on the strength of this we could assist in getting back Egyptian artefacts and the Elgin Marbles from the British Museum. My answer is certainly no because these artefacts and the marbles do not have the status of God.

Fruits of success

The standing of Zaiwalla & Co. increased steadily during the 1980s, but it was when, at the end of the decade, I went to see the new bank manager at the branch of NatWest where my firm had an account that I got to feel the firm had really 'arrived'. This was when we were occupying part of the first floor at 95A Chancery Lane and the ground floor was occupied by NatWest. It was customary for me to go and introduce myself when a new manager arrived at the branch, as was the case every three years.

When I went into the manager's office, I was surprised at the warmth and respect with which he received me. Straight away he told me that he was looking forward to meeting me because a few days before there had been a reception at the NatWest head office which was attended by the chairman, Lord Robert Alexander. When he told the chairman of his branch, he responded by saying, 'Yes, I know where that is. It is below Zaiwalla & Co. solicitors.' The bank manager was very impressed that he knew of our firm.

The tenth anniversary of the founding of Zaiwalla & Co. solicitors was celebrated with a party in 1992 hosted at the House of Lords by Lord Bruce of Donington. The guest list was considered important enough to be reported in the court and social pages of the *Times* and the *Daily Telegraph* newspapers. This reflected how far we had come and the quality of our standing in London. Included in it were many diplomats such as the ambassador of China, while among the legal and judicial stars who attended were Lord Irvine of Lairg and Lord Williams of Mostyn QC, the then chairman of the General Council of the Bar. The High Court judges who came were too numerous to name, but amongst the House of Lords judges were Lord Templeman and Lord Wilberforce.

It was a great party and this ten-year period for me was the most enjoyable of my professional life. Alongside, what was very important to me was the fun I had with my little children who were born in the early 1980s. To see them growing up was one of the best experiences I could possibly have. The good times started their decline in 1993 with the breakup of my marriage. There then followed a nightmarish twelve-year period, which I shall come to later.

4

From Side Table to High Table

Some events stand out as being of such seminal significance, either to oneself or the wider world, that their fine details remain etched forever in the memory. So it was with a dinner hosted on the night of 29 November 1991 by John Major, the British prime minister, at 10 Downing Street.

As the official residence of British PMs since 1735 and one of the most famous political buildings in the world, a sense of history looms large there. It has been occupied by almost all the great names of British politics from Robert Walpole onwards. William Pitt the Younger, Benjamin Disraeli, William Gladstone, David Lloyd George, Winston Churchill and Clement Attlee – and not to leave out Margaret Thatcher and Theresa May – have all lived at the iconic address. So, as a venue for dinners hosted by the PM, it carries great prestige and can serve as a powerful tool for getting 'the great and the good' onside. Almost whoever you are, an invitation to dinner at 10 Downing Street is something to be valued.

The dinner in question was held in the cabinet room. I was seated one place away from the PM. It was the first anniversary of his appointment after the Conservative Party had brutally ousted Margaret Thatcher from office. But what was remarkable about this particular dinner was the racial origins of the guests. Of the twenty-six people at the table, nineteen were Indian (including the sole woman attending). Given that also present were the Egyptian businessman Ashraf Marwan and two Greek shipping magnates, Adam Polemis and George Lemos (both were my clients), it meant only three of the guests were British by background – the chairman of the National Union of Conservatives, Sir Basil Feldman; the party's deputy chairman, Sir John Cope MP; and the economic minister, John Maples.

I had played a central role in organizing the dinner and for me it marked a moment when the Indian community had finally ascended to the top table of British life. It was a little less than a decade since I had opened Zaiwalla & Co. and I had cause to feel reasonably satisfied with the progress I had made. My decision to establish myself in the City of London rather than the Asian suburbs of Southall and Wembley had proved a success. In immigrant-dominated areas, black and Asian solicitors did County Court debt collection, immigration and crime. As a City solicitor I was able to do a far broader range of legal work and had been invited by the International Chamber of Commerce (ICC) to become a member of the International Court of Arbitration of the ICC in Paris.

What led to the Downing Street dinner was somewhat unusual, and the invitation came because of the Hinduja brothers. They, for their family business, had been wooing John Major as he rose through the Conservative ranks, becoming chief secretary to the Treasury and then chancellor of the exchequer in Thatcher's final government. As was their practice, in the autumn of 1990 the brothers held a Diwali party at their offices. There were around

500 guests, including the foreign secretary, Douglas Hurd, and Major himself as guest of honour. I met him there and it was to prove propitious.

A discreet dinner

A few weeks later Major became the PM and I received a phone call from Sir John Cope, whom I always found to be a fine and dependable man. He said he would like to see me at my office for a 'discreet conversation'. When he came, he told me that the Hinduja brothers wanted the PM to allow them to host a dinner for him where he could meet the Asian business community. Sir John said the PM was not very comfortable with this proposal, and so he had come to seek my thoughts on the matter. I said it would not be a good idea as it would potentially stoke jealousy in other parts of the Asian business community. A better idea, I said, would be for the PM to host the dinner himself at 10 Downing Street and invite business personalities from various communities rather than restricting the event to Indians. Sir John liked the idea but was unsure whether it would be practical. He asked me how the guests would be selected, how they could be deemed credible and who would vouch for them. I offered my services in creating and managing a suitable guest list.

The conversation with Sir John was revealing. It showed that the new government was keen to engage with minority communities, but equally that they didn't want to be taken for a ride by rich Indian businessmen with their own agendas. I was keen to underline, in an appropriately subtle way, that as an English-qualified solicitor my integrity in helping organize the event could not be questioned.

For my part, I was convinced the dinner would send a positive signal to the City of London that the British PM was prepared to meet Asians and other prominent business leaders from overseas for a serious exchange of views. I felt this would be a step in the right direction and would help open up the City of London – which was then largely still a closed shop – to the Asian community.

Within days the proposal took off. I had several meetings with both Sir John and with Sir Basil Feldman, who told me the PM liked the plan. I had always seen the need for the British establishment to truly reach out to the nascent multicultural Britain. Here was the opportunity.

I vowed to keep everything confidential and kept my word. Planning took around eight months. I took care to meet each of the invitees over lunch and obtained a promise from each of them that they would not gossip about the dinner. I warned them that if they mentioned their invitation before the event to any third party, they would promptly be dis-invited. Swraj Paul (now Lord Paul), known as a Labour Party supporter, told me over lunch at the Law Society that for personal reasons he did not wish to attend but still pledged to keep the event secret (which to his credit he did).

Looking back at that guest list, the names are fascinating. Among them were Laju Chanrai, a successful businessman who traded in textiles, edible oils and real estate. Anwar Pervez, who was worth £50 million and the owner of Bestway Cash and Carry. Manubhai Madhwani, worth £35 million, was in glass. Naresh Patel, worth £18 million, was the owner of Colorama Films. Prodip Guha was the vice chairman of Littlewoods. The one female attendee was Lakshmi Shivdasani, an Indian with interests in brewing and aluminium and the thirteenth richest woman in the UK.

In some ways, the odd one out was Vijay Mallya of United Breweries (which started Kingfisher Beer, now available in Indian restaurants in the UK) because his principal business was based in India, although he had commercial interests in the UK and his family lived there. A year or two later Tom Peet, who was in charge of Asian affairs at that time in the Conservative Party, called several times asking me to arrange a free helicopter ride for a government minister for his visits to a constituency and I would pass on the requests to Mallya who had offered his helicopter to ministers on occasions. I also recall Peet, just before the election in 1997, asking my views on the government rewarding Mallya with an honour.

Perhaps the most striking guests at the dinner hosted by the prime minister were the actor Amitabh Bachchan and his younger brother Ajitabh. I invited them partly because they were my firm's clients, but I also believed they would add some glamour to the proceedings. Amitabh was a Bollywood film star, while Ajitabh was involved in pharmaceuticals. Gopi and Prakash Hinduja were there, the family business having moved on from providing an informal banking service to the Shah of Iran's courtiers to having interests in oil and automobiles. Their wealth was estimated to be around £1 billion, making them the richest Asians in Britain and eleventh overall in the *Sunday Times* UK Rich List. The list of invitees was completed by a stockbroker, H.S. Narula, who had large interests in Libya; Narindar Saroop (of whom more later); and Dr Prem Sharma, father of Alok Sharma, who is today a Conservative MP and minister.

With fourteen Hindus round the table, it was thought appropriate to include as a guest G.D. Tandon, an expert on Hinduism, although religion did not feature in the evening's discussions. Nonetheless, his presence, and that of so many Hindus, showed how far the British establishment had come since the days of the Raj and, in particular, Winston Churchill.

Winston Churchill's 'problem' with Hindus

Back in 1945 Churchill is said to have expressed to his Downing Street aide John Colville, secretary to the cabinet Edward Bridges and air chief marshal Sir Arthur 'Bomber' Harris, head of RAF Bomber Command, that Hindus were a foul race 'protected by their pullulation from the doom that is their due'[15] and he wished Harris could send some of his surplus bombers to destroy them. During the war he also told Leo Amery, secretary of state for India and a contemporary of Churchill at Harrow School, that 'I hate Indians. They are a beastly people with a beastly religion.' Later he talked of 'Indians breeding like rabbits'.[16]

Amery's diary entry of 4 August 1944 records Churchill's reactions after the cabinet had discussed a letter to Gandhi: '… this let loose Winston in a state of great exultation … how once we had won the war there was no obligation to honour promises made at a time of difficulty, and not taken up by the Indians, and carry out a great regeneration of India based on extinguishing landlords and oppressive industrialists and uplift peasants and untouchables, probably by collectivisation on Russian lines.'[17]

This was too much for Amery, who noted: 'Naturally I lost patience and couldn't help telling him that I didn't see much difference between his outlook and Hitler's which annoyed him no little. I am by no means sure whether on this subject of India he is quite sane – there is no relation between his manner, physical and intellectual, on this theme and the equability and dominant good sense he displays on issues directly affecting the conduct of the war.'

So, at the dinner in the cabinet room at Downing Street almost fifty years later, Churchill's successor as prime minister was surrounded by the very class of Indian industrialists Churchill wanted Arthur Harris to bomb to destruction. Not only was John Major happy to dine with them, he made sure to accommodate the strict vegetarian dietary requirements of his guests. Spinach soup and potatoes were served, while for non-vegetarians there was brill.

---

15 John Colville's diary entry of 23 February 1945

16 Leo Amery: Diaries (1988) entry September 1942

17 Leo Amery: Diaries (1988) entry August 1944

A leak?

The dinner was an unqualified success. The only snag came four days later, when the supposedly private meeting made the national newspapers. Even the seating plan and menu appeared in the *Daily Telegraph*, along with mugshots of several of the guests, including me. It is said that the Hinduja brothers leaked the story and I was forced to deny that the dinner had been a fundraising exercise for the Conservative Party, telling the *Telegraph* reporter who rang me that Major did not use the occasion to seek donations, something which Laju Chanrai confirmed.

Nonetheless, the dinner provided me with a great personal boost. As chief representative of the guests, I helped the PM to the chair the evening and it was clear the PM and I had come to like each other. I found him to be a man of utmost honesty and integrity and during his years in Downing Street I used to be invited to take a table at the annual Christmas Ball in his Huntingdon constituency. When we met at events, we would always greet each other fondly, and while I never bragged about our relationship, unbeknownst to me, word quietly got around in the City and among cabinet ministers that I was a personal friend of the PM. I even started receiving invitations from British ministers to accompany them on their foreign tours.

They were not the only politicians now wanting to court me. Indian political leaders and government ministers would contact me, seeking personal meetings. V.C. Shukla, then the water resources minister, travelled to my country house in Sussex to meet me and asked me to arrange an appointment with him. Murli Deora, then an MP, and later energy minister, asked if I could set up a meeting with the PM, something I was able to do through Sir John Cope at very short notice. I also arranged for the famous godman Chandraswami to attend a brief meeting at Downing Street, the result of which was a photograph in his brochure showing him alongside Shukla and me.

On another occasion I arranged for an Indian MP named Mr Bhandari, son-in-law of the erstwhile law minister H.R. Gokhale, to meet the PM. This happened on a Sunday afternoon at the home of Shenda Amery, an internationally renowned sculptor who was a personal friend of John Major. It worked out as planned, and with Bhandari I also brought along H.D. Habib, chairman of Habibsons Bank in London, and my son Varun, who was then eight or nine.

While my personal closeness to the PM prompted Indian ministers to seek me out, this resulted in a serious downside which I had not foreseen and which I admit was an error of judgement on my part, creating a quasi-diplomatic role for me that overlapped with that of the High Commission.

One case that put me in a piquant position was my judicial decision as arbitrator in an international tribunal initiated by the Danish company Volund. The company was pursuing a multi-million dollar claim against an Indian government department over a power plant constructed under a Danish aid project to convert New Delhi's waste to energy. Volund had nominated me as their arbitrator. The principal issue at stake was whose responsibility it was to determine whether New Delhi's waste had sufficient calorific value to be used to generate power.

The Indian government nominated Judge Pathak, a former chief justice of India, who had finished his term as a judge at the International Court of Justice in The Hague, to the tribunal. Lord Mackenzie-Stuart, by then a former chief justice of the European Court of Justice, was the tribunal chairman.

After the hearing, the chairman produced a draft award that went against the Indian government. Pathak and I both initially agreed with the decision that it was the responsibility of the government to have determined this calorific value of the capital city's waste before agreeing to the construction of the plant. However, it became clear at a meeting at my office just before the award was to be published that Pathak was under pressure to change his decision. He said to me, 'I am never again going to accept an appointment as a party-appointed arbitrator.'

Out of sympathy I told Pathak that he could give a dissenting award, which would not affect the overall decision but might make his life easier. He agreed but the fact that I had preferred Mackenzie-Stuart's decision over Pathak's and my judicial decision in the international arbitration case had been unfavourable to India made me unpopular with the High Commission. Yet this was a decision I was absolutely bound to decide on the basis of evidence which had been presented.

A lasting outcome of the displeasure was that I was blacklisted by the Indian government, as per the information I have been able to glean, and remain so to this date. A decision that is particularly sad, given my contribution as a solicitor of Indian origin.

Private ambitions and public prejudice

My career has not been without such challenges. On some – thankfully rare – occasions I also faced overtly racist treatment in the City. But this was more than balanced by many supportive legal professionals, in particular the judges in the Commercial Court, who went out of their way to be courteous and helpful to me, and always did justice to my cases whenever I appeared. This was not the experience I had of industries such as insurance and maritime affairs in the City of London, where I often found supersized egos but small minds when it came to dealing with an immigrant solicitor.

In 1978 when I started my career, I would hear stories of the police rarely registering complaints from Asian or African immigrants. By the time John Major hosted that dinner in 1991, such institutional racism was rare amongst the guardians of the law. But notwithstanding the progress that had been made, it still struck me that few Indians had serious contact with the political leaders of the country. My primary goal became to help Britain evolve into a multicultural society. Unlike the United States, a country of immigrants, Britain is largely a country of natives, and I felt we Asians needed to understand this difference and gently move towards blending in with the majority community.

The other man who took the lead in making the UK's politicians aware that the Indians had arrived was Major Narindar Saroop. An ex-Air India employee, he had served in the British Indian Army in the 2nd Royal Lancers (Gardner's Horse) and Queen Victoria's own regiment, The Poona Horse. He saw himself as not just having integrated but assimilated into British culture, even cultivating a BBC-style, received pronunciation of which my father would have been proud.

I had first heard about Narindar during my years as a trainee at Stocken & Co. In the 1979 general election, he was selected by the Conservatives to fight the parliamentary constituency of Greenwich in London. After he lost to the Labour Party incumbent, Narindar used his contacts in the Conservative Party to start a private dining circle called the Durbar Club in 1981. Its aim was to introduce Conservative leaders to Asian high achievers. He invited me to be a member and I was appointed as one of his vice chairmen. Club meetings would be held at different venues, and Narindar would invite a government minister to speak. Margaret Thatcher, as PM, was a guest speaker at one club event while at another her husband Dennis addressed us.

The Durbar Club gave me great access to British political leaders, and I nurtured my contacts to give me a safety net in the event I was victimized professionally because of my Asian identity. These contacts meant that in 1983 I got to know Kenneth Baker, then Thatcher's education secretary. He introduced me to Tony Baldry MP, who was chairman of a government-supported education charity called the Prospect Trust. Ken advised that I should be appointed a director of the trust, which duly happened and led to my thirty-year ongoing personal friendship with Tony, who became a minister in Thatcher's and Major's governments.

Narindar Saroop is an excellent man with a heart of gold and helpful to anyone who seeks his assistance. But to many in the British Asian community he came over as a sort of 'Uncle Tom', so anglicized that they found it impossible to relate to him. Narindar's ambition was to be nominated to the House of Lords by the Conservative Party. With Lord Sinha of Raipur's hereditary title no longer in use, he believed there was an opening for a new Asian peer.

He was not the only one on manoeuvres. Zerbanoo Gifford, who like Narindar had fought and lost a seat in 1979, albeit for the Liberals, was aware that I was reasonably well-connected with the Conservatives, regardless of the fact that I had never been a member of the party. She wanted me to arrange a meeting for her with James Goodsman, who was then in charge of Asian affairs in the Conservative Party, indicating that she was prepared to defect if there was something in it for her.

The Conservatives knew that if they wanted to draw the Asian vote away from Labour they needed to do something significant, including appointing an Asian peer. So, I arranged a lunch for Zerbanoo with Goodsman at a Chinese restaurant in Woburn Place, near Holborn.

Zerbanoo is an eloquent, intelligent woman, and she impressed Goodsman. Unfortunately, she then mentioned to Shreela Flather, who had been the Conservative mayor of Windsor, that she had met Goodsman. Shreela duly complained about this to Prime Minister Thatcher at an event and even alleged that Zerbanoo was bad-mouthing the PM. I subsequently apologized to Goodsman for Zerbanoo's lack of discretion. Nonetheless, this scuppered any chance she had of being nominated to the Lords. Soon after, Shreela was nominated to the House of Lords by Margaret Thatcher's government and became the first Asian in modern times to get a peerage. Yet whenever I meet her at events, I get an impression she has never forgiven me for introducing Zerbanoo to Goodsman!

5

Bollywood, Bachchans and Consequential Damage

Nothing in my life matches what happened to me in the course of the early 1990s. I was happily married with two little children and had finally begun to enjoy the success which my legal training had brought me. I was something of an enigma in the English legal fraternity. I had a busy shipping and international practice with many clients from Greece and Singapore as well as India. Yet from that very satisfactory position I gradually found myself caught up in a high-profile libel case linked to the 'Bofors scandal', which turned my personal existence upside-down.

At the centre of this extraordinary set of events was one of Indian cinema's all-time stars, Amitabh Bachchan, and his businessman brother Ajitabh Bachchan – both of whom, of course, were to be guests at the dinner hosted by John Major in 10 Downing Street described earlier.

I first encountered the Bachchans in 1990, and very quickly Ajitabh and I formed a great rapport. He had a reputation as being a shy man, largely because the media compared him to his flamboyant brother Amitabh, with whom he was very close. In private, though, he was very different, and later I saw a side of him that many did not.

Both brothers were clever. Ajitabh, however, appeared to be a shrewd strategist and knew how to handle people. He had a way of getting things done. He knew how to move matters. He could keep a straight face, coming over both as convincing and innocent. He persuaded me to trust him and gave me the impression he was being honest when, for example, he said he was managing his brother's Bollywood earnings.

We developed a close relationship. He would refer to us as brothers, once even saying, 'We are like Siamese twins.' He would tell me we were joined at the 'cummar' (the Hindi word for hip) and call me 'Professor' because he said I was too straight and honest. It wasn't until much later that I would realize that while he pretended to be close to people, he was never really committed emotionally.

Amitabh, meanwhile, was a likeable character but very different from his brother. (His career was at something of a low at that time, although it was later to recover). He had a sharp memory and was always very courteous and respectful towards me. When I first met him, at the Taj Mahal Palace Hotel in Bombay – shortly after meeting Ajitabh – he was a leading Bollywood star, but I thought I ought to start the professional relationship with him on the right footing. When at that meeting he called me by my first name, I politely told him to address me as 'sir'. He accepted this was the right professional courtesy and thereafter throughout my interactions with him, he always addressed me in this way.

As we came to know each other better I was invited on several occasions by Amitabh to his home, where I met his mother and father, the latter a well-respected Indian poet. Amitabh's wife, Jaya Bachchan, was a charming lady and on one occasion she invited me to accompany her to a film centre where she was involved. She also arranged for me to have a private dinner with her and a well-known member of a leading Indian business group, the Parsi Godrej family.

But all of that was to unfold the more we became entangled together in the Bofors case.

Opening shots

The Bofors case became notorious in the 1990s (and still continues to make waves), embracing as it did accusations of bribery at the highest level against a cast of powerful and high-profile politicians and business people – including the Bachchans – across both India and Sweden.

At the heart of this long-running saga was the alleged corruption of the then Indian prime minister, Rajiv Gandhi, in respect of the purchase of field guns by the Indian Army from Bofors, the Swedish arms company and part of the Nobel Group.

In March 1986, a $285 million contract was signed between the Government of India and Bofors to supply the Indian Army with 410 firearms – 155mm state-of-the-art 'shoot-and-scoot' heavy artillery guns. A year later, a Swedish radio station claimed Bofors had paid tens of millions of dollars in kickbacks to a top Indian politician and key defence officials in order to seal the deal.

Sensationally, Prime Minister Rajiv Gandhi was suspected of personally benefitting from the bribe. The claims also included allegations that Amitabh Bachchan, a boyhood friend of Rajiv and later an MP from the Congress, had received the kickback on his behalf.

In brief, the Bofors scandal as it unfolded involved a European country, Swiss bank accounts, a Bollywood film star, politics and, above all, serious aspersions cast on the Indian prime minister. Unsurprisingly, it triggered a political earthquake in India, starting with Vishwanath Pratap Singh, finance minister and then defence minister in Rajiv's government, turning against him in a dramatic turn of events.

Singh was from Uttar Pradesh, India's largest state and the historic power base of the Congress. He had a reputation of being scrupulously honest, and while he had been a loyal party member, as finance minister he began to signal his independence through some much-publicized pursuits of tax-evading industrialists. Singh's actions made him popular with the public but not with big business, and so Rajiv moved him to the defence brief. In the event, this only escalated Rajiv's problems as Singh began investigating the Bofors deal. The consequence was they finally parted ways, and in the 1989 general election, Rajiv lost with Singh succeeding him as prime minister.

One of Singh's first steps as PM was to intensify the Indian government's investigation into the Bofors allegations, in an effort to establish that Rajiv and his friends had received the kickbacks. Singh was helped by the fact that the scandal had made headlines in Sweden. This northern European nation with an ethos of social democracy and high standards of business probity has been a beacon in the West, presenting itself as a country that not only cares for its own people but for peoples of the whole world. The affair was therefore causing appreciable damage to its previously pristine reputation.

In particular, it shocked the world that the Swedes were producing weapons of war and were prepared to grease the palms of politicians of a developing country to secure coveted defence contracts. It also unveiled the apparent use of Swiss banks as conduits in the deals. To top it all, the Swedish prime minister who had signed the deal with Rajiv Gandhi, Olof Palme, was mysteriously shot dead one night whilst jogging in the streets of Stockholm and his murderer was never found.

Getting involved

I had followed the events with interest, but only as a spectator. My role changed to an active participant when on 31 January 1990, the leading Swedish newspaper *Dagens Nyheter* ran a story entitled 'Breakthrough for Indian Bofors investigators, Gandhi's friend received the money'. It had already been reported that the alleged kickbacks had been sent to five secret Swiss bank accounts. The new story claimed Ajitabh Bachchan was the holder of a sixth account and had bought an apartment in Montreux, Switzerland with the money.

To my mind, it was Rajiv Gandhi who advised Ajitabh to get in touch with me. Rajiv and I had remained in correspondence after the success of Zaiwalla & Co., as mentioned previously. On another occasion, Rajiv had referred Sumatiben Morarjee, doyenne of the Indian shipping industry and a friend of the Gandhi family, to me for advice. Sumatiben headed India's first indigenous shipping company, Scindia Steamship, which had operated from the time of British rule of India.

With the Bachchans also being well-acquainted with the Gandhis, it was natural that Rajiv would want to help them. As an Indian lawyer in the City of London, with extensive experience of working with the Indian high commission, I was an obvious person to turn to. The task of making introductions was entrusted to Gopi Hinduja. By this time, I had ceased to be the Hindujas' lawyer. I was naturally intrigued to get a call from Gopi one morning inviting me to come for a meeting, as he wanted to introduce a new client who had some urgent business for my firm. So, I went across to his apartment and met Ajitabh Bachchan for the first time there.

The Bofors allegations had a devastating effect on the Bachchans. Amitabh had been given a Congress ticket to contest the Lok Sabha elections, but he had been forced to resign from his elected position because of public protest. Ajitabh and his wife Ramola, who were living in Geneva, had been asked to leave by the Swiss government on the basis that they were 'undesirable aliens'. The reasons hadn't been specified but Bofors must have had an impact. At our meeting, Gopi asked me to help Ajitabh sort out his family's UK immigration status – what appeared to be a fairly simple matter.

I met Amitabh in Mumbai. The brothers seemed nervous, but I told them that if the allegations were untrue, then we should start libel proceedings against the Swedish newspaper in London to clear their name. At first glance, this was a ludicrous suggestion. How, after all, could a Stockholm-based newspaper, published in Swedish, be sued in London? Surely there would be no jurisdiction in a British court over allegations made in Sweden about an Indian citizen?

However, I had thought of an innovative approach. I told the Bachchans that a suit would become feasible if we could show that at least one copy of the paper was available to read in London. My assistants trawled London's newsagents and managed to find one. Having thus secured physical evidence, on 2 March 1990 Zaiwalla & Co. issued a libel writ in the High Court.[18] The newspaper responded with an application to the court challenging the English court's jurisdiction.

The jurisdiction hearing was held before Mr Justice Davies on 25 March 1990. We had instructed the leading libel barrister Charles Grey QC, with Edward Garnier as his junior. (Garnier later became Britain's solicitor general and on his return to the Bar was instructed in 2016 by Zaiwalla & Co. in another case, when Irina Bokova, secretary general of UNESCO, sued the *Daily Mail* for libel.[19])

---

18 Bachchan v. Dagens Nyheter, No. 1990-B-1704 (HCJ) QB. 24 May 1990

19 Bokova v. Associated Newspapers Ltd [2018] EWHC 320 (QB)

Grey argued that with *Dagens Nyheter* available in London, Ajitabh had jurisdiction to file action in the English court. The Swedish daily was represented by libel litigation specialists Carter-Ruck, who were so well-known in the field that they were regularly mocked for it in the satirical magazine *Private Eye*. Their lawyers responded that in view of the fact that only a few copies had sold in London, the case should be heard in Sweden. We argued that London was widely recognized as the libel capital of the world, where, contrary to other places, justice was meted out in defamation matters. Therefore, action could be admitted even if a newspaper was not published in Britain. Mr Justice Davies was persuaded by our submission and held that the English court had jurisdiction. Suing in London had proved to be a smart move. I could see Ajitabh was impressed. Our initial success received vast press coverage in India.

Costs of involvement

As I soon discovered, however, this success in the English courts was not without its consequences. Even as I was savouring victory, a new Indian high commissioner arrived in London. The job of high commissioner to the United Kingdom is one of the most coveted in the Indian Foreign Service. When Prime Minister V.P. Singh came to power, he had appointed Kuldip Nayar, one of India's best-known journalists, to the London role. Nayar had no love for the Gandhis, having been imprisoned by Rajiv's mother, Indira, when she imposed the Emergency on the country fifteen years earlier in 1975. This was the only occasion since Indian independence that this provision was invoked.

When the new high commissioner arrived, it was normal for me as the mission's solicitor to make a courtesy call. I was therefore relaxed as I made the short journey from my office on Chancery

Lane to India House on Aldwych. On such occasions I always took another person with me, so notes could be kept of any discussions.

Initially the meeting went well. Kuldip Nayar was very friendly. He gave me tea and samosas and we talked for close to an hour. It was only towards the end that he raised concerns that I was acting for the Bachchans. 'You are a good man,' were his precise words. 'Everybody respects you. You are working so hard for India. We like you. But why are you acting for those "rogues"?' as he put it. 'We like you acting for the Indian high commission. You don't need them.' With that his tone got sharper. 'I will give you seven days to decide whether you want to act for the Bachchans or continue to work for the High Commission of India.'

Clearly, I had not anticipated the full ramifications of accepting the Bachchans as clients of my firm. At the same time, I was acutely aware that I could ill-afford to fall out with the new high commissioner. Although we had a busy and valuable practice with non-Indian clients, their work (largely involving Greek and Dubai ship owners) tended to be sometimes sporadic. By contrast, the Indian government was one of our most important long-standing clients, and this had contributed significantly to my firm's standing in the English legal profession. We had been solicitors for the high commission from 1982, every year handling about seventy to eighty shipping arbitration and other contract cases where the Indian government had accepted English arbitration to determine disputes under contract. I was aware that without this work, Zaiwalla & Co. might well lose its footing in the profession and with that its growing reputation.

I returned from this meeting reeling. The idea that the Indian high commission should dictate to me whom I should have as a client was monstrous. As a man of principle, I knew I should reject Nayar's ultimatum, but to lose the Indian government's work would be a serious blow. Choosing between the high commission and the

Bachchans was one of the most difficult and important decisions I had ever had to make.

The evening after the meeting with the new high commissioner in London, I met Ajitabh and shared my concerns. I expressed my anger but also spelt out what being sacked by the Indian government would mean for my firm. Ajitabh visibly panicked at the thought that I might decide not to work for his family. He said, 'New Delhi has confidence in you, trusts you and they don't want anybody else.' By 'New Delhi', I assumed he meant the Gandhis, although he took care never to say so. I told him I had a week to decide and he replied, 'Leave it with me. I will come back to you tomorrow.'

The next day Ajitabh came to my office as usual and told me he had discussed the situation with 'New Delhi', who said my integrity was trusted immensely and that I should say goodbye to the high commission. In return, they would set me up in a business so that I would never have to work again.

This was a stunning offer and I had to think very carefully about the matter. In the end – even though I did not seriously believe Ajitabh would deliver on his promise (more on this later) – I did eventually choose to stick with the Bachchans, but for a different reason. I had accepted instructions from the Bachchans when Rajiv Gandhi was still the prime minister. So, I considered that it would be wrong for me to drop the Bachchans as a client simply because the new regime in India disliked them.

Two or three weeks after our previous meeting the high commissioner asked me to see him again. Over tea and biscuits, I gave him my decision that I would continue to act for the brothers. They had been referred to me by Delhi and I believed it was wrong in principle for the high commission to dictate to me whom I could or could not represent. I said, 'There is no conflict. An Indian is suing a Swedish newspaper in England. You should in fact be supporting him to clear his name. Why are you instead getting upset?'

Nayar listened to me politely and told me that while it was my decision, it was a bad one. 'How can you do this to the Indian government?' he asked me. 'We have made you here.' Years later I met him again at the Delhi residence of Fali Nariman, the eminent senior advocate and my colleague at the International Court of Arbitration in Paris. When we discussed the Bachchan case, Nayar said, 'I tried to tell you to fudge it.' That was simply not true.

Looking back, I know that as a Parsi I have always had some very firm principles. Perhaps then I was even more a man of conviction than I am now; I felt strongly about the issue whatever the fallout. I returned to my office after our meeting and a week later there arrived a two-line telex from the high commission informing me my firm was no longer the Indian government's solicitors. At that point we were working on around seventy cases, including for the Central Bureau of Investigation in Delhi, but were told to drop everything, lock, stock and barrel.

I used to be a regular at the high commission's functions. Everyone at India House was friendly and I was treated with respect and a degree of importance. All the invitations stopped. I had taken a very big risk and I knew I had lost my bread-and-butter client.

Sometime later the law secretary, Dr P.C. Rao, telephoned me from Delhi saying he regretted the high commissioner's decision and asked me to continue acting for the Indian government in a major international arbitration my firm was handling for ISRO, the Indian Space Research Organization. ISRO was facing a claim of several hundred million dollars from McDonnell Douglas, an American aerospace manufacturing company, in connection with one of its space satellites, INSAT-1B. This concluded with McDonnell Douglas dropping the claim after the final hearing of international arbitration proceedings had commenced in London.

The following period was a challenging one for Zaiwalla & Co., but we managed with our few other clients.

Ajitabh later encouraged me to sue the Indian high commission as they had stopped paying my overdue fees. He said, 'Sarosh, you must not let them go, I insist you must collect.' There was a £353,000 claim, over half of which constituted counsel's fees incurred in government cases, which Zaiwalla & Co. was liable to pay. Ajitabh pushed me to lodge a court claim against the high commission and he paid me £200,000 to cover the cost of doing so. I won the case, recovered my firm's fees and in his judgement, Mr Justice Gatehouse expressly mentioned that my 'conduct was beyond reproach'.

The high commission immediately arranged to pay my outstanding fees after the judgement was obtained from the High Court. There was no appeal. I was expecting this to happen because the law ministry in Delhi had consistently told me whenever I had asked that because the payment of outstanding invoices had become political in India, it was not going to be easy to obtain it unless there was a court judgement. India has a democratic constitution and the majority of cases which clog its courts are those where the government is the defendant.

The battle commences

Meanwhile in the High Court, *Bachchans v. Dagens Nyheter* gathered speed. On 12 July 1990, we inflicted a significant defeat on the Swedes. The paper had opposed Ajitabh's application for an order that the hearing be held before the court went into summer recess on 31 July. The paper's plea was that the case must be heard in Stockholm first. The court rejected the demand and fixed a date for commencement of the libel trial.

As we prepared for it, I explained to the Bachchan brothers that libel action works the reverse of most other legal processes. Ajitabh had filed for defamation, but he was not required to prove he had received no kickbacks from Bofors. On the contrary, under English libel laws *Dagens Nyheter* had to establish their allegation was true. The paper had a track record of investigative journalism and around that period Swedish media were full of stories exposing illegal arms sales to Eastern Europe, the Middle East, Vietnam and Australia. But such investigations counted for nothing. *Dagens Nyheter* would have to come forward and show why their allegations against Ajitabh should be believed. Unlike in the United States, there was no public interest defence in libel in British courts, a law which has since changed. Had there been public interest defence, I would have had to prove the newspaper had written the article out of malice.

The Bachchans would later come up against the greater freedom Americans provide the press, but for the time being, all that was needed was for Ajitabh and Amitabh to take the stand and deny they had received any kickbacks. What they said in the witness box and how they conducted themselves was vital.

I also explained to them that the case would hinge on what the Swedes presented. Their key witness was an Indian journalist, Chitra Subramaniam Duella, then with the Indian daily the *Hindu,* later with the *Indian Express* and the *Statesman.*

Chitra had been supplied some 350 documents by Sten Lindstrom, the head of Swedish police who had investigated the Bofors allegations. The documents included payment instructions to banks, open and secret contracts, handwritten notes, minutes of meetings and an explosive diary kept by a Bofors official. Lindstrom had stumbled on them by accident when his team was searching Bofors's offices and found a set of documents with instructions to Swiss banks that the name of the recipient should be blacked out. An accountant had asked why anonymity was necessary since the payments were legal. 'Bofors was unable to explain and then we found more and more documents leading to India,' Lindstrom later recounted.[20] His decision to turn whistle-blower was a result of frustration. He said, 'I knew what I was doing when I leaked the documents. I could not count on my government, Bofors or the Government of India to get to the bottom of this.'[21] When the Bachchans' trial took place, Lindstrom had not revealed that he was the source and so *Dagens Nyheter* could not call him as a witness.

The trial was set for 19 July 1990 in court 11 of the High Court. It was clear that this was no ordinary case. From early in the morning a large crowd of Indian teenagers gathered outside in the Strand, holding up placards and jostling with each other to catch a glimpse of Amitabh Bachchan. He had flown to London to testify and face cross-examination for the sake of Ajitabh, travelling with their mother, Teji, who had once worked as an assistant to Jawaharlal Nehru, the first prime minister of India.

The London-based Indian journalists who had also gathered in force had extensively previewed the event as a real-life version of the sort of courtroom scene which often forms the climax to a Hindi film. As one put it, Amitabh's arrival was like the greatest of Indian stars lifted from the tinsel world of Bollywood into the real-life world of legal drama.

What neither the crowd nor the journalists knew was that my team and the lawyers for *Dagens Nyheter* had been hard at work to get ready for the trial. We had acquired information, which remains confidential for legal reasons, about one of the witnesses who was to give evidence for the Swedish paper. This was so damaging that it effectively made it impossible for Carter-Ruck to prove justification, which was their defence. They decided they had no choice but to

---

20 'Bofors "Deep Throat" removes veil', New Delhi: *Business Standard*, 25 April 2012

21 'Bofors arms deal: "No evidence Rajiv Gandhi took bribe"', India: BBC, 25 April 2012

settle. A clue was provided by the fact that in addition to solicitors from Carter-Ruck and their counsel David Eady, the paper's Swedish legal adviser, Peter Danowsky, had flown in to London to agree to the deal. But none of the journalists covering the story noticed this.

In a big trial we normally arrive forty-five minutes early to say hello to our opponents. It is very civil and there is no reason for it not to be. After exchanging documents and statements, you know what they are going to say, and they know what we are going to say. In legal actions these days there are no courtroom surprises of the sort you see in films or read about in Perry Mason books.

On this occasion, though, there was a surprise. At the door of the court, a Carter-Ruck solicitor approached me, and I realized the settlement was on. Amitabh and Ajitabh were next to me as we spoke; they could only communicate with Carter-Ruck through me. Carter-Ruck stated that they were willing to settle and agreed to apologize to Ajitabh in court and pay a small sum in damages.

As is standard practice when such settlements are made, a statement is read out in court which is agreed between the two sides. I inserted a comment to the effect that the allegation against the Bachchans had been made by someone close to the then prime minister of India, V.P. Singh. That was the killer point.

The insertion read, 'A remarkable feature of this case is that the defendants received the information upon which they based their story from sources close to the present Government of India.' I knew this would point the finger at Singh and help the Bachchans. It was also true.

Reporters gathered in the wood-panelled courtroom noticed I was conferring with Carter-Ruck. As an *India Today* correspondent described it, 'English and Swedish lawyers discussed strategies in conspiratorial whispers.' The truth only became clear when Judge MacPherson entered the courtroom, the crowd settled down, and David Eady, appearing for the defendant, rose to speak. The fact that he addressed the court first rather than Grey was an initial indication that something unusual was afoot. Since Ajitabh had brought the case, Grey would have been expected to open it and then let Eady respond.

Instead, and to gasps from the gallery, Eady read out an apology from *Dagens Nyheter* to Ajitabh for libelling him. He explained that this was being tendered on the authority of the newspaper's editor, Christina Jutterstrom, and its Swedish legal adviser, Peter Danowsky. The statement said that as a result of 'further information' obtained by Danowsky from Switzerland that morning, he and Jutterstrom were 'now completely satisfied that they were misled earlier this year in trusting information from persons directly involved in the investigations into the Bofors transaction on behalf of the Indian government'.

India Today would later describe Eady as offering 'an apology that amounted to an abject surrender to Ajitabh'.[22] Judge MacPherson ruled that damages be paid to Ajitabh. After an adjournment, the court reassembled to hear from Charles Grey. He said the allegations by *Dagens Nyheter* had not only caused distress to Ajitabh but 'also caused embarrassment to Rajiv Gandhi', and in order to soothe this distress Ajitabh had been awarded 'substantial' damages and costs. As is usual in such settlements, the figure I had negotiated was not specified. It is usually a reasonably modest sum, but the public were not to know that.

As the judge walked out of the chamber Amitabh fended off the hordes of autograph hunters to give his mother a huge hug. He told the gathered journalists, 'I came here looking for a fight. But this film ended with the credit titles. The Bachchan brothers have won.

22 'Swedish newspaper apologises for naming Ajitabh Bachchan in Bofors case', London: *India Today*, 15 August 1990

For four and a half years nobody believed us. Finally, the truth has come out.'

In fact, the truth about what had happened behind the scenes to force the Swedish paper to settle did not come out and never will. *India Today* reported that 'informed sources said Ajitabh's counsel submitted a report by a leading British investigative agency saying that the entire story about the sixth Swiss bank account was fabricated'. The report claimed that no one – not even the relevant Swiss magistrate – would have known exactly which accounts were frozen when the *Dagens* story appeared. The Swiss magistrate who ordered the freezing of the accounts on the basis of the Indian first information report (FIR) went on military duty the day after issuing his order and returned only three weeks later, the agency reported.

For my part, client privilege means I can never disclose the events that forced *Dagens Nyheter* to settle or the details of the 'conspiratorial whispers' in court 11 on the morning of the trial.

The triumphant Bachchans accompanied me back to my office. Amitabh had brought along with him Vir Sanghvi, a prominent Indian journalist, and gave him the story. I saw at first-hand how to manage the media. Sanghvi called editors of various newspapers all over India from my office and Amitabh gave interviews, which were plastered all over the Indian press. After that, it was a familiar ride in Ajitabh's Lexus to my home in Wimbledon, where the Bachchan brothers, Renoo and I celebrated over a happy dinner.

In New Delhi, the Bachchans' enemies did their best to put a negative spin on the story. As *India Today* reported, '... official sources admitted that the apology and the Swiss authorities' rejection of the Indian letter rogatory seeking details of those suspected to be holding numbered bank accounts with money from the Bofors pay-offs were setbacks. But they insisted that the London case was a victory against a foreign newspaper, not against the Indian government or investigative agencies [which] are still confident of a breakthrough. CBI Director Rajendra Shekhar led a team to Switzerland to deliver a new letter rogatory and has been given a free hand to hire the best lawyers.'

A second libel case followed.[23] We had decided to go after India Abroad News Service (IANS), which, like the Press Trust of India, was a wire service operating out of New York and New Delhi and reported news without comment.

At the trial, Amitabh, Ajitabh and his wife Ramola said under oath that they had been made victims by Indian prime minister V.P. Singh. The jury reached a unanimous decision in our favour and the award for damages was £110,000. However, IANS did not have the money to pay and closed its office in London. The owner was a US-based person of Indian origin and the Bachchans wanted to enforce the order and teach him a lesson. So we applied to enforce the judgement in New York,[24] hiring Chalos, Brown and English, a local law firm.

The American lawyer, Peter Skoufalas, and I appeared together in the New York Court, but in America the environment was very different to Britain. The *New York Times* and other newspapers closed ranks in opposing our application, citing the First Amendment of the US constitution to protect freedom of speech, and the defence became a matter of public interest. I could see the decks were stacked against us and after a hearing that lasted half a day we lost. There was no further libel action.

A few years later, I was invited by the governor of Maharashtra to Raj Bhavan, his palatial residence in Mumbai, for tea, and I took along my son Varun. The governor, Dr P.C. Alexander, had been the

---

23 Bachchan v. India Abroad Publications Inc., No. 1990-B-1484 [High Court of Justice, Q.B. 12 June 1991]

24 Bachchan v. India Abroad Publications Inc. 154 Misc. 2d 228, 585 N.Y.S.2d 661 (Sup. Ct. N.Y. Co.1992) [13 April 1992]

principal secretary to Indira Gandhi when she was prime minister. He knew me well because he had also been the high commissioner for India in London when I won a case for the state of Tamil Nadu in an English court. This was to facilitate the return of the Pathur Nataraja idol which the Indian government believed had been unlawfully smuggled out of India.

Over tea, the governor told me that V.P. Singh was his house guest and would like to meet me. Over three hours, I had the pleasure of meeting the man whose wrath the Bachchans had earned. I found Singh to be a sincere man. He claimed he knew nothing about his government dismissing my firm from acting for the high commission but did disclose that as finance minister, he had received a message from the Indian ambassador in Germany that a large kickback was received in the purchase of a submarine by the Indian Navy.

'I went to my prime minister,' he said, 'And Rajiv Gandhi told me to leave it with him. I accepted that, but no action was taken. Sometime later I received a message from the Indian ambassador in Stockholm that in the Bofors guns deal, another large kickback had been received by a high Indian political personality. I went back to Rajiv and he again told me to leave it with him. So, I could not keep quiet and I had to go public.'

Getting into the shipping business

After the London libel trial, Ajitabh kept his promise of finding the money to set me up in business. When he had first mentioned it months earlier, I had not taken it seriously. However, he had come back to it a few days later while driving me home (as he often did at that time, then staying with my wife and me for dinner). He asked me how much would be needed to set up a business that would provide a reasonably good income for me for life. He also asked whether I had any suitable projects that could be funded. As it happened, I did have one in mind.

Sometime earlier, I had been approached by a family friend, a Parsi called Mehernosh Khajotia, who had formerly captained merchant ships and managed Constellation Ship Management. It was the London subsidiary of the South East Asia Shipping Company, a prominent Mumbai-based shipping group owned by the Parsi family of Khushrow Dhunjeebhoy (a well-known personality even today at the Mumbai race course).

Mehernosh was a similar age to me and lived in a modest house near Hounslow with his wife Zinya and their small children. He could not have been earning a lot, but he was a good talker and a flashy character who favoured dark glasses, white trousers and coloured shirts, a garish Parsi style of dressing.

One afternoon he dropped in at my office with a personal project that he said only I could make happen. He had been working with Dadi Balsara, a rich non-resident Indian businessman, but after two years of leading Mehernosh up the garden path, he had turned him down.

The mention of Dadi made me sit up – I knew him. He was another Parsi, even more colourful a character than Mehernosh and with a personal life which read like a Bollywood screenplay. He had been the in-house astrologer at the Taj Mahal Hotel in Mumbai, where one day he read the palm of the widow of one of the richest men in Singapore. They fell in love, married and settled in the island state. When she later died, Dadi returned to India, took a suite in Delhi's Taj Mahal Hotel and from this base started various businesses, launching Himalayan water, among others. I had got to know Dadi after a dinner hosted by John Major in 1990. Dadi came to introduce himself and told me that he would like to be invited to future such high-profile events. He claimed to be one of the richest men in the world. He invited me to Singapore, and the next time I was there for a client's case he took me to lunch at a swanky restaurant. 'That is my regular seat,' he said, pointing to a chair. He always talked like that, ever out to impress with his worth and importance.

While much of Dadi's talk was bombast, I enjoyed his company and I had been fascinated to learn that Mehernosh had tried to start a business with financial support from him. And since Mehernosh did not tell me why the proposal was refused, I was curious to know what it was about and whether it would work. I had every reason to believe that despite his claims of vast fortunes, Dadi probably didn't have spare money to finance it in the first place.

Mehernosh had told me that he had been looking for $5 million from Dadi, but when he came to me he was looking for three times as much. 'Find me $15 million,' he told me. 'We will make money. You will never have to work again. I will manage it and we will share all benefits and profits I make equally.'

The plan was that we would become ship owners. We would buy old ships, hire them out and earn from freight charges. That, though, would not fetch significant profits. The big money, Mehernosh claimed, would come from selling the ships when the market went up.

Having told Mehernosh originally that I had no chance of finding that kind of money, suddenly, thanks to Ajitabh's offer, my circumstances had changed significantly – the money might be available after all. I discussed it with Ajitabh, who came back to me the next day. 'That's approved,' he said. 'You did not let us down'.

Receiving a reward for winning a case is not unheard of. The money is recorded in the firm's books and tax paid on it as applicable. So, if either Rajiv Gandhi or the Bachchans rewarded me for winning the latter's case, this would have been perfectly above board. And I was used to clients promising me future riches once a case was over, even if my experience was that these promises came to naught. (The only exception was a Pakistani rice trader who offered a $50,000 reward, and this was paid because it came as part of the $900,000 cargo damage claim settlement that came into Zaiwalla & Co.'s client account.)

Some six or eight weeks after our victory, Ajitabh came for his usual evening rendezvous at my office and said, 'Sarosh, I have told you I will keep my word. The Bachchan family thanks you for what you have done. The money has arrived.' He didn't say from where it came. He just told me, 'These are our personal funds. This $15 million is Bachchan money and we are keeping our word. You have cleared our name, our family name. We will put it in the business of your choice and you will receive the income from it.'

There was clearly a contradiction. Originally, he had told me Delhi had agreed to this money. By 'Delhi' I understood him to mean Rajiv Gandhi. If Delhi was Gandhi, then was not the $15 million also Gandhi's or the Congress party's money? In the legal action in London, the court was told the Bachchan wealth came from Bollywood and IPCA, a pharmaceutical company in India owned by the family. It did not come from Bofors. So, when Ajitabh said it was Bachchan money I did not pursue the matter. Whose money it really was would have dramatic consequences later.

At this point though, the question was not the source of the $15 million but where it would be invested. I outlined Mehernosh's project and Ajitabh's response was that it seemed fine and he requested a meeting. Once Ajitabh and Mehernosh met, sure enough the money was produced. Knowing I had no previous experience in business, Ajitabh said he would manage the business for me and I agreed. In effect, we went into a partnership. Mehernosh said he wanted 40 per cent and the rest was mine, but with Ajitabh taking the responsibility of managing my share of the business, he asked for 40 per cent in his name so that he could control Mehernosh. The result was that on paper I ended up with only a 20 per cent share; with Ajitabh becoming the de facto majority shareholder. In any case, I was not party to discussions with Mehernosh when the sharing arrangement was agreed. Besides the 40 per cent equity interest, Mehernosh's company, Constellation Ship Management, was to receive over $200,000 per month for managing our ships.

A $100 company called Delta Shipping was incorporated in the Bahamas. Dennorkse Bank, a Norwegian shipping bank with a branch in London, lent $15 million to match our investment, and the business was soon up and running. I would go for some meetings but played no active part in running the company and had no powers. I was content with this arrangement because at that time I trusted Ajitabh without any hesitation. In any case, I had no choice because the money never came to me, it went directly into Delta Shipping. Mehernosh and Ajitabh ran the business and got along very well.

Mehernosh was an energetic, pleasant person with plenty of ideas. As a qualified seagoing captain, he always had an ambition to be a ship owner and was determined to organize everything. It was just after the first Gulf War and so was the right time to buy ships as prices had fallen. The first two ships were purchased from Greek companies and the third from a Korean one. The first Greek ship, *Lokris*, cost $3.5 million and was renamed *Avon Delta,* while the second one cost $4 million and was renamed *Nile Delta*. Both were handy-size ships, able to carry around 23,000–24,000 tons. The third and much larger vessel was a Panamax costing $22 million called *Good Leader,* which became *Ganges Delta*. She could carry 100,000–120,000 tons.

As a silent partner, I was supposed to have fewer worries. It seemed all I had to do was attend dinners. Despite having made my reputation as a shipping lawyer, Delta Shipping's legal requirements were entrusted to a different law firm because Mehernosh wanted it this way and I had no objections.

A surprising turn

My first inkling that something was amiss came some months later when I got a call from Sinha Reshamwala, who had an Indian shipbroking company in London. I had always felt a bond with him, for just as I was the only Indian who owned a law firm in the City of London, Reshamwala's company, Faircastle, was the only Indian independent shipbroker.

What Sinha told me came as a shock. 'Sarosh,' he said, 'You are a rich man now. I did not realize you would do this.' When I asked him what on earth he was talking about, he said, 'I am talking about ballooning and the kickbacks you received when you bought *Lokris*. As you know, Sarosh, this is a closed market, so we know what is going on.'

'Ballooning' is when you buy a ship for a certain amount, but you tell the seller to give an invoice for a higher sum for the lending bank's purposes and you take the difference. I knew some Greeks used ballooning to secure higher bank funding. Sinha revealed that *Lokris* actually cost much less than $3.5 million, as I had been told. The implication would be that Mehernosh must have pocketed the rest.

I immediately spoke to Ajitabh, but he told me to ignore such talk. I now suspect Ajitabh knew what was going on and was a participant too. I would never have agreed to be a part of such malpractice, but then I was kept entirely in the dark and knew nothing of it. I accepted Ajitabh's advice, but soon after the $22 million vessel *Good Leader* was bought, Mehernosh acquired a palatial house in the very upmarket Virginia Water near London for £2 million (or possibly more).

He told me he had recently inherited some money from an elderly aunt in Australia, but I didn't believe him and demanded a meeting with both my business partners. Mehernosh was furious about my allegations and Ajitabh again suggested I let it be. Instead,

I put my foot down. I don't like people not being straight with me. After that I would send notes to Mehernosh asking him to tell me about Delta Shipping's transactions. He would send my letters back unopened and then stopped talking to me altogether.

In 1993 Ajitabh came to me and said it was best if legally he took over my share in Delta Shipping, so I would not have to have further dealings with Mehernosh. Perhaps I was naïve, but I had not invested any of my own money and so agreed to the proposal and retired from the partnership.

Mehernosh had proved to be a complete let down, changing diametrically once the seed money had arrived. But despite all the fuss, my relations with Ajitabh had remained strong. We were still joined at the cummar and he continued to come to my home for dinner.

Not long after, Ajitabh told me he was closing down the shipping business but that he would invest the money in London properties in our joint names and share the benefits equally. I had no option other than to believe him and said fine (although this was never to happen). I have had no communication with Ajitabh since that last meeting back in 1993. I was still under the impression it was Bachchan money. Later, I was to discover whose money it really was. For now, though, I was to learn a far more shattering truth about my marriage.

My world crumbles

Despite its turbulent start, Renoo and I had what could be termed a happy marriage. Once the children came along life was fun and we were a close-knit family. Despite being an outsider, I was achieving considerable success in the mainstream British legal profession. Renoo was a great mother to our children. We both wanted them to attend the best schools and be educated privately. So our son went to King's College School, and our daughter to Putney High. We had three or four brief holidays a year in places like Austria, Croatia, Ireland and Switzerland. Every winter we would go to India to see our parents. At our home we had a butler and an ayah, who apart from helping look after the children also did the cooking. We were very content.

Or so I thought.

In April 1992, Renoo demanded a divorce, telling me she wanted to lead an independent life. She told me she wanted me to move out of the matrimonial house. This came out of the blue for me without any prior hint or discussions. I was devastated and went into an utter state of shock. I visited a nearby church in Wimbledon by myself in those days and just sat there, not knowing what to do. I wouldn't make a scene at home with the children around. I made the mistake of never telling anyone. Although I knew so many people, I felt they were acquaintances and not the true friends I could share my pain with.

In August 1992, instead of going with the family on our annual two-week summer holiday in Austria and Croatia, I was by myself in Delhi at the Oberoi Hotel. I started suffering from a severe irregular heartbeat and I had difficulty breathing. The hotel called a doctor, who referred me to the Gupta Nursing Home, where I was given injections to attempt to stabilize my heart. Just after midnight the doctor told me that I might not survive the night and advised me to leave a note for my family. Instead I just prayed. I prayed to God to look after my children and guide them. I found I was not afraid of death. I found out how important my faith is. This was a life-changing moment. As Bahá'u'lláh, founder of the Bahá'í faith, said as his first counsel, 'Possess a pure, kindly and radiant heart, that thine may be a sovereignty ancient, imperishable and everlasting.'[25]

---

25 *The Hidden Words of Bahá'u'lláh*, Baha'i Publishing Trust, 1949

This will connect any individual with God. Religion is only a label. God is Divine energy.

In the morning the first person to visit me was Murli Deora, an Indian MP from my original home city of Mumbai, whom I had got to know well as a result of Bofors and who later became petroleum minister in Dr Manmohan Singh's government. The Oberoi had told him where I was, and he came running to see me. He also told my brothers, who came from Mumbai. The next day Amar Singh, who later became a leading politician, arranged for me to be taken to Escorts Hospital, a specialist heart centre. There I was treated by Dr Naresh Trehan, one of India's top cardiologists. I was admitted to the intensive cardiac care unit and was there for seven days. My confidence and my health both seemed shattered and I was left feeling weak and embarrassed.

When news of my divorce came out, which had become very acrimonious towards the end, those who I believed were jealous of me became a part of my ex-wife's support group, attacking me publicly and damaging the good standing I had worked so very hard to achieve. Disinformation was spread that I was having an affair with Ajitabh's wife Ramola. This was wholly untrue. I had no affairs during my marriage. It is often said that law is a jealous mistress. Once you are involved with law, there is no room for anyone else.

I became something of a recluse for some time. I would work hard at the office and stay late before going home. I bottled up my emotions, unable to shout or scream like some can. It was a horrible time. Farokh Udwadia, an eminent Mumbai-based physician and a distant relative, advised me to keep reciting the Zoroastrian prayers Ashem Vohu, which in English translates to: *In righteousness lies real happiness. It is God's finest gift. Happy is he who is righteous for righteousness sake.* I also took the advice of a cardiac consultant in London to take up transcendental meditation.

My association with the Bachchans had one more surprise in store for me. In 1997, more details finally emerged about the possible source of the $15 million. I learnt through a source close to Gopi Hinduja that the money had allegedly come from Congress party funds, which were entrusted to Ajitabh.

This means that I was lied to. I was furious. I rushed to Delhi to discuss this with Sonia Gandhi. I got to know her well only after Rajiv's death. We were introduced by Murli Deora at a party he hosted in Mumbai for Mark Tully, the legendary BBC correspondent.

I was impressed with Sonia. She spoke well, was likeable and sincere. The first time I went to call on her after Rajiv's passing away, she said, 'Rajivji had so much regard for you. He liked you very much. Rajivji was always talking very highly of you. I would like you to become a Rajiv Gandhi Foundation trustee.' When I suggested it would be better if she got somebody in India for this purpose, she was not upset, and I continued to go to her official residence at 10 Janpath to see her. But following the revelation about the source of the $15 million, this was not a social call.

When I was fighting the Bachchans' libel case, I perhaps did not appreciate quite how crucial a matter the Bofors scandal was for the Congress. It had cost Rajiv the 1989 general election. By winning the libel action and establishing that Rajiv had received no kickback, I had helped rescue the party's reputation. Most people now accepted he was innocent, and he was on the verge of returning to power in 1991 when he was assassinated. That is why Ajitabh had received the money from the party's funds to give to me as a reward. But he didn't tell me this, insisted it was Bachchan money and, of course, never gave it to me in any case. When I conveyed all this to Sonia, she was visibly upset but remained silent.

As I left 10 Janpath, I saw why Ajitabh had always tried to keep me away from Sonia, including preventing Renoo and me from attending a reception hosted by Prince Charles at St. James

Palace for her when she was visiting London after Rajiv's death. He claimed it was the high commissioner who drew up the guest list, but he wanted to stop me getting to know Sonia personally. He was keeping me away.

In the days that followed my meeting, I drew comfort that although I never did get the money Ajitabh had obtained, at least I had done the right thing in sharing the information with Sonia.

I had no intentions of punishing the Bachchans. If the source of the $15 million was corrupt political funds, then I was glad I did not receive it. Throughout my life I have firmly believed in forgiveness and to leave punishment to the universe. I was also never after easy money.

Two weeks after our meeting, I read reports,[26,27] published in India, that Sonia and the Bachchans had fallen out. It was clear to me that what I told her had led directly to her breaking relations with them.

The Bofors saga had also entangled me in a political uproar in India, with my name bandied about in Parliament. Rene Felber, the Swiss foreign minister, leaked a memo to a journalist that had been handed to him by his Indian counterpart, Madhavsinh Solanki. This note recommended to the Swiss government that it close its inquiry into the Bofors kickbacks. When this news reached India, Solanki admitted in Parliament that he was given a sealed envelope to give to Felber, but said he was unaware it contained a Bofors memo. Solanki further elaborated he was in his seat on the plane when 'a well-respected Indian lawyer in London' gave him the envelope and requested him to give it to the Swiss foreign minister.

There was a presumption in the Indian press that this lawyer was me. Naturally, the Indian parliament raised questions about the

---

26 'The B-i-G Freeze', New Delhi: *Outlook*, 8 November 2004

27 'A tale of two families', Mumbai: *Mumbai Mirror*, 23 September 2018

propriety of its foreign minister carrying a sealed envelope, without knowing its contents. I knew nothing about it. There was no way I would have got security clearance to board a plane on which I was not travelling, let alone deliver anything to anyone in it. To find my name being baselessly flung around in the Indian parliament and press was stressful and it was the kind of publicity I could do without.

The final chapter of the saga came out in Mumbai around 2010, some two decades after it had started. Mehernosh had returned to India with his family. I was visiting Mumbai when a common friend of mine, Suresh Mankad of P&I Services India, told me Mehernosh wanted to see me. It was the first time we had spoken since our acrimonious split over Delta Shipping Company. Over lunch at the Oberoi Hotel, which Mehernosh hosted, although I wasn't aware of it, Mehernosh must have known he was terminally ill. He said sorry for what had happened between us. I accepted the apology but asked what happened to the money. He told me Ajitabh had lost $500,000 of it but had kept the remaining $14.5 million. He added, 'Has Ajitabh not told you that he took back $14.5 million?'

I had cleared Ajitabh Bachchan's name, but, if what Mehernosh said was true, it was he who profited so handsomely. Meanwhile I had lost my work with the Indian government which I cherished. Now I had to start all over again.

It was China, India's northern neighbour and rival, which would help revive me and my career.

Panama Papers post-script

Perhaps significantly, Amitabh Bachchan has in 2017 faced questions on Indian television about his involvement in the Panama Papers. This episode involved the leak to the press of sensitive files containing incriminating confidential information about a number of high-profile overseas companies. This has led, among other outcomes, to the former Pakistan prime minister, Nawaz Sharif, being sent to jail consequent on information obtained in the papers by the Pakistani government. Amitabh's name featured in the Panama Papers in a way which suggested that he was involved in purchasing ocean-going vessels through Panama companies (although I am not aware of the truth of Amitabh's involvement in this). The only time Amitabh and I had a serious meeting of any sort about the Delta Shipping project was at the instance of Ajitabh, who had told me that Amitabh needed to be briefed. While on way to holiday with my family in Goa in 1992, I had stopped over in Delhi to meet Amitabh briefly to discuss the project and its profitability.

6

China Calls

My life has been marked with chance encounters, many of them producing very happy results.

Word had got out in legal circles that my firm was no longer acting for the Indian government and we had started proceedings against various of its entities to recover our outstanding invoices.

In the summer of 1991, I was invited to a lunch event in the House of Lords. I found myself sitting at the same table as Ji Chaozhu, China's ambassador to the United Kingdom. He could not have been more high-powered. Educated in the United States, he had been Chinese Prime Minister Zhou Enlai's English interpreter, accompanying him to the 1954 Geneva Conference over Indochina and on many other international trips.

For most of the next two decades, he was a close aide to Zhou. He was also a frequent interpreter for Mao Zedong, often appearing on his right on the reviewing stand at Tiananmen Square during public celebrations, when English-speaking dignitaries were present. He was the interpreter for Mao for the last two official visits with such dignitaries in 1976, just a few months before his death.

At the lunch table we got talking and exchanged business cards. I was intrigued when he read my name and immediately said, 'Yes, I know about you.' Somehow, he was aware that my firm had acted very successfully for the Indian government and that we had only recently ceased to act for them in the English court. I must also suppose he knew my name because I was quite well known for being the first non-European solicitor to establish a firm in the City of London, plus Zaiwalla & Co. had featured in many English law reports by then.

As the conversation developed I mentioned that although I loved travelling, I had never been to China. To my great surprise, the ambassador suggested I should visit China and share my experiences in order to help them get their commercial legal system going. By this time, the 'opening of China' under Deng Xiaoping had taken place and I had followed events with interest. I told him I would love to take up his invitation, and he said he would arrange a visit to Beijing.

In my early years I had never really got to know anyone Chinese well. My only contact had been as a child growing up in Bombay, when I had met a few Chinese people who ran some of the most popular restaurants. In the 1950s and 1960s when Indians, on rare occasions, ate out, they almost invariably liked to go to Chinese restaurants. There they could eat pork which was not a dish much cooked in most homes. It helped that the Chinese had tailored their cuisine to match Indian tastes.

However, having taken a keen interest in politics from the age of eight, I had closely followed the efforts by Indian politicians led by Nehru to cultivate close links with Communist China. I grew up hearing the media talk of '*Hindi-Chini bhai bhai*', or Indians and Chinese are brothers. But in the 1950s and 1960s China was isolated. The United States had refused to recognize the regime in Beijing. It was pretending that the island of Taiwan (controlled by its client Chiang Kai-shek) still represented all of China and allowed it to retain the country's seat on the UN Security Council.

Relations between China and India began to fray in 1959 when India gave the Dalai Lama refuge after he had to flee Tibet. Then in 1962 a border dispute saw China launch a devastating attack, crushing the Indian Army in a series of battles on the north-east frontier between the two countries. The China war shattered Nehru and he did not recover from it, dying less than two years later. It also had a collateral impact on my generation. Alarmed by the ease with which the Chinese had humiliated our armed forces, it was decided that all college students would have military training in a newly formed National Cadet Corps. So, for my first two years at college I spent some early mornings being drilled by sergeant majors.

My first trip to China

I didn't know whether the Chinese ambassador was serious, but a few days later I discovered he was very reliable. I received a call from the Chinese embassy inviting me to lunch. Over this, the ambassador told me he would be happy to sponsor my trip. Although he did not say exactly why, I am sure he chose me because I had the only non-white law firm in the City and because we had worked for the Indian government.

This was a very interesting break.

By this time, I was already spending a lot of time overseas for work. I would go to places where English solicitors would generally not venture. So, I was happy to spend time doing unpaid advisory work in China, meeting people and seeing in what way I could contribute in the development of an international legal system similar to that in the West.

The Chinese wanted me to spend a week in their capital. I was very busy, so I said I would go during the Christmas holidays, when the courts were closed. I went in December 1991 and the Chinese government looked after me very well. I was put up in the Beijing Hotel, where in those days guests of the state normally stayed. There was a welcome balance of meetings with tourism. I thought it would not be right for China to pay for my flights, even though they had invited me. I paid for myself to fly economy class via Hong Kong, then still a British colony. The Chinese ambassador organized everything else: meals, hotels and sight-seeing trips.

I was greeted at Beijing airport by two government officials from the China Council for Promotion of International Trade (CCPIT). They were Madam Zhu, who later became the head of CCPIT in Shanghai, and Dr Tang Jinlong, now the head of Tang Law Group in China. Both have remained my good friends over the years.

The Beijing Hotel was located very close to Tiananmen Square, which in recent years has undergone a very impressive face lift. The hotel was well-maintained with a glamorous red carpet.

Overall, this was a completely different China to what it is now. It was the old China which I had read about and seen on television. I'm so glad I saw it, as that China has gone, never to return. It has changed so rapidly that when I go today, it surprises me. Then everybody was in a blue-grey uniform and both men and women had short hair. There were millions of bicycles on the road and very few cars. There was just one make of car in any case, and it was reserved for the Chinese Communist Party officials. There was one shop where they sold English pastry.

I was in Beijing for a week while the rest of the world was celebrating Christmas. I realized that China was different to any other country I had visited before. There were no Christmas celebrations, no evidence of Christmas at all, in fact. On Christmas Day people were working as normal.

Wandering around the city one evening, I heard Western music being played and saw old people ballroom dancing in the streets. Unlike in India, there were no vagrants and the streets were clean.

The food provided a revealing insight into China in 1991. Every evening there was a banquet hosted for me where, through interpreters, they wanted to know the workings of the Western legal system. Once everyone was seated around a large round table the speeches began in Chinese, with translations for me. As soon as the food came, the Chinese, who until then had paid much attention to me, would start eating, ignoring me completely. This was because in those years they had possibly never seen that sort of expensive food before, certainly not in such quantities. I had this experience throughout my stay in Beijing during this first visit. Despite China claiming to have removed poverty, luxury food was beyond most people's ambitions.

Nowadays there are plenty of Chinese millionaires but there was no sign of them in 1991. When you went to offices there were often no tables and chairs of the kind I was used to, just Chinese-style furniture. That was the case everywhere, even in government and lawyers' offices. It was only later in the 1990s that things began changing.

I was keen to know how much they earned and found most people received only about $50–75 a month. Even the top people would get no more than $75–100 a month. The difference would be that if you were a clerk, your whole family would be in one room and use communal toilets with everyone in that building. There was a one-child policy, so families were small. If you were of a higher rank, you would have a one-bedroomed flat. If you were higher still you would have a two-bedroomed flat with your own en-suite toilet and possibly a car.

Everybody had accommodation provided by the state. Everybody had a job. Everybody was literate and there were newspaper posters which everybody read to find out what was going on in their country. There was one shop which sold goods of interest to only foreign visitors, the Friendship Store. It is still there today, although much improved. There were two types of local Yuan currencies in China then, one for the foreigners and one for the local Chinese. In the Friendship Store, only the foreigners' Chinese currency would be accepted. All the main cities had a Friendship Store and it was the only place you could buy things like butter and cheese because the Chinese were, until recently, lactose intolerant.

I had my own problems with food on this first trip because I am mostly vegetarian. I do not eat meat, fowl or shellfish. I discovered Chinese food in China is very different from what I had eaten in Bombay or London. Food was often cooked in pig fat and much of it was chicken or prawns. Later, I got to know how to order but on that first trip even if I asked for vegetarian food, they would give me Chinese sea cucumber. At the banquets I would give some excuse and eat only one or two vegetable dishes out of the countless options presented. The only McDonald's was at the opposite end of Tiananmen Square, a long walk from my hotel. I used to go and have a fish fillet there or go to the only Western hotel in Beijing at that time, The Sheraton, and have some potato chips.

Even if their cuisine caused problems, I came to admire the Chinese. It was clear to me that they genuinely wanted a long-term friendship and working relationship with me, and I wanted that too. I was touched by the enthusiastic and warm welcome I received in China at every meeting the government organized for me.

People were honest and straightforward. They were also dedicated to their jobs and would not hesitate to work long hours for their country. On my visit to see Mao's mausoleum in Tiananmen Square, I accidently dropped a bundle of Chinese renminbi. A guard came running after me with a gun round his shoulder and tapped me on mine. To my surprise, the next thing he did was to hand over the currency. I said to myself that this might not have happened in Hong Kong, India or indeed anywhere else.

It was soon evident that the Chinese government was keen to use my experience as an outsider starting a law firm in the City of London. There were only four law firms in Beijing, including one called Great Wall, and I visited them all, explaining how we operated in London. The lawyers in these Chinese firms weren't actually legally qualified but were simply PR men given the title of 'lawyer' by the Communist Party. Clifford Chance had just established an office in Beijing in cooperation with C&C law firm, another of the four Chinese firms, but their objective was simply to provide legal services to Western companies wanting to invest in China.

During my discussions with the representatives of the government I was asked many questions about the legal system in the UK and in the West generally. For the Chinese to turn to an English solicitor for advice may seem strange. By the time I went, the Americans should have been well ensconced in China. Nixon's visit to China in 1972 saw America finally recognize the communist regime. American engineers certainly came. Yet over the next twenty years, American legal firms failed to set up shop and this worked in my favour.

For me, this visit was a memorable one. The Chinese were very courteous towards me and were tremendous hosts. I soon realized that they respected me as being of Indian origin and made this clear to me, time and again. China as a whole seemed to respect India as one of the great ancient civilizations. If you go to the Summer Palace and see the paintings of Buddha and his disciples, you can see a link between the cultures of India and China.

I had been concerned that my Indian background might have been a hindrance. But during my trip I realized that China had invited me to their country for an informal consultation precisely because I had over ten years' experience of working for India. The

India–China dispute was completely irrelevant. It didn't affect me at all.

Having travelled worldwide, I have found China is the only country where an Indian is not discriminated against. A white man is favoured to an Indian man in most countries. The Chinese word for a white man is 'devil'. In the Middle East if you have a white assistant, they will salaam to him, pay respects to him. In Kuwait, you may have a British passport but if you're born in India there's still a police check. I later went to Kuwait on a Chinese international arbitration case matter and despite having a British passport I had to wait for the police check to come through at airport immigration. I was made to wait in a room for fifteen to twenty minutes before I was allowed in. I had been there two or three times before. Every time I found Indians and Pakistanis were badly treated. Even in Hong Kong, between a white man and a brown man the Hong Kong Chinese will defer to the white man because of their colonial past. But in China I found that everybody trusted Indians and said enthusiastically, 'Indu, Indu.' Even cycle rickshaw drivers called me 'Indu' with a smile.

Setting up in Beijing

By the end of my first visit, the Chinese assured me of government support if I were to start a Beijing branch of Zaiwalla & Co. I wasn't very sure that I should, chiefly because I felt I couldn't afford it. Although the firm was doing well, our main work was in shipping and the Indian government had just ceased to be our client. But then on my return to London, the Chinese embassy informed me that they would like to use my firm's services in London. My firm then opened an associate office in Beijing towards the end of 1993.

What I came to realize was that the Chinese trusted the Indians. I was made particularly aware of how my Indian origin eased things for me in 1995, when Jiang Zemin (then the general secretary of the Communist Party, effectively the executive head of the government) came to London. During his visit, I was called to the embassy and introduced to him by the Chinese ambassador, Ma Yuzhen. He told Jiang Zemin that I was representing China in the UK arbitration cases, and Jiang Zemin said to me in English, 'I'm glad you're representing China, that an Asian is representing China.'

During our conversation, the Chinese leader also told me, 'China does not want to dominate the western countries, but China wants to be treated with respect.' I asked which three countries he considered most important and powerful. He named the United Kingdom as one, besides the US and Japan. I asked why the UK, and what about Germany? His answer was, 'Major decisions are taken by the UK in Whitehall and then executed by the USA.' In other words, British mind and American muscle. I was also surprised that he could speak English at all, albeit slowly.

Our Beijing office was run by a Chinese man, Professor Sung. It was quite expensive buying computers and all those things, but I could see the potential for work and decided to invest the money. My faith in the Chinese was justified because from the start they gave me high-quality legal work.

I started going to China fairly regularly from the autumn of 1992, and over the next ten years I must have gone over sixty times.

At the height of my professional activity in China I would travel about once or twice a month. The Chinese would call me there for meetings because they wouldn't send people to London except for the arbitration hearing. They took care of the airfare and the British Airways staff at Beijing airport got to know me very well. I would stay for a week and then come back.

I was making so many journeys that in 1994 I rented a serviced flat in the Asia Pacific building in Beijing at Ya Balo near the diplomatic area. All the residents were from overseas and it was a short walking distance from Tiananmen Square. It was not expensive and there was a shop in the apartment block. As if to make me feel more at home, on the ground floor was an Indian restaurant called Omar Khayyam run by a Singaporean Indian who had a photograph of Satya Sai Baba, a venerated Indian saint. There was also a restaurant called Taj Pavilion started by a Parsi from Dadar, Mumbai named Mehernosh Marfatia. He now has a Chinese wife and a son called Kersi, a Parsi name.

Supporting UK trade missions

My standing in China was also helped by my friendship with John Major and my contacts with the higher reaches of the ruling Conservative Party. Suddenly I was not just any old solicitor but a British solicitor of Asian origin who had access to the high table of British politics.

This became evident in October 1994 when I was invited to be part of the British team the trade minister, Sir Richard Needham, was taking to China. I had got to know Needham quite well, and he very kindly came to my office for a chat over tea, even when he ceased to be a minister. I went on about four or five of his official trips to India, including one on the Concorde, the only time the famous aircraft flew there, and stayed for six days in India visiting Calcutta, Madras, Bombay and Delhi.

On this occasion Sir Richard phoned me up and said, 'Sorry, Sarosh, the trip is cancelled because of some problems in Hong Kong. The Chinese have cancelled it.' The official reason given was China's inability to agree on dates. But when I asked the Chinese ambassador in London, he confirmed what Needham had said but added that the British were behaving badly.

What had upset the Chinese was what Chris Patten was doing as governor of Hong Kong. A close political ally of John Major, Patten had played a crucial role in the 1992 election and was earmarked to become chancellor of the exchequer after it. In his autobiography written after he lost the 1997 election to Tony Blair, Major describes how during the 1992 election Patten was 'a rock of calm in a tempestuous sea' and told Major, 'I'm here to fall on my sword on your behalf, prime minister.' Though Major won unexpectedly in 1992, Patten lost his Bath parliamentary seat. He turned down a peerage and Major offered him the governorship of Hong Kong to oversee the British colony's handover to China in 1997.

Patten decided he would spend the last years of British rule in Hong Kong bringing democracy to the island. The local Chinese in Hong Kong rather liked Patten's reforms but the mainland Chinese – having noted that the British had done nothing to promote democracy in the previous 150 years they had owned the colony – were not pleased. They saw it as the British living up to their reputation of being 'perfidious Albion'. Beijing's mood could be seen in the Chinese media. They called Patten by colourful names such as 'strutting prostitute',[28] 'tango dance', 'serpent' and 'triple violator'.

By now I was well versed in working for Chinese state clients and quickly sensed I could act as a facilitator. I told Ma Yuzhen, I could speak to John Major's colleagues about this and he was happy for me to try.

The Chinese concern was that Patten was trying to sabotage the handover. China also suspected the British believed Thatcher had undersold Hong Kong, although I was told by the British side that the suspicion was unwarranted. With the support of the new Chinese

---

28 'Holding Out in Hong Kong', Hong Kong: ChinaFile, 12 June 1997

ambassador, Ma Yuzhen, I arranged for a meeting at my offices at 33 Chancery Lane. At this meeting, 10 Downing Street was represented by Lord Feldman, who at that time was the chairman of the National Union of Conservatives, and Lord Hesketh, the leader of the House of Lords and a close confidant of John Major. The Chinese side was represented by Ma Yuzhen and another person. The meeting went on for two or three hours, I had ordered sandwiches but both sides said they preferred just fruit.

There were polite but very frank discussions. Without any bureaucrats present, everybody could speak freely. The Chinese were under the impression that Britain was backtracking on the agreement and didn't want to give up Hong Kong, and that was the reason why it was creating trouble by introducing democracy to the colony. They received an assurance from the British side that this was not the case. So it was that over fruit in my office, a second channel of communication was established between Britain and China. At the end of it they agreed they would carry on direct, high-level conversations to remove any misunderstanding relating to the Hong Kong handover.

The secret second-channel talks clearly went well for in May 1995, Michael Heseltine, president of the Board of Trade in the British government, made the first cabinet-level visit to China in three years. I was invited to join Heseltine as part of his ministerial accompanying delegation. He went as the head of what was described as the biggest British trade mission to that country, hoping to improve Sino–British relations and help reduce the £800 million trade deficit with China.

As with all such trips, several contracts had been lined up to be announced during Heseltine's week-long visit, including a $100 million joint venture by Bass to expand its brewing interests and a telecom deal by the British company, GPT. Beijing in turn was keen to give the impression that it had drawn a line under the row over Hong Kong's political future and trade matters. The fact that Heseltine would meet Li Peng, the Chinese prime minister, was seen as significant.

In the year preceding this there had been trade missions to China by the US, Germany, France and Canada, during which claims had been made that billions of dollars' worth of contracts, joint ventures and letters of intent had been signed. Compared to that, the British trade mission to Beijing, Shanghai and Guangzhou was a low-key affair. However, UK's investment of $578 million in China by the end of 1993 headed the European league, with more than 600 British joint ventures in China.

Heseltine was keen to persuade the Chinese government to allow the British to open a consulate in the southern city of Guangzhou, mainly to handle trade matters. The British had first suggested this in July 1994, but with Hong Kong creating a problem it was still 'under study' by Beijing. Heseltine also had 150 businessmen in tow representing companies like British Gas, Lucas, Rolls-Royce, British Telecommunications and a string of other big organizations across all sectors of industry. One of the 150 was my firm, Zaiwalla & Co.

It was a great experience to be there. It gave me an immense standing in the legal and high-level business world. Heseltine took a 747 Jumbo Jet with business-class seats only and the British flag on it. At the start of the day he would say 'Good morning, stars', by which he meant stars of the UK. We were from all over the UK. If I was perhaps the only lawyer there, I was certainly the only brown face. This wasn't about diversity. I was on the trip because I was close to the British prime minister and the Chinese government was my client.

If Michael Heseltine was happy to have me there as part of the British team, Sir Leonard Appleyard, the British ambassador to China, did not give the same impression. My suspicions were increased by a bad experience I had in Shanghai. We were travelling from there to Hong Kong. Heseltine was going to meet us there as we were told he was taking a helicopter ride to meet the president of China, who was returning from Africa. We were staying in a big hotel in Shanghai. On this trip we travelled in a large convoy of twenty or more cars, with local police outriders. Before we left the hotel, I told the British embassy staff I was going to get something from the hotel lobby. By the time I returned, by an unfortunate oversight the convoy had set off without me. I had to call on all my customary determination and resourcefulness to get myself to the airport on time.

I was in a panic. The British embassy had my passport. As this was an official trip, we did not have any visa problems; the British Embassy staff, with the help of airport security, would just escort us into the VIP lounge and whisk us through passport controls and customs. But now I was stranded and the manager of the hotel realized I was worried about how I would get to the airport. I didn't know anybody in Shanghai. I said I would take a cab, but he said, 'You'll never make it, sir. Your flight is scheduled to leave in one hour and there are millions of bicycles on the road.'

Fortunately, the day before at the official dinner there were British and Chinese flags on the tables. I'd been given permission to take two of them with me as a souvenir. I also had with me the brochure produced for the trip. It featured pictures of Heseltine and all the delegates, including me. I told the taxi driver I would hold the flag and the brochure out of the cab window to make it look like I was an official and as I did so he honked his horn regularly and drove at full speed.

We made it to the airport, but I immediately faced more problems. I couldn't speak Chinese and I didn't know the whereabouts of the VIP terminal where our plane had landed. I went into the main terminal and walked to the immigration counter. I tried to look very confident and when the officer said, 'Passport?' I said, 'No passport,' and showed them the brochure with my photograph. They shouted, 'Identity, identity!' but I had no way of responding. Then they called the security head who could speak a little English. He said, 'Give me something, some identity.' I remembered I had a London Royal Automobile Club plastic membership card with me, so I gave it to him. Incredibly, this proved enough for me to exit immigration. They phoned ahead and the jumbo was still there; the airport authorities immediately drove me to the VIP terminal before it left.

If the British travel arrangements had caused me problems, I had also caused a problem for the Mayor of Shanghai on this trip. He was hosting a dinner reception for Heseltine and his team. A short, slight man, we were introduced to him in a queue and shook hands. Michael Heseltine was first, I was after him. I always shake hands with a firm grip and as I did so, the Mayor fell down. On my second visit with Michael Heseltine the following year, the same mayor was there and, unsurprisingly maybe, they all remembered me.

This second visit took place in May 1996 and on this occasion, we faced competition from a rival English attraction. The English football team was due to play China in the coming week at the Workers' Stadium, and demand for tickets was high.

This trade mission was billed as the biggest ever, with about 180 leading British businessmen (and, according to the mission brochure, a grand total of two businesswomen). It was just thirteen months before Hong Kong's sovereignty reverted to China, and the British were keen to portray the visit as a success.

For me, one of the many accompanying Heseltine, the greatest honour I received was when we were staying in the China World Hotel. It was a rather stylish modern hotel and we reached it at night. The next morning, Ma Yuzhen, who had retired as an ambassador and become the vice foreign minister, came in his official flagged car, and said he wanted to meet one of the delegation members – me! We talked for half an hour and he also introduced a local client to me.

On this second trip I mentioned to Heseltine what I perceived to be the British ambassador's somewhat unfriendly attitude towards me on their previous visit. Sir Leonard Appleyard was still the ambassador, and so Heseltine went out of his way to include me and make me feel important. The ambassador gave a dinner for a few people at his home and I was invited. Heseltine even ensured the seating plan changed so I was next to Sir Leonard, whom I found to be a very pleasant person.

The Chinese way to work

What struck me from my time in Beijing was how hard the Chinese worked. When I travelled there it was usually for short trips, so we used to work till two in the morning. The Chinese staff in clients' offices never complained. We used to get takeaway food and eat it while working. In one arbitration case in the mid-1990s, I needed some documents regarding an event which had taken place five or six years before. I asked for them very late and was told they were in storage. But by 7 a.m. the next day they were delivered to my hotel. This would rarely or never happen in most countries. Perhaps because of the strong political leadership the Chinese can move quickly. If I told the right person, things happened.

The Chinese didn't know the western world, but they were willing to learn. If Indians don't know something, they still sometimes pretend to know, whereas the Chinese will confess their ignorance and say that they want to learn.

I always found the Chinese to be very good hosts. They continued to take my informal advice on how to make China more attractive for foreign inward investment. When I first went to China the companies were almost all completely government-controlled. They wanted to set up western-style companies but didn't want domination by the West. My advice was to allow western law firms to come in but make sure that 50 per cent of the firm is Chinese-controlled because the aim should be to educate the locals.

I learnt that when the Chinese meet a foreigner for business, they always come in a team of five or six, sometimes even more. Only one or two would speak English and outsiders could easily make the mistake of assuming those individuals were the ones in charge. The Chinese business culture was to negotiate hard but once an agreement was reached and sealed, they would always keep their commitment. Oral agreements were not considered binding and would be treated just as a step for further negotiations. However, the placing of a company's seal along with the signature was most important to make an agreement binding.

The Chinese give absolute priority to their national interest. The best example of this was when we were acting for China National Petroleum Corporation in their legal dispute against LG-Caltex of South Korea. This was an oil and gas project and I discovered the Chinese had three levels of engineers working on it. The top level consisted of American and British, the second layer Chinese Americans and the third layer local Chinese.

One of these engineers, a Chinese American from Texas, told me, 'Sarosh, remember that you are in China and while they need you, you'll be fine. Once they don't need you, you will be out. You just wait and see. They will learn from you how to do things and once they do, you won't last. The first layer to go will be the whites because they are the experts. The second layer is people like me, Chinese-American, here to teach the Chinese. Once I've taught them, I will be out. They'll only do that when the local Chinese are able to learn the job.'

In my ten years working in China I was to discover he was spot on. The Chinese called me to work for them because they wanted to learn from me. I see nothing wrong with that. This was a very practical approach. They called me 'law master' and still when I go to China, they host a banquet for me.

Once they had learnt from me, the work slowed down. I have no regrets about this. It was a great honour and privilege that the Chinese government trusted me and made me a part of their team.

In 1991 China had a Communist Party legal system, which was not capable of functioning for international purposes. So, during the second half of the 1990s, they started developing a legal system which the world could understand. The Chinese then started sending their students to study law at top international universities and by the early 2000s they were returning as qualified lawyers. My experience in the 1990s was that if you want justice in China, it depends on how much they need you. If you are needed, the courts will decide in your favour. If not, you are on your own. I did not experience any corruption but there were subtler forms of state control.

Working in China made me aware of the contrast between the two giants of Asia. Indians carry a tremendous amount of colonial baggage. They had been conquered and ruled by a foreign power from thousands of miles away. The Chinese suffered humiliations at the hands of the same European powers, but they were never conquered or ordered to learn English.

In one respect, Indians and Chinese are similar. Both are very vocal when they get angry, shouting and screaming. We used one Chinese lawyer in an arbitration my firm was handling for the China National Petroleum Corporation (CNPC) and the China Petroleum Technology Development Corporation (CPTDC). He was sitting at the table talking with one of my client's Chinese team. Suddenly they started shouting at each other and he stormed out of the room, slamming the door – which then fell down. This was not untypical.

Key cases

My work involved major international arbitrations, six of them from Beijing-based corporations and one from Shanghai. All the cases were difficult, but we won or substantially won them all for our Chinese clients.

The first instruction my firm received from the Chinese government was to act for China Petroleum Engineering & Construction Corporation (CPECC) in an arbitration in London. The dispute had arisen from a contract CPECC had obtained from the Kuwait Oil Corporation. Interestingly, a political friend close to 10 Downing Street told me that this contract was brokered by Downing Street in exchange for China not exercising its veto in the UN Security Council over the US liberation of Kuwait in 1991. I learnt from this that the Chinese government was willing to adopt practical approaches with other countries but that it would expect to get something back if it gave anything up.

The CPECC project was in the wake of the first Iraq war and involved the construction of a gathering station for the Kuwait Oil Corporation by CPECC. It had led to a dispute with an engineering company, Cummins. The arbitration went on for a year or two and CPECC was partially successful. The Chinese government was happy with my firm's services and more work followed.

On one of my many visits to Beijing while acting for CPECC, I was told that the Chinese government had another large ongoing London international arbitration. They had appointed one of London's biggest law firms, Linklaters, to act for CNPC (whose chairman is always China's petroleum minister). In this arbitration CNPC was defending a claim of around $300 million, brought by LG-Caltex over the construction of a gas tank in Maoming. Midway, CNPC decided to transfer this international arbitration case from Linklaters to my firm. It was to turn into my biggest case for the

Chinese – a multi-million-dollar joint venture, and my client was facing a claim for damages.

The case, as the English Court of Appeal judges pointed out, raised 'new and important points in relation to Sections 67 and 73 of the Arbitration Act 1996'[29] and it was to go, ultimately, to the House of Lords (the UK's apex court at that time) for judgement. Our immediate task was to express concern over whether the sole arbitrator appointed by the parties, Bruce Harris, could properly continue. The Chinese side had lost confidence in Harris because of the manner in which he had been making procedural orders. They believed he was a qualified lawyer when they gave their consent to him being appointed because his CV stated that he had worked at the London law firm Richards Butler (now merged with Reed Smith).

When they learnt that Harris was not a qualified lawyer but had worked only as a legal executive at Richards Butler, they were concerned. My first instruction was to apply to the English court for his removal. The hearing came up before Mr Justice Mance, who refused the application on the grounds that the application ought to have been made at an earlier stage. Nonetheless after hearing this, Harris changed his CV, deleting references to him having worked at Richards Butler.

There followed a two-week hearing before Harris, who made an award dismissing the claim on the grounds that he had no jurisdiction. The Chinese team in Beijing were delighted. The claimant, represented by Holman Fenwick and Willan, another well-respected solicitors' firm, challenged the arbitration award

---

29 LG Caltex Gas Co Ltd v. China National Petroleum Corp Contigroup Companies Inc (formerly Continental Grain Co) v. China Petroleum Technology & Development Corp [2001] EWCA Civ 788

dismissing the claim. The case then went before Mr Justice Atkins in the Commercial Court on a jurisdictional point and we won.[30]

LG-Caltex appealed this judgement and their appeal was successful. We applied to the House of Lords for leave to appeal but it was refused. This meant the claimant – and the claim – could start all over again. But in the meantime, LG-Caltex had also started another arbitration for the same claim before a different arbitration tribunal under a different chain of contract relating to the same project. This meant that the Chinese party had to defend the claim before a different tribunal. This went on for some time and after the arbitration hearing was completed, the arbitration tribunal took more than six months to produce its decision. In the meantime, both parties sensibly decided to resolve the dispute.

My one concern was my firm was owed money from CNPC for the LG-Caltex arbitration. There was an outstanding invoice of around £350,000, including about £180,000 in counsel's fees. The claim that the China Petroleum Technology & Development Corporation (CPTDC), CNPC's subsidiary, was defending had been settled amicably between the parties, but my Chinese clients were unhappy that after winning, the claimant could start another arbitration for the same claim. At this time, an unfortunate event in my London office involving a colleague who had misappropriated large funds from the firm's bank account had led to a financial crisis for Zaiwalla & Co, of which more later. This meant I had to close the Beijing office.

With no funds to continue, I had no option but to tell my clients about my firm's financial difficulties. I was honest, telling them I was going to downsize the firm and they should consider going

30 LG Caltex Gas Co Ltd v. China National Petroleum Corp Contigroup Companies Inc (formerly Continental Grain Co) v. China Petroleum Technology & Development Corp [2001] 1 WLUK 403

elsewhere. At this point the Chinese clients decided that they did not need to pay my invoice. Maybe they thought the firm might not survive and so there was no need to pay.

I decided that the only way to get CPTDC to pay up would be to go to China. I made three journeys to Beijing to do so, paying for each trip myself. My plan was to see my Chinese clients face to face. With the help of Steve Buckley, minister counsellor at the British embassy in Beijing, I met the Chinese deputy minister for commerce about recovering my firm's unpaid fees.

On each of my visits the Chinese client met me with utmost courtesy and friendliness but made no commitment to make payment. Whenever I wrote to them, it was met with no response.

Then I read in the *Times* that the Chinese prime minister, Wen Jiabao, was coming to London. Tony Blair was the British prime minister then, so I wrote a personal letter to him with a copy to his wife, Cherie, whom I had known professionally for many years. I pointed out that his election manifesto said he would support small- and medium-sized businesses, and asked if he could intervene with the Chinese prime minister about my firm's unpaid invoice.

The official reply from 10 Downing Street said it was a private matter and the PM couldn't help. I wrote back to Cherie Blair and said I was disappointed with the prime minister's reply to my request. To my surprise, I then received a very short-notice invitation to an official banquet being given in honour of Wen Jia Bao. This was typical of Tony and Cherie Blair's kindness and understanding shown to me over the years.

I accepted and donned my black tie in good heart, but when I arrived I realized I was on a fairly remote table, far from the senior politicians. Thankfully the British ambassador to China, Sir Christopher Hum, a lovely man, came to my rescue during a break and said, 'Mr Zaiwalla, I understand that you have a problem you want to discuss with the prime minister?' I immediately understood what was intended.

He took me straight to the Chinese PM, where Sir Christopher said, 'Prime Minister, this is Mr Zaiwalla, he's a friend of our prime minister. He wants to talk to you.' With these words, he left, and Wen Jia Bao and I spoke for a while through interpreters. He told me that he knew of our firm. I explained how my firm had saved CNPC and CPTDC from a substantial part of the claim against them and I had not been paid for my legal services. I said, 'Do you mind if I send you a copy of the outstanding invoice?' He agreed to receive it, and so the next morning I personally delivered my firm's outstanding invoice to his hotel, The Mandarin in Knightsbridge.

The very next week I got a call from my client in Beijing asking to see me about the invoice. They duly paid, although I was happy to negotiate a discount to maintain good relations. For the Chinese, keeping face is important, and as over the years we had undertaken almost £3 million worth of work for them, a reasonable deal seemed in order.

My ten-year involvement with the Chinese was a good and enjoyable experience. My firm during this period was instructed by many Chinese state-owned clients, including Bank of China; Minmetals, a minerals and metals trading company headquartered in Beijing, and COSCO, the Chinese shipping company. When the vice chairman of the Bank of China was in London, I was honoured that she visited my firm for a lunch appointment with me. With the one exception, Chinese government clients always paid the bills promptly. They had widened my horizons enormously.

India–China relations

While acting for China, I got to travel and visit various cities across the country while tracking down evidence for my clients. My great regret was that the Indian government did not take up an offer that the Chinese made through me to have back-channel talks to solve their long-standing border dispute.

Following my success as a facilitator over the Hong Kong issue, the Chinese ambassador in London, Ma Zhengang, suggested we do the same thing with India. This meant setting up a second-channel, confidential meeting between the political leaders in China and India to find a practical resolution at a senior level to settle the border dispute.

'We can produce evidence that there are no minerals or anything in the Himalayan territory which China claims,' the ambassador told me. He added, 'What we want is a proper borderline to be drawn between the countries. China wants the original border of Tibet to be the border with India. The line drawn by the British Raj as the border between Tibet and India cannot be considered the proper border. We are not claiming any Indian territory but what is Tibet should come back to us.'

I had several meetings with him and he provided me with a lot of documents. Subsequently, he and I prepared a detailed note to be passed through me to the then Indian foreign minister, Jaswant Singh.

The ambassador reiterated the Chinese position that the India–Tibet border originally drawn by Henry McMahon, the then foreign secretary of British India, and signed by him and Lonchen Satra on behalf of the Tibetan government at the 1914 Simla Convention, was unacceptable. While India regards the McMahon Line as a legal national border, China rejects it and the Simla Accord. It contends that Tibet was not a sovereign state and therefore did not have the power to conclude treaties. Chinese forces briefly occupied this area during the Sino–Indian War of 1962.

However, according to a 1959 diplomatic note signed by Zhou Enlai, the former Chinese prime minister, China does recognize a

Line of Actual Control that closely approximates to most of the McMahon Line along the eastern side of its border with India.

I told the Chinese ambassador that for India to part with any territory would not be acceptable for the Indian people, especially after the 1962 border war. I also brought to his attention the fact that at the time the border as drawn by McMahon was agreed by Tibet and India, Tibet had a government. Therefore, there had been a legal and binding acceptance by Tibet and India of the location of the border. This, in turn, would be binding on China. In my conversations with him, the ambassador accepted that all these points could be discussed.

One issue that I specifically raised was the possibility of the Chinese leasing to India a corridor passing through their territory. This would enable Indian pilgrims to visit the Hindu pilgrimage sites in China at Mansarovar and Kailash. The ambassador indicated that it could also be discussed in exchange for India ceding some of its territory in the Himalayan mountains, where no one lived and there was no evidence of any mineral deposits. He said China would enter into settlement discussions with an open mind.

I gave the note which I had prepared, with the ambassador's input and approval, to Maneka Gandhi, who confirmed to me that she had passed it on to Jaswant Singh. (As it happens, Maneka was at that time my client and had been a minister in the Vajpayee government. Maneka was suing Katherine Frank and her publishers about allegations of sexual impropriety by her late husband Sanjay Gandhi in a book about Indira Gandhi. We settled it in Maneka's favour and they paid the costs. The book was withdrawn, re-edited and reissued.[31])

---

31 'Maneka Gandhi wins suit against author, publisher of *Indira: The Life of Indira Nehru Gandhi*', London: *India Today*, 31 December 2001

When I met Jaswant Singh at an event in the Washington Hotel in London a few months later, he said to me airily, 'I have given your note to my department to consider.' Nothing happened. Had the Indian government taken this seriously, China would have had to respond, and they could have resolved the matter. For China in those days the focus was on economic development and not military might. Full employment for its population was the order of the day, and I did believe China was genuinely keen on sorting out the border dispute with India and with that entering the Indian market.

One of the benefits that emerged from my friendship with China was that their subsequent ambassador in London, Ma Zhengang, encouraged me to start an Asian Business Breakfast Club with the aim of encouraging the formation of an Asian Economic Union, similar to the European Union. The inaugural planning meeting was held at the Savoy Hotel, which the ambassador, Tony Baldry MP and I attended. Baldry and I then started the Asian Business Breakfast Club as joint conveners.

With the assistance of the business group London First, we would invite around forty-eight guests. The breakfast would usually be held in the members' dining room at the House of Commons. I would invite half of the guests and London First would invite the other half. We would usually find a sponsor to cover the cost of the breakfast events. The Chinese ambassador sponsored a breakfast event at his embassy and so did the Malaysian ambassador at his. At my request, Bloomberg Television hosted and internationally televised a breakfast for the then Mongolian prime minister, Rinchinnyamyn Amarjargal, when he visited London. (Amarjargal is still in the Mongolian parliament and a leading member of the Democratic Party.) This started my Mongolian connection.

The Mongolian affair

At the beginning, I used to travel to Mongolia via China, but now I fly there from Berlin on Mongolian Airlines. Mongolia is very different to China. What impresses me is that the Mongolian language uses a lot of Sanskrit words. My general impression is that the Chinese are a little tense whereas in Mongolia everybody appears to smile and is much more relaxed. Mongolians are also much more spiritual.

In 2015 I was invited by Puntsag Tsagaan, chief of staff to the president of Mongolia, to travel to Ulan Bator. He told me Mongolia had a difficult case on which they had consulted many local and international lawyers. The general advice had been that the case was not possible to pursue because the debtor company had been dissolved and the claim was seventeen years old. They were up against a wall.

On the day I arrived in Ulan Bator, Tsagaan invited me for dinner with the general director of Erdenet Mining Corporation, which owns one of the world's largest copper mines. Erdenet was 51 per cent owned by Mongolia and 49 per cent by Russia. It had a claim against Kazakhstan for $20 million. This arose from a deal involving the shipment of copper ore to that value to a government-owned Kazakhstani company, which would then return the copper in rods to Erdenet after processing. However, after receiving the copper ore, the rods never came back to Erdenet because the company was privatized and taken over by the son-in-law of the president of Kazakhstan, who had since passed away. For several years the Mongolian government used diplomatic channels to press Kazakhstan to pay Erdenet's claim. No settlement resulted.

On the second day of my visit I met Erdenet's team at its offices, including its chief in-house counsel, Bolor Erdene. I went through all the diplomatic notes and in the file found a note of discussions between the countries' presidents where the Kazakhstan president had promised the Mongolian president that if this claim could not be resolved, it should be settled by an international court. But which international court?

The International Court of Justice in The Hague would not have jurisdiction because it can only decide disputes between states. In this case, Erdenet, although majority-owned by the Government of Mongolia, was a corporate entity. The International Court of Arbitration of ICC Paris was also out of the question because there was no mention of arbitration. Erdenet told me that suing the Government of Kazakhstan before the Kazakhstan court would be a hopeless proposition. What to do? Even if we found a court in a country which could be prepared to accept jurisdiction, there would be a bigger hurdle of limitation, which appeared impossible to overcome as the claim was old. On the face of it, Erdernet's claim was hopelessly time barred and against a non-existent debtor.

Fortunately, I noticed that the note recording the conversation between the two presidents was only four years old. So I came up with an idea of starting proceedings in the English court. This was on the grounds that in the Commonwealth of Independent States (CIS), which included Kazakhstan and Mongolia, the English Commercial Court is treated as an international court. In the Commercial Court in London today, around 40 per cent of the disputes relate to Russia and CIS countries.

So, at the end of my second day, I advised the general director and Tsaagan that Erdenet's only way forward was to bring the claim before the English court. I made it clear that the chances of success were slim but there was a possibility of settlement because the family of the Kazakhstan president was involved, who would probably prefer that the trial should not go ahead.

I managed to obtain leave from the English High Court to issue proceedings. The Kazakhstan government appointed English lawyers and they made an application challenging the jurisdiction of the English court. The application came before Mr Justice Cook and the court held that it did not have jurisdiction.[32] On my advice, Erdenet applied for leave to appeal. This application was considered by Lord Justice Clarke and accepted. In his reason, he made some very helpful comments. The result was that just before the appeal hearing, Kazakhstan arranged with a third party to buy out the principal claim of $20 million. So, through my intervention, Erdenet succeeded in recovery of their claim despite it being so aged.

32 Erdenet Mining Corp v. Kazakhstan [2016] EWHC 299 (Comm) (02 February 2016)

The Zaiwalla family: Parents Ratanshaw and Nargesh; brothers Bomi, Dara, Dinsoo and Khushroo; and little sister Zenobia. (Sarosh is on the far left, front row.) Ratanshaw, a solicitor with an office in south Bombay's Readymoney Mansion, was an Englishman in every respect apart from his skin colour.

With British Prime Minister Margaret Thatcher and ex-wife Renoo. Thatcher was a guest speaker at a Durbar Club event, when Zaiwalla was its vice chairman in the late 1980s.

IMAGES COURTESY OF THE AUTHOR.

With Indian Prime Minister Rajiv Gandhi in New Delhi, 1988. Zaiwalla was in India's capital to attend the prime minister's birthday celebrations.

The Asian Business Breakfast Club in action at the House of Commons, 2001. The club was started with the aim of encouraging an Asian Economic Union, along the lines of the European Union.

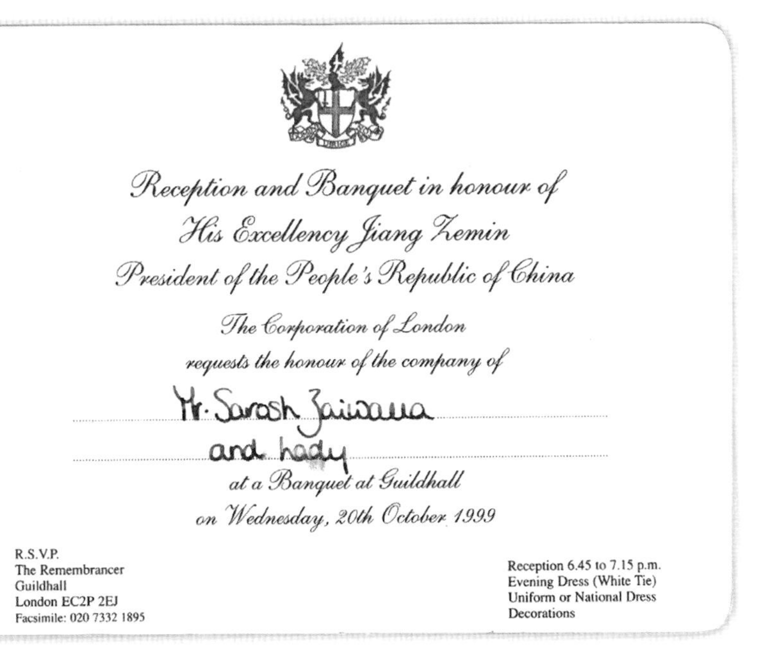

Reception and Banquet in honour of
His Excellency Jiang Zemin
President of the People's Republic of China

The Corporation of London
requests the honour of the company of

Mr. Sarosh Zaiwalla
and Lady

at a Banquet at Guildhall
on Wednesday, 20th October 1999

R.S.V.P.
The Remembrancer
Guildhall
London EC2P 2EJ
Facsimile: 020 7332 1895

Reception 6.45 to 7.15 p.m.
Evening Dress (White Tie)
Uniform or National Dress
Decorations

Invitation to attend a banquet for Chinese President His Excellency Jiang Zemin, in 1999. Zaiwalla enjoyed a special relationship with China and had set up an office in Beijing in the 1990s.

Zaiwalla with his Beijing office team and guests, 1999. Zaiwalla & Co. was one of the first English law firms with a branch in China.

LETTER FROM RT. HON. LORD WILBERFORCE - 21.2.89

Feb 20.

Dear Mr Zaiwalla,

Many thanks for sending the judgment in The Diamantis Pateras (Hellas) Marine Enterprises Ltd. It is certainly a great tribute to Lord Justice Bingham and also to you for your persistence and skill in producing the victorious argument. Congratulations!

Yours sincerely

Richard Wilberforce

The Hon. Mr Justice Morison
President

Employment Appeal Tribunal
Audit House
58 Victoria Embankment
London EC4Y 0DS

Telephone 0171 273 1029

20 November 1996

Dear Mr Zaiwalla,

"C"

Zaiwalla & CRE v Elstub & Others

Thank you for your further letter of 8 November 1996.

You ask me for a further statement.

It seems to me that the transcript shows the circumstances in which your complaint of race discrimination came to be mentioned in the proceedings before the Commercial Court, and I have nothing to add on that point.

Once I had become aware of those proceedings, I was greatly troubled about the potential problems that might arise in relation to the then current arbitration. I expressed those concerns, as the transcript shows. I was of the view that it was important that you should put before the Court sufficient material to enable me properly to consider the position. I was concerned about the implications which such proceedings might have on the doing of justice in the arbitration.

I should add that, as far as I am concerned, I do not consider that you behaved improperly in telling me, reluctantly, as I recall, of the problem in the first instance; nor in the way you responded to my request for material. It was on the basis of this material that you asked for, and were given, leave to amend your Notice of Motion. Although your allegation of bias against Mr Harris did not prevail, it was not a frivolous amendment. If I had regarded it as such, then I would have made a different order for costs.

I am sorry that the way you behaved in my court, which I regarded, and still regard, as quite proper, has led to contempt proceedings against you, particularly as I expressed the view that I should be properly informed of the material, rather than that the issue be swept aside, or dealt with on a half-considered basis.

Yours sincerely,

Thomas Morison

Zarosh Zaiwalla Esq.

Letter dated 20 February 1989, from the Rt. Hon. Lord Wilberforce, a House of Lords judge, congratulating Zaiwalla on winning an argument.

Letter the from Hon. Mr Justice Morison, dated 20 November 1996, in which he supported Zaiwalla in the contempt proceedings in the racial equality case.

The Hon. Mr. Justice Colman

ROYAL COURTS OF JUSTICE
STRAND, LONDON, WC2A 2LL

Tel: 0171 936 7132
Fax: 0171 936 7421

1st July 1996

To whom it may concern

I have known Mr S Zaiwalla and his firm for at least twelve years. For the first nine years of that period, when I was Queen's Counsel at the Commercial Bar, I worked closely with Mr Zaiwalla personally on numerous commercial cases in litigation and arbitration. In so doing I had ample opportunity to form an opinion of his legal ability and professional integrity. As to the latter, I have, in the course of my work, read many pages of inter-solicitor correspondence in which Mr Zaiwalla and his firm participated.

I can say without qualification that I found Mr Zaiwalla' work of high quality throughout and I never encountered any conduct by him personally or his firm which would possibly have been fairly described as transgressing professional standards or in any way lacking in integrity. More specifically, I found that Mr Zaiwalla had good litigation judgment in two particular respects. He always recognised a bad point for what it was and he had a remarkable ability for extracting winning points out of situations which at first sight seemed to be utterly hopeless. Perhaps for this reason his firm's litigation success rate was unusually high.

I can also say that he was a robust litigator in the sense that if a point was there to be taken he would take it if he saw it to be in his clients' overall interests. In this connection, I have occasionally heard expressions of criticism typically from old school tie solicitors in City law firms similar to those referring to the "style" of Mr Zaiwalla in litigation expressed in paragraph 3 of the summary of the telephone conversation on 6th September 1989 and I have often wondered whether those criticisms would ever have been expressed about the same conduct on the part of another old school tie solicitor not of racial minority origin.

Letter from the Hon. Mr Justice Colman, a High Court judge, dated 1 July 1996, testifying to Zaiwalla's professionalism and integrity.

V. V. Veeder QC

Essex Court Chambers
24 Lincoln's Inn Fields
London WC2A 3ED

Telephone: (Int + 44) 171 813 8000
Facsimile: (Int + 44) 171 813 8080
Internet: 100662.2602@compuserve.com

To whom it may concern

21 June 1996

Mr Sarosh Zaiwalla

I have known Mr Zaiwalla for over twenty years, almost from the very beginning of my practice at the Bar in 1971. I knew him first as an Instructing Solicitor and a Solicitor acting for adverse parties, particularly in shipping disputes; and over the last ten years, I have known him as a respected figure in the field of international commercial arbitration, both in England and abroad. In the latter capacity, I know him as a senior figure in the ICC Court of International Arbitration and an active supporter of the London Court of International Arbitration.

I have a great regard for Mr Zaiwalla, personally and professionally. I know him to be most able as a commercial lawyer and international arbitrator; and I believe him to both effective and assiduous in representing his clients. As a Solicitor, he is an opponent to be feared; and as a professional colleague, a person who has my admiration and respect.

V.V. Veeder

V.V.Veeder QC

Testimonial from V.V. Veeder QC, dated 21 June 1996.

16 JUN 1993

10 DOWNING STREET
LONDON SW1A 2AA

THE PRIME MINISTER

15 June 1993

Dear Mr. Zaiwalla,

Thank you for your generous letter of 11 June. I am most grateful for your kind comments.

Racism is something I simply will not tolerate. I do very much believe that the state of race relations in Britain today is generally better than at any time in recent history. I am keen to play some small part in ensuring racial harmony develops further.

Yours sincerely,

John Major

Letter, of 16 June 1993, from British Prime Minister John Major, sharing his thoughts on race relations and fostering racial harmony in the UK.

Letter from British Prime Minister Tony Blair, who wrote to Zaiwalla, on 13 February 1998, reassuring him that Derry Irvine, Lord Chancellor of the Court of Appeals, would look into his complaint against the conduct of three judges.

10 DOWNING STREET
LONDON SW1A 2AA

THE PRIME MINISTER

13 February 1998

Dear Sarosh,

Many thanks for your letter of 27 January enclosing one you sent to Derry Irvine on 23 January.

I know Derry will look long and hard at what you say.

With best wishes,

Yours ever

Tony Blair

With the Russian ambassador, His Excellency Alexander Yakovenko (left) and Alexander Kramarenko, the deputy ambassador, at a lunch hosted in Zaiwalla's honour, 10 August 2015.

Zaiwalla met with the Dalai Lama for a one-on-one chat about Tibet, in 2004.

With Ban Ki-moon, UN secretary-general, at the UN headquarters in New York, 2007. Zaiwalla first met him on a flight to Nairobi, when he was South Korea's foreign minister.

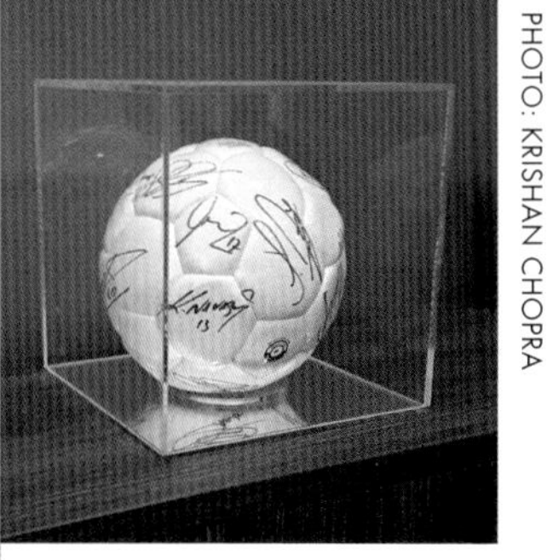

PHOTO: KRISHAN CHOPRA

A football signed by the Real Madrid team and presented to Zaiwalla by Argentinian legend, Diego Maradona.

The author in his Chancery Lane office, March 2019.

7

'My Boys Don't Trust Indians'

By the early 1990s, Zaiwalla & Co. had built its reputation as a specialist maritime law firm. I wanted to expand its shipping department further. While for a time the Indian government had provided a great deal of maritime work, I had cultivated the private sector by getting more Greek and other non-Indian ship owners as clients, including the shipping magnates Lemos, Halcousis, Polemis and Hadjantonakis and other Greek ship owners from Piraeus, Greece.

These vessel owners were members of various London protection and indemnity (P&I) clubs, which covered their legal costs and other liabilities. Vessel owners, under the terms of the cover, could choose their own solicitor. In reality, they usually left this choice to the club.

The two big shipping companies in India during those years were the Great Eastern and the Essar Shipping. Whenever I was in India, I would make a point of dropping in at their offices. In due course, I got to know K.N. Seth, vice chairman of the Great Eastern, to the point where I considered him to be a personal friend. During my meetings with Seth we would discuss the possibility of Zaiwalla & Co. being instructed to do their work in London, but on each occasion his comment was that their P&I club, the Britannia Steamship Mutual, was against using my firm. This was naturally disappointing, so after a while Seth suggested I should seek a meeting with the club's chairman, Ken Patterson, to discuss whether they might change their attitude – after all, I had made a good reputation for myself generally in the market.

In fact, I had already met Ken Patterson previously at a lunch at his office with the Mumbai shipping lawyer S. Venkateshwaran, better known as 'Venky'. So I went over to his office and asked if my firm could be approved by his club to accept instructions from its members under freight, demurrage and defence insurance cover (FD&D), which was essentially legal fee insurance cover for their shipowners' cases. Patterson heard me out but was non-committal.

Some five or six months later, on another visit to Mumbai, I met Ravi Ruia, vice chairman of the Essar Shipping Company. I had previously helped him with some personal legal matters in London, and he was very pleased with the service he had received. So, reasonably enough, I asked if Essar would consider instructing Zaiwalla & Co. in their shipping cases in London. He immediately said that he would and even as I was having tea with him he sent a note to this effect to the head of his shipping department, one Captain Kumar. He then spoke to Kumar and arranged for me to go to see him in his office.

It was all looking very encouraging when Kumar then instructed me in a dispute concerning one of their vessels, the *Nand Ekta*, in a time charter party dispute. Naturally I was delighted, but I had celebrated too soon. A few days later Kumar called me to say that there was a problem as Britannia Steamship Mutual had not given their approval to my firm being instructed.

I went to see Ken Patterson again, seeking an explanation. He told me bluntly there was very little possibility of Britannia ever approving Zaiwalla & Co. to act for its members. When I asked why, his blunt response was astonishing. 'My boys don't trust Indians,' he said.

I could hardly believe what I had heard. I returned immediately to my office and rang Kumar in Mumbai. He said that Essar would stand by its decision and told Britannia as much. This is how Indian business culture is different. If an owner of a company tells the head of a department to instruct a particular firm, then that head of department will ensure that those instructions are followed. However, this was considered so outrageous that Britannia sent representatives to Mumbai on two separate occasions for the specific purpose of persuading Kumar to withdraw Essar's instructions to our firm. Moreover, Britannia then advised Essar that, in the opinion of its legal department, the shipping company had no chance of success in the *Nand Ekta* arbitration case.

I took a different view. I reassured Essar that it had a reasonable prospect of success. A week before the final maritime arbitration hearing I was proved right when the other side capitulated, and Essar succeeded.

When I rang Britannia to let them know, the junior employee handling their file at the club, Charles Elstub, abruptly told me that he was only allowed to speak about the case to my assistant, Joe Hurley. Hurley was a white junior solicitor in my firm. I told him this was unlawful, and that I felt Britannia's conduct was racist. Our conversation ended abruptly but I was determined not to let the matter drop. I wanted to be treated with the respect which British law demanded.

My immediate step was to write to Ken Patterson to inform him about this latest insult, reminding him of his own remarks: 'My boys don't trust Indians.' I also requested an apology and asked for an undertaking from him that he would not take such an approach again. If he did not, then I warned that I would be compelled, in accordance with the law, to complain to the UK's Commission for Racial Equality (CRE).

Matters get more serious

In response to my letter Patterson came to my offices but refused to withdraw what were, in my opinion, his racist comments or give the undertaking I had sought. I had expected him to tender an apology or explain that he had not intended to be offensive. If he had done so, that would have been the end of the matter. Instead, he was visibly angry at my threat to report the matter to CRE, saying that if I did so, it would mark the end of my firm in the City and the likelihood of it doing any further maritime cases. He said he and the club would ensure that it would happen. I asked him not to make such threats. He nevertheless repeated them, his face turning red with rage. I replied that I would do what was right.

As he was leaving my office, we shook hands, but he reiterated his earlier threats in no uncertain terms. If I complained to the CRE, it might well be the end of my firm as far as maritime work was concerned.

I found the whole encounter deeply distressing because I had never come across such fury and hostility from an English professional. I swung into action in response, contacting and speaking at length to Angela Rumbold, the Conservative MP from Mitcham & Morden in South West London. She was also the chairman of the One Nation Forum, an organization which advised the government on diversity and of which I had been invited to become a member. She then spoke with the prime minister, John Major, revealing what I had encountered. I also wrote to the PM about Britannia's conduct.

Major's response to this by a personally addressed letter to me was striking. '*Racism is something I simply will not tolerate,*' he wrote. '*I do very much believe that the state of race relations in Britain today is generally better than at any time in recent history. I am keen to play some small part in ensuring racial harmony develops further.*'

Encouraged by the support of the One Nation Forum and the prime minister – and despite Ken Patterson's threats – I decided to make my formal complaint to the CRE. This was not for any personal gain but because I felt it was my duty to do so. I believed Britannia had breached race relations laws with Patterson's remarks and it should be held to account for that. Added to that, at a personal level as an Indian, I must admit that I had found profoundly offensive the generalized suggestion that we were all untrustworthy in some way.

The CRE accepted my case and decided to start County Court proceedings against Britannia. This decision was made by the CRE alone. I was made a formal second claimant but the CRE would be responsible for all legal costs, including my own. Charles Elstub was the formal second defendant, even though, to my mind, he was simply following his superior's instructions and was innocent of racism. But again, that was the CRE's decision, not mine.

Building the case

What followed was a horror story that reflects the power which the old boys' club still had in the City of London at that time. At no point did Britannia seek to contact me to find an amicable resolution. Although this was surprising, it was, in my opinion, also indicative of their attitude towards Indians and race generally.

Britannia's lawyers did not deny Ken Patterson's remark. But it then became a matter of semantics. They argued in Britannia's defence that the reason the club would not approve of their members instructing Zaiwalla & Co. was not because I was an Indian by race but rather it was because of my 'Indian style' of handling cases. I was surprised by this amazing justification for the comment. This was an absurd defence given that I had trained, qualified and practised in London as an English solicitor for more than fifteen years. I had never even practised in India.

In its defence in the race-relations proceedings, Britannia relied on affidavits served in court by two maritime arbitrators and two individual Indians. These affidavits in due course came into the public domain, as they were read before the Court of Appeal and the County Court on the issue of costs after Britannia withdrew its contempt proceedings against me (described below). Three of the affidavits considerably upset me because I considered all the witnesses to be both well-wishers and friends. At least they pretended to be, but I can imagine that they had their own personal motives for supporting the club.

The first was made by maritime arbitrator Bruce Harris of the London Maritime Arbitrators Association (LMAA), who was well aware of my firm and its successes – he featured in my biggest Chinese case involving the CNPC (as described previously). The second was John Maskell, partner at Norton Rose, another leading maritime law firm.

Not long before Harris gave his affidavit, he had attended my firm's tenth anniversary reception in the House of Lords, which also had distinguished legal and judicial luminaries present. He had also earlier attended a Christmas reception at my firm's offices in Chancery Lane in December 1991, where the chief guest was the then attorney general, Sir Patrick Mayhew QC MP. At these events Harris had complimented me for the standing that I had achieved in maritime arbitration circles, a consequence of my successes in the English courts challenging awards. Let me make it clear that I never bore, nor will I ever bear, any ill will towards Harris. Even now, whenever I have met him, I have always gone out of my way to greet him.

In his affidavit in the race-relations proceedings, Harris described an incident in an arbitration case before him which concerned disputed events relating to a procedural issue at a meeting between a Mr George, a partner at Ince & Co., and me. Harris made it clear that he believed George's account of events and implied the problems had been caused by my 'Indian style'. He went on to conclude that my professional shortcomings could, in his opinion, be summed up in a single phrase as 'lack of judgement'. I felt this breached the rule of confidentiality, which requires non-disclosure of events that occurred during an arbitration hearing. I cannot judge his motives for doing that.

Harris went on to state, 'I do not think Mr Zaiwalla's general approach to the cases I saw was practical or commercial ... If I was now working for the club, I would never voluntarily instruct Mr Zaiwalla, and if a member asked that Mr Zaiwalla be used on a particular case, I think I would try to dissuade the member. That would be because from my experience of Mr Zaiwalla, it is likely that a substantial amount of unnecessary unjustifiable costs would be incurred ... I would expect any club with experience of him to take such a view and I think that he was sufficiently well known amongst clubs and other solicitors in our field that this approach would be regarded as pretty general.'

Through this evidence, he was putting the boot in and supporting Britannia in the race-relations proceedings.

Harris is not a qualified lawyer but had worked previously in a P&I club. He was also highly selective in what he brought to the court's knowledge, leaving out any reference to successes I had achieved in cases in which he himself had been involved.

For example, he neglected to mention a notable case involving the ship *La Pintada* where my firm represented the president of India on an issue of compound interest for late payment of demurrage. I had personally appeared before him at the arbitration hearing. Harris, as a sole arbitrator in this case, produced an award against my client. Harris felt so confident that his award would be upheld that he attended the court hearing when the award was challenged – arbitrators are neutral and it is unusual for them to be present in court when their awards are challenged. When the award was remitted back to him, he produced the same award but with a postscript emphasizing that he was doing so with even more enthusiasm. When the matter came back before the Commercial Court, Mr Justice Staughton, by means of a 'leapfrog' procedure, referred the case directly to the House of Lords. In what was a test case, my submission was accepted 5–0; as this was a test case, it saved the Indian government a liability of more than £5 million. As it happens, the only time Tony Blair's name appears in the law reports is in the first decision of Mr Justice Staughton in the *La Pintada* case (where he was instructed by my firm along with Derry Irvine QC).[33]

So, I felt a sense of fairness would have called for Harris to have brought to the court's attention in his affidavit my track record of such successes as an English lawyer. He chose not to. He would also have been aware that my firm was acting for many ship owners with the support of other London P&I clubs, and that the West of England P&I Club and the UK P&I Club had occasionally approved my firm being instructed by members who were Greek ship owners.[34]

Meanwhile, by contrast, John Maskell displayed the gentlemanly qualities for which the City of London is internationally renowned.

---

33 La Pintada Compania Navigacion SA v. President of India (The 'La Pintada') [1983] 1 Lloyd's Rep. 37

34 La Pintada Compania Navigacion SA v. President of India (The 'La Pintada') [1984] 2 Lloyd's Rep. 9

He invited me for lunch and told me that as the head of his firm's shipping department he was under pressure to produce an affidavit in support of Britannia. He apologized to me for being compelled to give such evidence, asking for my understanding as the club referred a lot of cases to his firm. He added that most people recognized and respected my abilities as a lawyer but admitted there were some who did not want more 'Sarosh Zaiwallas' around. I thanked him for letting me know and said that I understood his position.

One of the two Indian witnesses was Venky, the Mumbai shipping lawyer. He said that my firm had instructed him to appear as an advocate at a maritime arbitration hearing in Mumbai and argue a legal point that he did not want to argue. He said this was evidence of my 'Indian style'. I found it perplexing. English barristers are frequently asked to argue points of law against their better judgement but which are based on instructions from solicitors. Perhaps this may be considered an 'English style'?

The other Indian witness, the Great Eastern's K.N. Seth, had some time earlier sought my assistance to purchase a distressed vessel called *Sonid*, again chartered to the president of India. It had a government cargo on board which had been unable to get to an Indian port because its owners went bankrupt. Seth sought to criticize me through his affidavit. Seth had never been a client of Zaiwalla & Co., but as he was on the board of Britannia, he could hardly be considered an independent witness. However, during one of my visits to Mumbai he discreetly sent a message through a common channel to let me know that he would not be appearing in court to give evidence at the race-relations hearing.

Gaining support

My response to these affidavits was to contact eminent judges and QCs to give evidence in my favour. Lord Wilberforce, Lord

Mackenzie Stuart, Sir Roger Buckley, Sir Michael Kerr, Sir Anthony Colman and V.V. 'Johnny' Veeder QC – all provided fulsome testimonials.

Lord Wilberforce, one of the outstanding English judges of the twentieth century, wrote, *'I have found Mr Zaiwalla to be an experienced solicitor of high quality and capacity, especially in commercial matters. From the personal knowledge of him which I have acquired, I believe him to be a person of integrity and good reputation.'*

Johnny Veeder, a leading QC in the international arbitration field, wrote in his statement, *'I have a great regard for Mr Zaiwalla, personally and professionally. I know him to be most able as a commercial lawyer and international arbitrator; and I believe him to be both effective and assiduous in representing his clients. As a solicitor, he is an opponent to be feared; and as a professional colleague, a person who has my admiration and respect.'*

Several maritime arbitrators gave statements in my favour for the race proceedings. Clifford Clark, one of the founders of the LMAA and the doyen of the London maritime arbitration community, said, *'Zaiwalla always had a firm grasp of the reference and maintained a professional attitude on all occasions. I can't remember him not taking a good point, and he usually conceded any bad points. He held no animosity on the occasions when an award went against his clients.'* He went on to say, *'If Mr Zaiwalla has attracted criticism ... it is perhaps because he has been so successful in the London legal/arbitration scene, and because he is unprepared to allow injustice to prevail.'*

In his statement, Sir Anthony Colman, a sitting High Court judge, said he had found that I had good litigation judgement and a remarkable ability for extracting winning points out of situations which, at first sight, seemed to be utterly hopeless. Sir Anthony further commented, *'I have occasionally heard expression of criticism, typically from old school tie solicitors in City law firms, similar to* [the Defendant in the race-relations proceedings] *and I have often wondered whether those criticisms would ever have been expressed about the same conduct on the part of another old school tie solicitor not of a racial minority origin.'*

For its part, the case concerning the vessel the *Lips*[35] before the House of Lords was a typical example of my out-of-the-box thinking about the correct interpretation of the law. My client was again the president of India. The ship owners had claimed exchange loss because the freight and demurrage had been calculated in US dollars and made payable in sterling in London. It was paid late, and sterling had fallen in value in the meantime. As I habitually did, I made my submissions on law in an affidavit without consulting counsel. The Commercial Court accepted my legal submissions as to the proper construction to be placed on the meaning of the term in the contract. However, the Court of Appeal unanimously rejected it.

In the House of Lords, I instructed Anthony Diamond QC to appear for my client and the ship owner instructed Anthony Grabiner QC (now Lord Grabiner). After Diamond had completed his opening submissions, Lord Mackay of Clashfern, the Lord Chancellor, reminded him that he had not dealt with the submissions I had put forward in my affidavit. Diamond turned around to me and told the court that 'with the greatest of respect to Mr Zaiwalla, I am unable to support those submissions'.

It was then Grabiner's turn to advance his submissions on behalf of the ship owners. When he had finished, Lord Brandon, one of the Law Lords, asked him to deal with the view of the law stated in my affidavit. Grabiner replied that as Diamond had not put those arguments forward, he had no obligation to do so. At this, Lord Brandon appeared agitated and said that the House of Lords, as the

35 President of India v. Lips Maritime Corp (The 'Lips') [1987] 2 Lloyd's Rep. 311

highest court in the land, had a duty to deal with what it considered to be the correct legal interpretation.

The House of Lords later delivered its judgement in the president of India's favour based on acceptance of my submissions on law. However, it did not award costs because the president's counsel had abandoned my submissions.

A few weeks later, Lord Mackay, the Lord Chancellor, accepted my invitation to attend Zaiwalla & Co.'s Christmas party, the first time a sitting Lord Chancellor had visited a solicitor's office. When he arrived, the first thing he did was to congratulate me on my client's success in the *Lips* case. Many years later, in October 2017, I received a telephone call from Lord Mackay inviting me to have lunch with him at the House of Lords. He told me that he always remembered the *Lips* and *Gladys* cases, where I had fought and succeeded in the House of Lords with what was then considered a novel legal approach to English law. This was a typical example of the British establishment appreciating the great and the good.

The *Gladys*'s case[36] involved an issue as to whether the strategy that I pursued before the Commercial Court was, as alleged by my opponent, an abuse of process. It was therefore a controversial issue. The House of Lords, by a decision of four to one, held that what I had done as part of strategy for my client was perfectly legal and correct. Even the dissenting judge, Lord Goff of Chieveley, in his usual courteous manner, said in his judgement, '*I have to say that I find this a most remarkable way of proceeding. I have never heard of such a thing being done before. That is not, of course, of itself a good reason for stopping it; but it is a very good reason for examining it very carefully indeed.*' In three of these, I was successful against the earlier advice of leading Queen's Counsel. In the fourth case,

36 Metal Scrap Trade Corp Ltd v. Kate Shipping Co Ltd (The 'Gladys') (No.1) [1990] 1 Lloyd's Rep. 297

involving the vessel *Anticlizo*,[37] the Court of Appeal enthusiastically gave leave to appeal, but the House of Lords held that it had no jurisdiction to consider.

Besides my victories in the House of Lords, Bruce Harris would have been aware of my success for clients in cases before maritime arbitration tribunals. I was instructed by the Food Corporation of India (FCI). It was dissatisfied with two earlier judgements of Justices Lloyd and Bingham on the legal construction given to the term in the contract 'entry at customs' for the purpose of time allocated to a charterer to discharge cargo, in this instance involving the vessel *Albion*. At the Indian port, there was a prior entry and a final entry, and the vessel could only discharge the cargo after the final entry at customs, which would occur after a health check of the vessel and the crew. The FCI faced a liability of several million dollars because there was always congestion at Indian ports.

Upon being instructed, I researched the issue and took the view that the distinguished judges, both of whom went on to the House of Lords, had made the wrong decision. This was because the correct argument on law, with supporting evidence of Indian law, had not been placed in the earlier cases before the court on the FCI's behalf.

I recommended to my client that despite the two High Court decisions, they should fight the same issue again in arbitration. I appeared personally as an advocate and put forward my newly formed submission of law and suggested to the tribunal that the judges had got their decisions wrong. At this, the chairman of the tribunal, a senior LMAA arbitrator, became very agitated and said that I had no respect for the judiciary and that the tribunal was not going to allow me to put forward such an argument on law. I responded by telling him it was wrong to express a view before

37 Food Corp of India v. Anticlizo Shipping Corp (The 'Anticlizo') [1988] 2 Lloyd's Rep. 93

having heard me out fully and he might therefore consider stepping down. He got angry and walked out in the midst of the hearing, after directing a few abusive words at me.

A stunned silence ensued, but I remained calm. I had learnt early in life that whatever the circumstances, one is always to remain cool and act with humility and courtesy. I knew too that this incident would be made public in the maritime arbitration community, by those who did not want an outsider around, to show me in a bad light.

Michael Dean QC was appointed as the new chairman and the arbitration hearing was resumed a few weeks later. He was much more patient, telling me that he saw some force in my argument, but that the tribunal was bound by the earlier decisions of the High Court. He made an award against the FCI but very fairly set out my argument in the arbitration award. We then appealed to the Commercial Court and my client was successful before Mr Justice Webster.[38] This caused ripples in the London P&I clubs. There then followed a further arbitration on the same issue concerning the vessel *Nestor*.[39] With all guns blazing against me and my client, I once again appeared as solicitor advocate, and when the award went against the FCI, we appealed to the High Court. There, to everyone's surprise, Mr Justice Leggatt said that my interpretation of the contract term was correct, 'not by comity but by inclination'.

The vessel owner, who was represented by Holman Fenwick and Willan, appealed the High Court judgement. The appeal application came out before Lord Justice Bingham, who had earlier decided this issue against the FCI. After hearing counsel for both sides, he

---

38 President of India v. Davenport Marine Panama SA (The 'Albion') [1987] 2 Lloyds Rep.365

39 President of India v. Diamantis Pateras (Hellas) Marine Enterprises (The 'Nestor') [1987] 2 Lloyds Rep.649

gave a short judgement to the effect that after considering new legal submissions, he was of the view that his earlier decision was wrong.

A week or two later, Lord Wilberforce called me to establish if it was correct that Lord Justice Bingham had done this. I said it was, and he asked me to send a transcript of the judgement, which I did. I then later received a handwritten letter in which he paid tribute to Lord Justice Bingham and then to me for my 'persistence and skill in producing a victorious argument'.[40]

I felt a sense of fairness would have called for Harris to have brought to the court's attention in his affidavit my track record of such successes in my capacity as an English lawyer. He chose not to.

The Fletamentos case

In the meantime, I had further dealings with Harris, appearing before him on behalf of a Spanish shipping company called Fletamentos Maritimos. Fletamentos was referred to me by Jose Alcantara, a leading Spanish maritime lawyer, who was at that time president of the Spanish Maritime Association. Alcantara had first been introduced to me years before by Cedric Barclay.

Alcantara had called me and said that Fletamentos had earlier instructed a large city firm with which it was unhappy, and he had recommended that it instruct my firm instead. Fletamentos was particularly concerned about the independence of the arbitration tribunal, of which Harris was a member and which had made some adverse orders in the past against them that they considered to be unfair.

When I appeared before them, it seemed to me that Harris and his colleague Mark Hamsher were displeased that I had

40 Lord Wilberforce's letter, dated 20 February 1989, is reproduced in the colour plates.

been instructed. I had asked for disclosure of documents from the other side, but the arbitrators summarily dismissed my request. I challenged the arbitrators' decision in court. The challenge came before Mr Justice Morison in the Commercial Court,[41] a brilliant judge who went on to become president of the Employment Appeal Tribunal.

The other side managed to fix a quick emergency hearing of my client's application. I applied to the court for more time and sought an adjournment. For this purpose, I appeared before Mr Justice Morison, who said, 'Mr Zaiwalla, you are quite well known, and you can do it yourself.' I had a two-day hearing in open court before him (opponent counsel was Alistair Schaff) and at the end of it, he commented that the arbitrators had behaved in an odd way.

I said, 'My Lord, there may be a possible reason. One of the arbitrators, Bruce Harris, has given evidence against me in race-relations proceedings commenced on my behalf by the Commission for Racial Equality.' The judge turned red and said, 'Tell me more about it.' I then gave the judge a short gist of the allegations Harris had personally made against me in his affidavit in the race proceedings.

My client's application did not succeed but at the conclusion of his judgement, Morison said:

> I very much hope that the maritime arbitration community recognizes the importance of welcoming into it those who, by racial origin, come from countries from which much of the legal commercial business originates; otherwise London will lose its position as the preferred choice for the resolution of international disputes such as the present one, which has no connection with

41 Fletamentos Maritimos SA v. Effjohn International BV (No.2) [1997] 1 Lloyd's Rep. 295

this country other than the parties' wish to have their disputes resolved here.

It was a bold and courageous statement by the judge, Thomas Morison, although it may well have helped prevent his promotion to the Court of Appeal. It also led to the Britannia P&I Club launching proceedings for contempt of court against me for having disclosed to Mr Justice Morison during the hearing for Fletamentos that Bruce Harris had given an adverse affidavit against me. A finding of contempt of court can lead to a person being sent to prison, and it is a very serious allegation to make against a solicitor (who is an officer of the court). It was clearly a pressure tactic on the part of the defendant P&I club.

The club expected me to cave in, but I was determined not to give them that satisfaction. I knew I was acting correctly in bringing to the attention of the CRE what I considered to be the racist conduct of Britannia.

I also had in mind that as a pathfinder, I must show silent courage so that other non-white professionals, finding themselves in a similar situation, would continue to run on that path. I have a collection of verses in poetry from which I occasionally gained strength. One such verse was, *'Be not afraid of anyone, no matter what his size, if danger threatens, call on me and I will equalize.'* My deep faith in Divinity I had had since childhood remained and I was certain that God would look after me and protect me.

I went back to Mr Justice Morison, who wrote letters to me to be placed before the judge at the contempt hearing. He said I had done nothing wrong and had produced evidence in relation to Bruce Harris's involvement at his insistence and request. On seeing the judge's letter just before the start of the contempt hearing, Britannia offered to withdraw their contempt application.

However, as Judge Morison had not given the relief that my Spanish client had wanted, the client appealed;[42] and the appeals court bench was made up of Lord Justices Simon-Brown, Morritt and Waller.

Right from the start of the hearing, one of them made it clear that they were unhappy with Mr Justice Morison's comments. It was felt that he should not have included them in his judgement. It seemed to me from the start of the appeal hearing that the Court of Appeal bench was intensely hostile towards me personally and was using the appeal as an opportunity to criticize me in such a way as to favour the defendants in the race-relations proceedings. One of the judges said during the hearing that the court had never come across racism in the City of London and I was just creating trouble.

Since I was not personally a party to the appeal, I had no opportunity to rebut those accusations. I asked my client's counsel, Murray Pickering QC, to bring to the attention of the judges the evidence in my favour but he refused, saying he was acting for Fletamentos, not me. I was concerned that the Court of Appeal might say something adverse against me in its judgement, but Pickering told me it was highly unlikely as the court knew that it had not heard my side of the story.

I was right to be concerned. While the Court of Appeal expressed a concern not to 'pre-judge' any of the issues in the race-relations proceedings, nevertheless in its judgement it went to the extent of praising Harris for making his affidavit. The court had not seen the glowing testimonials from the judges, QCs and arbitrators produced in support of the CRE's claim, debunking what Harris had said. The court was, however, aware of the imminent start of the race-

42 Fletamentos Maritimos SA v. Effjohn International BV (No.2) Court of Appeal (Civil Division) [1997] 2 Lloyd's Rep. 302

relations trial some two weeks later. It knew that Britannia's defence depended on what was described as my 'Indian style'.

In short, the Court of Appeal had decided, without hearing me, to hand the club a 'silver bullet' for use in the race-relations proceedings. The Court of Appeal was also not aware that at the time Harris made his affidavit, I had taken four cases before the House of Lords on behalf of my clients. Three of those cases, which concerned the vessels *La Pintada*,[43] the *Lips* and the *Gladys*, had required special leave to appeal from the House of Lords. In all three of these, I was successful against the earlier advice of leading counsel and had to apply for special leave to appeal to the House of Lords. In the fourth case, involving the vessel *Anticlizo*,[44] the Court of Appeal enthusiastically gave leave to appeal, but the House of Lords held that it had no jurisdiction to consider.

The hearing opens

Britannia P&I, not surprisingly, made good use of the Court of Appeal's judgement in the Fletamentos case, as the judges must have expected it would do.

The case had initially been reserved by Circuit Judge Hallgarten QC to be heard before him in the Central London County Court. He had also notified the parties in advance of the hearing that he had decided to hear the matter without lay assessors. This was despite race-relations proceedings requiring two lay non-white assessors to be present. It was certainly unusual, but Hallgarten was part of the maritime old boys' club, coming from chambers known for shipping law cases. He would not alter his decision to sit without

---

43 President of India v. La Pintada Compania Navigacion SA (The 'La Pintada') [1983] 1 Lloyd's Rep. 37

44 Food Corp of India v. Anticlizo Shipping Corp (The 'Anticlizo') [1988] 2 Lloyd's Rep. 93

lay assessors, and when I asked the club's solicitors to consent to my request that Hallgarten recuse himself, they refused to do so.

I appealed on an emergency basis to the Court of Appeal and a different bench of the Court of Appeal presided by Lady Justice Elizabeth Butler-Sloss ordered Hallgarten to be removed and the case to be relisted before another judge.

The evening before the case was due to be heard, Britannia's lawyers sent me a notice to inform me that their legal costs were around £600,000. They said they would be claiming it personally from me if I did not consent to abandon the race-relations proceedings. This was an example of bullying me into submissions.

At that point, I was not worried as any cost liability would be borne by the CRE. I was not aware, however, that the club's solicitors were already in contact with CRE and that it had agreed to withdraw. In fact, I was to find out only on the morning of the hearing that CRE had decided to drop the case. This was done on a 'drop hands' basis, which means no costs are payable by either side. In other words, Britannia would not be claiming costs from the CRE for abandoning the race-relations proceedings, despite the fact that the decision to commence them was taken by the CRE and not me personally. Although I was party to the proceedings, the communications between Britannia and the CRE were not copied to me by the club's lawyers. I had been kept in the dark.

I was shocked. The CRE representative told me the decision had been taken at a high level, by which I understood to mean by the commission's chairman, Herman Ouseley. When I questioned him further, the CRE representative told me that they considered the club's defence to have been proved by the evidence of what the Court of Appeal had said in its judgement in the Fletamentos case. This was seen to be enough to back up the claims of my undesirable 'Indian style'. I therefore had no opportunity to explain to the CRE that the observations were made without seeing my evidence or hearing submissions from me. The Court of Appeal judges had put the boot in – in effect, favouring the defendant in the race-relations proceedings – at the hearing of an unrelated matter, in which neither I nor Britannia were parties before them.

Although the CRE was the principal claimant in the case, I had instructed a QC (as I would be put through a gruelling cross-examination) and was ready for the trial with my witnesses. My counsel advised me that the Court of Appeal's judgement was a death blow to my chances. He also said that if I continued with the proceedings, I would have substantial costs liability for a four-day trial. He added that if I insisted on continuing with the proceedings, he would consider standing down and I would have to appear myself before the court.

I was faced with a stark choice. I could have continued the case but without the CRE's financial support, and with my counsel's reluctance to argue that the CRE's claim had merits, I had no option but to agree to drop my complaint. I was also bullied into agreeing to pay £25,000 for the defendant's cost when in a race proceedings commenced by CRE the complainant should face no personal cost liability. The day after I did this, the Indian assessor who was sitting with the trial judge asked me why I settled, saying, 'You would have won. The judge was in your favour. This was a clear case of discrimination.'

The aftermath

Today, all I can say is that what happened is in the past and I would not suggest that Britannia is guilty of racist behaviour now. The changes that have intervened have been enormous, but right then I experienced the personal stress of taking on a London P&I club establishment. Looking back on the whole episode from the vantage point of a far more liberal and open twenty-first century City of

London, I had suspicions as to what prompted the CRE's decision to drop the case. I feel deep political currents may have been at work. John Major, the prime minister, was expected to lose the general election and Tony Blair was likely to succeed him. But there is no means of knowing whether this is true. The subsequent changes have been enormous, but right then I experienced the personal stress of taking on an establishment.

I felt sufficiently aggrieved to complain to the new Lord Chancellor, Derry Irvine, about the Court of Appeal judges. I also sent a copy of my letter to the new prime minister, Tony Blair, who personally replied to me: '*I hope Derry will take a long and hard look at what you say.*' I received a letter from the Lord Chancellor saying he had initiated an inquiry into the conduct of the three judges.

For his part, Herman Ouseley was later – and perhaps surprisingly – to receive a peerage. Britannia's counsel at the case, Charles Faulkner QC (a former roommate of Blair's) was himself made a lord just after the formation of the 1997 Labour government. In 2003, he succeeded Derry Irvine as Lord Chancellor.

A few months after my CRE case was dropped, Justice Morison came to one of my events specially to meet me. He told me not to withdraw my complaint against the Court of Appeal judges. He said that the judiciary was broadly divided on my complaint. Half the judiciary felt that the Lord Chancellor had no jurisdiction to investigate the conduct of the judges as they were independent. The other half considered my complaint to be sufficiently serious for the investigation to go on. Two other judges, including one Court of Appeal judge, told me in an informal conversation that the Court of Appeal had acted very unfairly towards me. One of them gave me, with what he said was sadness, an apology for the rough and unfair treatment I had received from his brother judges.

The final denouement of this story came in Kuala Lumpur against the backdrop of a Commonwealth Law Conference. The

Lord Chief Justice Woolf was leading the official British delegation, of which I was a member.

There was a session on tampering of the Malaysian judiciary by the Malaysian government. Lord Woolf was aware of my complaint to the Lord Chancellor, and I told him I was going to speak out at this session about what happened in my case. I also told him that on the previous day, Robert Sayer, president of the Law Society – the body that represents some 80,000 solicitors in England and Wales – who was also part of the delegation, had told me while discussing the Kamlesh Bahl case (more of this later) that I should forget about there ever being racial equality for non-white solicitors. (Sayer later achieved notoriety when he was charged by the Crown Prosecution Service for inventing a false identity as a country vicar and forging a passport; the case was not proceeded with on the grounds of Sayer's ill-health.[45])

Lord Woolf suggested to me that I should remain silent, promising to invite me for a cup of tea when we returned to London so we could find a way to reach a solution. I agreed and decided not to speak about my experience at the conference.

The Lord Chief Justice kept his promise and invited me to see him at his office in the Law Courts. He told me that he had taken note of the miscarriage of justice in the race-relations proceedings and the possibility of unconscious racial discrimination in the judiciary against me. He assured me that steps were being taken to eradicate it, saying, 'Your complaint to the Lord Chancellor was well understood.'

Lord Woolf then requested that I close the complaint so that the matter could end and I could move on having made my point. I agreed. I knew when to stop. Obviously, the fact that all the judges

---

45 'Solicitor leader struck off for fiddling funds', London: *Legal Cheek*, 27 July 2015

knew about what had happened was, in a way, an achievement and would go some distance to eradicate the rare occasion of unconscious racial discrimination in the British judiciary. Lord Woolf was true to his word and since then, the English courts have moved actively to bring about diversity in the legal profession. It was only after my race-relations proceedings that the City of London also took note of the need to do the same.

A record of success

While Bruce Harris had attempted to cast doubt on my effectiveness in acting for my clients, I am glad to say that my record spoke for itself then and continued later.

Very recently, according to the highly respected magazine The Lawyer, two of the most important cases heard by the Supreme Court in the last ten years involved my firm acting for one of the parties.

One of these high-profile cases was *Hashwani v Jivraj,*[46] which had raised an interesting question: Could an arbitration agreement provide for a term that the arbitrator or arbitrators should belong to a particular religious community? As the European Equal Treatment Directive, now embodied within the UK's 2010 Equality Act, forbids discrimination on grounds of religion, we succeeded in the Court of Appeal.[47] This caused a flutter in the international arbitration community, with both the International Court of Arbitration of the ICC, Paris and the London Court of International Arbitration (LCIA) applying for and being given leave by the Supreme Court to support the appeal against the Court of Appeal's decision as interveners.

The Supreme Court subsequently overturned the decision but Sir Richard Buxton, one of the Lord Justices who had heard

---

46 Jivraj v. Hashwani [2015] EWHC 998 (Comm)

47 Hashwani v. Jivraj [2011] UKSC 40

Sadruddin Hashwani's appeal, and who had retired by the time of the Supreme Court judgement, wrote an article in *The Law Quarterly Review* (volume 128, January 2012) in which he referred critically to the impact of lobbying by powerful arbitration institutions. It is extremely rare for a retired Lord Justice openly to criticize any decision of the Supreme Court. This article was brought to my attention by Lord Justice Aikens, one of the Court of Appeal judges who had heard the appeal, at a London Maritime Arbitration Association (LMAA) annual dinner.

The second notable case was that of *Bank Mellat v Her Majesty's Treasury*.[48] My firm acted for Bank Mellat, one of the largest Iranian banks. It had decided to appoint us to replace Stephenson Harwood, one of the top London firms, after it had lost before the High Court and the Court of Appeal.

This case concerned the listing of Bank Mellat by the Treasury under Iran's nuclear proliferation sanctions. This was the first case where the Supreme Court went behind closed doors to consider sensitive intelligence evidence. The bench of nine judges of the Supreme Court held by a majority of five to four that the UK government had acted both unlawfully and irrationally in listing the bank.

Kamlesh Bahl – a related case

Shortly after my dealings with the CRE the Kamlesh Bahl case erupted, attracting much media interest and hinging on many of the same issues of prejudice against members of an ethnic minority.

Bahl, an East African Asian, had been appointed chairman of the Equal Opportunities Commission by the John Major government

48 Bank Mellat v. HM Treasury Supreme Court [2013] Lloyd's Rep. F.C. 580

and went on to become vice president of the Law Society. The convention is that after a term as vice president, that person then succeeds the president. This would have made Bahl the first woman, and the first Asian woman, to achieve this.

However, as the millennium began, matters did not proceed according to plan. Lord Griffiths, a former law lord, was asked by the Law Society to investigate bullying claims against Bahl. He found that she had used 'bullying tactics' and 'usurped' the role of the secretary general, Jane Betts, who was the head of the Law Society staff. The confidential Griffiths Report said her behaviour had 'at times, been demeaning and humiliating and at other times, offensively aggressive'. The report named five members of staff whose versions of events were preferred by the Griffiths tribunal to that of Bahl. Within days, the Law Society voted to suspend her and in March 2000, Bahl resigned, saying she was a victim of a 'witch-hunt'.

She went on to say, '*I believe the price I have had to pay for trying to reform the Law Society has been to be labelled a bully. I went in with a mandate for reform and this is what has happened. I have been fighting single-handedly against a massive establishment that doesn't want me, an Asian woman, to be there. I believe I have been treated unfairly throughout this whole episode – it has been a witch-hunt. It has put me under the most enormous stress.*'

Bahl decided to take the Law Society to the Employment Tribunal. On 29 November 2000,[49] the hearings began. Her supporters included the Society of Black Lawyers, who claimed the case highlighted institutional racism within the legal profession, while her QC, Robin Allen, said that as one of the best-known Asian women in the country, she had been an outsider when she arrived at the Law Society. 'When outsiders ruffle feathers and stumble they

49 Bahl v. Law Society [2003] 7 WLUK 994

are kicked when they are down,' he said. 'That is what happened to her.'

Seven months later, the tribunal ruled that the Law Society was guilty of race and sex discrimination against Bahl (although these findings were subsequently overturned in the employment appeal tribunal, a decision upheld in the Court of Appeal).[50]

After the initial ruling, Bahl urged the Law Society 'to take every step to ensure that no other woman or no other person from an ethnic minority ever has to go through a fraction of what I have had to go through in the last two years'.

When the Law Society made a substantial claim for costs with a view to making Bahl bankrupt, she came to me for help. That was the irony because when she was chairman of the Equal Opportunities Commission, she had refused an invitation from me to lunch; however, I saw merit in the case.

I referred her to Lord Dholakia and we had a public meeting in a committee room at the House of Lords. I had just become chairman of the British Organization for People of Indian Origin (BOPIO) and chaired the meeting. As well as MPs and peers such as Lord Parekh and Lord Patel of Blackburn, it was attended by organizations including the Sikh Forum, the Gujarati Congress, the National Council of Hindu Temples and the Goan Association. Bahl explained her treatment by the Law Society and the subtlety of institutional racism. Lord Parekh spoke on the potential danger of disguised racism creeping into British society, and I made my vital point about British Indian pathfinders owing it to the younger generation to assist in eliminating the remaining ill of racism.

At this meeting, Lord Dholakia called on the Law Society to help remedy the situation, saying that otherwise Asian solicitors would immediately create an Asian Law Society. Following this,

50 Bahl v. The Law Society (and others) [2004] EWCA Civ 1070

the Law Society's financial claim against Bahl was withdrawn and those responsible for the action moved on. The new head of the Law Society assured Asian solicitors that steps would be taken to eradicate unconscious racism.

Both the Britannia and the Bahl cases illustrated the problems a minority, and in particular, an ethnic minority, can face in professions like the law. Breaking through glass ceilings is not easy. It was only after my race proceedings against Britannia that both the City of London and the Royal Courts of Justice started recognizing unconscious institutional racism and taking steps to remedy it.

I drew an important conclusion from my experience, and I drew comfort from it. It was that the British sense of fair play was evident. It ensures that any person who feels victimized can in the end find justice, albeit sometimes not in the way they first planned and not without a struggle.

Thankfully things have now changed, with diversity becoming an acceptable word. I do not think that racism was endemic in the maritime arbitration community, although I saw there were some exceptions. The LMAA remains a much-respected organization. I have fond memories of giants and founder members of the association such as Cedric Barclay, Clifford Clark, Albert Morris, Reginald Bishop, Ralph Kingsley and Donald Davies. There was also Alec Kazantzis, a non-practising barrister and an arbitrator of Greek origin. He was an honest and kind man, and an excellent arbitrator. While the race-relations proceedings were going on, he came over to my offices to meet me – he was concerned about the effect that those proceedings would have on my practice. At the meeting, Kazantzis said from his own experience that one could take the P&I clubs on and hope to survive. With the grace of God, I did.

8

Trials and Tribulations

The twelve-year period from 1992 until 2004 was a good and a horrible time, personally and financially.

The breakdown of my marriage in April 1992 led to divorce in the summer of 1995. This meant I had to give up my former family life. We had been living in a luxurious house in Wimbledon, then valued at £450,000 and now worth up to £3 million. It would go to my ex-wife, who later sold the property and bought two houses with the proceeds. The children stayed with her and I would take them at the weekends to my Sussex home, which in the divorce proceedings was independently valued at £180,000 (and which I kept).

One positive development, however, was that I became a friend of a kind Irish lady and through her found a one-bedroom flat to rent on Eaton Place, a prized London location. This changed my life. As a single person I would often be invited to dinners at neighbours' houses, and so, despite my marriage problems, I began to meet the cream of London society. Meanwhile, through my relationship with John Major I would be invited to events such as the Summer Ball and the Blue Ball. British government ministers would invite me to accompany them on their foreign visits as part of trade delegations and I was even the invited guest of the government when the Royal Yacht *Britannia* visited Dubai, Bombay and Madras on its final voyage in 1996.

Dubai's ruler, Sheikh Mohammed, was so surprised to see a brown face as part of the British team that a few weeks later he personally invited me to Dubai for a dinner hosted by him for Nelson Mandela, who was then the president of South Africa. The following year, he invited me to a dinner he was hosting for the Australian prime minster.

The dinner in Dubai gave me a unique opportunity to meet Nelson Mandela and his wife, Graça. I went with my then English girlfriend Annie Geddie, who was from Plymouth but had lived as a child in Zimbabwe when it was still Rhodesia. Her father had worked in the Rhodesian air force and then lived in South Africa, so she was equally keen to meet Mandela. Mandela and I spoke for a long while and he suggested that I should make contact with his London solicitor, which I did upon my return to London. I presented Mandela with a book, *India: Colours of a Continent*, by Angela Colman, which my firm had published in memory of my late father. Over dinner, I was pleased to see Mandela turning over the prints of the paintings in the book.

My biggest mistake – employing Andrew Milne

My divorce, unfortunately, had a knock-on effect on my professional standing. Before my divorce I was treated by the legal fraternity as an enigma, even a star. But by late 1992, I realized that my ability to manage my firm was being damaged by the stress of my marriage ending and the resulting heart irregularities I was suffering. So, in early 1993, I decided to recruit a solicitor with experience of working in one of the large, so-called 'Magic Circle' firms to support me.

I contacted Chambers & Partners, the legal recruiting agents who now publish the well-known legal directory of the top 500 UK law firms. I spent half a day with Michael Chambers working out the precise candidate I needed. He recommended Andrew Milne, who had previously worked at Clifford Chance. Chambers told me that in the previous year Milne had got himself into a bankruptcy situation – he actually owed approximately £1.2 million to more than a hundred creditors – and was making an individual voluntary arrangement (or IVA). He felt that if I could help him sort it out, he would be a useful and loyal employee. After interviewing Milne, I decided to employ him. With my modest support, his bankruptcy was subsequently annulled under the IVA, with his creditors receiving eight pence in the pound.

I appointed him with the primary responsibility to look after the administrative side of the firm. In due course, I agreed that to the outside world he would be described as a managing partner, although he remained at all times on a wage as a salaried partner. Milne told me that he had researched Zaiwalla & Co. and, given its good reputation, believed that with proper management it would become 'a goldmine'. The arrangement was that in addition to his wages he would receive a bonus of 30 per cent of the annual net profits for his management.

I soon found Milne to be a very good organizer. I never got to know him well socially, but he gave the impression of being a pukka Englishman. He insisted I should wear an Hermes tie, took me to Gieves & Hawkes on Savile Row for my suits to be made and would get someone to polish my shoes. When I travelled by car he would open the door for me. He said I deserved the best and I began to trust him immensely, giving him authority to sign the firm's office account cheques. In hindsight, this was a big mistake. He proved to be a complete disaster.

Every month he would show me the firm's monthly profit and loss account, tell me the profits and present me with a cheque for signing, which purportedly represented his 30 per cent share. I would sign the cheque in good faith, not seeking independent verification of the accounts.

It was some years before my eyes were opened to the real situation. Milne came to inform me that my Sussex house needed to be mortgaged for a large loan from the bank. I had thought the firm was cash rich, but he told me if I didn't agree to the mortgage, wages could not be paid, and the firm would collapse.

I made a dash for the auditor's office, where I discovered that Milne had been taking money without my knowledge or authority. The next morning, I found Milne had cleared his office. I immediately sent one of my firm's solicitors, Smeetesh Kakkad, to meet Milne at his home and explain to him that I would be prepared to come to a reasonable arrangement with him, following which if some of the monies were returned, that could be the end of the matter. Milne sent a message back saying that if I went to the police, he had information on me which would destroy me. I had no idea what this information might be.

I sacked Milne for misconduct and the matter went to arbitration. The High Court appointed Sir Brian Neill, a retired Court of Appeal judge, as the sole arbitrator. He decided that while I could not get back the amounts for which I had signed cheques, Milne was ordered to pay back the other funds he had helped himself to. The arbitrator made an award of £525,000 plus interest and costs for Milne to pay me. My claimable legal costs were around £225,000, including my counsel Justin Fenwick QC's fees. As it was, Milne was made bankrupt and ended up paying me and his other creditors nothing.

Worthy of an honour?

It later became clear how Milne would try to blackmail me. Sometime earlier, just weeks before the 1997 general election (in which John Major's Conservatives were voted out from office), Lord Feldman, chairman of the National Union of Conservatives, came to see me. He told me that Prime Minister John Major was inclined to award me a CBE for my services to the country. This was for the part I had played in 1994 to resolve the friction between Britain and China over the handover of Hong Kong and the work I had been doing to promote good trade relations with India and China through my high-level contacts in these countries.

I asked Milne to join the meeting, thinking he would be pleased by the news. To my surprise, Milne became aggressive with Basil Feldman and put on a big drama, saying I should refuse the CBE as this was too lowly. He said I should instead receive a peerage or at least a knighthood for the number of cases my firm had succeeded with in the English court, including the House of Lords, for overseas clients. This had contributed to the development of English law, brought in foreign earnings and created jobs.

He persuaded me to stay quiet and let him do the talking. In hindsight, I believe Milne was trying to prevent me from receiving anything because an honour might increase my standing and assist me in taking any legal action against him if and when his theft was discovered.

Basil Feldman returned the following week. He told me that he had spoken about me with Major during their weekly meeting. While the PM was not in a position to offer me a higher honour, he had spoken with the Lord Chancellor, Lord Mackay of Clashfern, to consider nominating me from the Lord Chancellors department for something more significant than a CBE, and Mackay had agreed. For this to happen, Basil told me that I should nominate someone who could give him at least ten names of eminent persons who could act as referees. I chose Milne to take on this role.

Of the ten nominees that Milne secured eight were eminent personalities from the legal profession. Two, Tony Baldry and

Keith Vaz, were MPs. As it can take up to two years for honours to be approved, and given that John Major subsequently stood down, nothing further was heard of the proposal at this time. In the meantime, I had discovered about Milne's misappropriation of Zaiwalla & Co. funds.

The Tony Baldry matter

On 5 December 1999, soon after the arbitration award was made against Milne, an article about me appeared in the *Sunday Telegraph*. It was a sleaze story of exactly the type that had helped end the Conservative Party's period in office two years before. The newspaper said Tony Baldry, who had been minister of state at the Ministry of Agriculture, Fisheries and Food, had recommended me for an honour but failed to declare a 1994 loan I had made to him of £5,000.

It was Milne who was behind the *Sunday Telegraph* article. His motive I believe was simply to thwart any chance of me being awarded any public honour – and to seek revenge.

Yet, the facts were simple. Tony had been in financial difficulties at the time and came to me as a personal friend asking for a temporary loan to help cover the school fees of his two children. I agreed, saying that whatever interest it cost my firm, he would repay. This he duly did, and while I gave it no further thought, Milne had kept photocopies of both the cheque which I gave Tony and his own post-dated cheque for return of the loan.

On the same day that the article appeared, Milne wrote to William Hague, the new Conservative leader. After introducing himself as a former partner of Zaiwalla & Co., he claimed he was writing to 'put the record straight'. However, his letter was full of inaccuracies.

'I have personal knowledge of the matters which have been reported in the *Sunday Telegraph* today as I was Deputy Senior

Partner of Zaiwalla & Co. when the loan was made to Mr Baldry,' he wrote. This was manifestly untrue not least because Milne was a salaried partner and certainly not the 'Deputy Senior Partner'.

Milne went on to claim that William Hague had attended a 'promotional breakfast for Zaiwalla & Co.' at the House of Commons. This was also not true. He was referring to the Asian Business Breakfast Club of which Tony Baldry and I were co-conveners and which the Chinese ambassador always attended.

Milne alleged that Tony was not really a friend of mine at all, adding that 'for one of the meetings to negotiate the loan he came in an official ministry car', with the driver 'kept waiting for some time while the negotiations took place'. Milne claimed Baldry was seeking the loan because 'his girlfriend was very extravagant and had "cleaned him out"', and that he initially wanted to borrow £20,000. This was also not true. Perhaps most unforgivably, Milne wrote that 'Mr Zaiwalla had made other payments to politicians and had a reputation as a moneylender'. This was wholly fabricated, just like so many other allegations made by Milne in his letters to Hague and to Elizabeth Filkin.

It was clearly intended to hurt me the most. The Indian moneylender is a racial stereotype, a figure mocked by the British when they ruled India, and nearly always portrayed as a villain in Bollywood movies, a man often shown with a huge distended paunch who preys on the weak. Milne was implying I was trying to corrupt the British system in the way that Indians in India do. He went on to say that I 'had apparently been very short of money', but did not attempt to resolve the contradiction as to how I could at the same time also be a moneylender – something I was not.

In this letter, Milne also alleged that the Asian Business Breakfast Club did not have a constitution, officers or list of members, but rather 'it is merely a marketing label for Zaiwalla & Co'. If it was then it was unbeknownst to me.

Milne had already raised some of these issues directly with Tony Baldry in 1998, during our arbitration. Tony must have felt he had heard the last of this, but then the *Sunday Telegraph* article appeared bringing it all back up again.

The very next day after its publication, Baldry himself referred the matter to Elizabeth Filkin, the parliamentary commissioner for standards, to investigate, saying he would 'withdraw from the proceedings of the House until these matters are resolved'. He strongly refuted the allegations of corruption.

Baldry wrote:

> The facts are straightforward. I have known Sarosh Zaiwalla for a number of years as a friend. Some years before I became a minister we worked together on a charitable trust called The Prospect Trust. We didn't see much of each other during the time I was a minister but when details of my divorce were published in the newspapers, Sarosh got in touch with me, as he too had experienced a divorce in similar circumstances. We met from time to time thereafter, socially as much as anything, to give each other mutual friendship and support.
>
> It is true that he made me a loan. There was a Loan Agreement document signed and witnessed, which I hope can be produced which sets out the terms of the loan … I hope that it will be possible to produce the loan document as it will show not only the dates and the amounts, but the fact that I did pay interest on this loan. I asked Sarosh Zaiwalla if I could borrow £5,000 and my recollection is that it was agreed that I would borrow £5,000 for a short period of time, but that I would pay back the sum together with the amount of interest he would lose by not having that money on deposit. When I repaid the loan, it was repaid with interest. I hope that it will be possible to produce a copy of the Loan Agreement. I myself did not keep a copy as once the money had been repaid I saw no necessity so to do. I

would stress that at this time my only relationship with Sarosh Zaiwalla was one of mutual friendship. I had absolutely no contact with him in my capacity as a government minister. As far as I am aware, his firm at that time was dealing primarily in shipping matters and international commercial arbitration and had no dealings with the Ministry of Agriculture where at that stage I was a minister.

The only reason that Sarosh Zaiwalla lent me this money was out of friendship but, as I have explained above, it was a loan that was made without commercial detriment to his firm, with it being agreed that I pay the cost to them of my using the sum of money over a short period of time. The Loan Agreement was witnessed by another partner [a reference to Milne] in the firm. That partner was subsequently dismissed for misconduct. There was subsequently arbitration on the Partnership Agreement where a former High Court Judge found that this same former partner should repay a substantial sum of money to Zaiwalla & Co. It was he who took possession of the Loan Agreement and it may be that when he left the firm, he took this document, together with other papers. However, I am sure that Sarosh Zaiwalla will use his best endeavours to find a copy of the Loan Agreement if it still exists and is in his possession.

Moreover, as this loan went through his firm's accounts, I am sure they will have a record of the day on which it was lent, the amount that was lent, and the day on which it was repaid, and the amount which was repaid. I understand that it is said that I should have declared this loan to my Permanent Secretary at the time. I considered this to be a small loan, as between friends, over a short period of time. I was confident that at the end of the loan period it could be repaid. I do not consider that at any time it made me in any way beholden to Sarosh Zaiwalla and indeed in due course the sum together with the agreed interest, was repaid. I certainly didn't appreciate at the time that there

> was a suggestion that there was a requirement to report such a loan to the Permanent Secretary or to enter the same in the Register of Members' Interests. It is of course a matter for you and the appropriate authorities of the House to decide whether I got this matter wrong.

On 22 December, Milne also wrote to Elizabeth Filkin the following:

> I would particularly ask you to look into his booking breakfasts at the House of Commons in the name of a non-existent organisation, the Asian Business Breakfast Club, which is simply a marketing label of Zaiwalla & Co., in order to get around the rules for such bookings. I would also ask you to look into whether it was proper for Mr Baldry to have given a reference for Mr Zaiwalla to receive a CBE, at a time when he hardly knew Mr Zaiwalla, as part of the price for the loan which he received. I would also ask you to look into whether it was proper for Mr Baldry to have used a ministerial car to attend the offices of Zaiwalla & Co. to negotiate the loan. I would also ask you to look into each of the other ten separate matters which I raise in the letter to Mr Hague.

In forwarding the letter he had written to Hague, Milne told Filkin, 'I am sure that Mr Hague will not forward it to you as requested. I would ask that the contents stand as a formal complaint against Mr Baldry.'

The central question was whether Tony Baldry, after receiving the loan, had (as one of the ten referees) recommended me for an honour.

Filkin's report, issued on 21 March 2000, did not uphold Milne's complaint, concluding that '*Mr Baldry was not required to register the loan from Mr Zaiwalla because the concession he received did not exceed the threshold of £215. Although clients of Zaiwalla & Co. were from time to time invited to the breakfasts I have received no evidence that Mr Baldry booked the dining rooms "to get around the rules for such bookings" or that the Club was "simply a marketing label".'*

Tony was therefore able to continue his distinguished career, being appointed Second Church Estates Commissioner in 2010 and knighted in 2012 for public and political service. He was made privy counsellor by the Queen, and after his retirement from the House of Commons in 2015, the dormant title of High Steward of Banbury was revived for him, and he was also appointed a deputy lieutenant of Oxfordshire. In 2016, he was awarded the Langton Award for Community Service by the Archbishop of Canterbury 'for his community service, especially as an advocate for the continuing contribution of parish churches to the common good'.

The 'Brown' case and Keith Vaz

For my part, my trials and tribulations were not over. In 2000, the *Sunday Telegraph* journalists moved on from scrutinizing Tony and started looking at my relationship with the Labour MP Keith Vaz.

Milne told them he was prepared to swear an affidavit that I had financial links with Vaz and suggested they speak with Brian Brown, a former clerk at my firm, as a source on this.

However, for the journalists there was a problem – in 1994 Brown had been discovered stealing from my office. It was Milne himself who had apprehended Brown and extracted a voluntary confession that he had taken £44,000. The police were then called, and Brown was charged and subsequently convicted and sent to prison for four years.[51]

---

51 https://publications.parliament.uk/pa/cm200001/cmselect/cmstnprv/314/31408.htm

The journalists knew that Brown's prison record represented a significant impediment and so – to provide corroboration about the Vaz allegations – they obtained recordings of a conversation between Brown and Milne. The transcript of the conversation was provided to Elizabeth Filkin by Milne, purportedly as evidence confirming Milne's allegations that Keith Vaz MP had received £2,000 from me. The following transcript was reproduced in the subsequent select committee report. Brown had no idea he was being recorded.

Andrew Milne (AM): Brian, it's Andrew Milne.

Brian Brown (BB): Hi.

AM: I have been contacted by the *Sunday Telegraph* and I am really rather concerned at what you may or may not have been saying to them. They say they are going to run some story and I am very anxious to find out what you have said to them about Mr Vaz.

BB: I haven't said anything.

AM: Were you discreet?

BB: I haven't said anything. What they asked me about I didn't know. Simple as that. I haven't heard from them for four weeks.

AM: I was contacted by them quite recently and I was really rather concerned. I didn't want my name to get into the paper about this sort of thing. It concerns the £2,000 that you handed over to his assistant.

BB: Well, supposed to have. It's not something that I remember. That's what I told them.

AM: That you had chosen not to remember.

BB: Not that I had chosen not to remember. That I didn't remember.

AM: You certainly did hand over an envelope at some stage.

BB: Or so I am told, but I still don't remember it.

AM: I am quite anxious to get our story straight on this because I have been telephoned a number of times.

BB: I am interested to know where you got the number from.

AM: I asked them how you might be contacted after they mentioned your name two or three times. They eventually gave me the number. What do you do now?

BB: That's irrelevant.

AM: I am anxious to get our story straight.

BB: I have no story. They got nothing from me, nothing from my family and that's the end of it. I have heard nothing from them for four weeks.

AM: You were discreet in what you said to them.

BB: I told them I couldn't remember. Which is exactly it.

AM: I have a vivid recollection that you did hand over an envelope with £2,000 in it to Mr Vaz's office.

BB: Well that wasn't asked of me. I was asked about a bloke called Baldry. Vaz never came up into the conversation at all.

AM: You were asked if you had given Baldry money – which you hadn't done.

BB: That's right. Because it was 1987, er 1997.

AM: Oh, I see. That's comforting. I was asked about Mr Vaz though which I did find concerning because I do remember you did give him – or someone from his office – an envelope.

BB: Oh, yes. I remember that quite vividly, he was up there quite a lot.

AM: They asked me various other names which I found concerning. Do you remember the name of Vaz's assistant who you actually handed the cash to?

BB: No, because it was to him personally.

AM: You handed the £2,000 to Mr Vaz personally.

BB: Well, however much it was, it was to him personally. I don't remember any assistants.

AM: Did Keith say thank you?

BB: I couldn't tell you.

AM: Can't remember that?

BB: No.

Brown only discovered that the recording had been made when the *Sunday Telegraph* informed him that his conversation had been passed on to Filkin. He was not happy about 'certain methods employed by the *Sunday Telegraph* to coerce a statement from me about events of which I knew absolutely nothing'.

As a result, he had 'declined all invitations to speak to them and that will remain to be the case'.

However, while he stated he was never present at any discussions, meetings or other transactions between me and Tony Baldry, he did add:

> I do, however, recall that a payment of I think £1,000 was made to Mr Vaz by Mr Zaiwalla for what I seem to recall was described as being for an "office fund". I do not, however, remember the date upon which the payment was made though it was whilst Mr Zaiwalla's practice was housed at 95A Chancery Lane which I suppose makes it prior to May 1994. I have been informed by the Sunday Telegraph reporter that a statement by a third party (whom I assume to be Andrew Milne) stated that I was initially requested to hand Mr Vaz a cheque which was refused, and the payment was requested in cash which I withdrew from the firm's bank and handed in an envelope to Mr Vaz. This may or may not be the case, I simply cannot be certain though I

> suspect that it could be the case. I was certainly not involved in any discussions which led to the payment being made nor was I made aware whether the payment was a gift or a loan.

The truth is as follows. Keith used to come to our office. We were friends, not least because he was the first Asian MP in modern times, and to all of us British Asians, Keith was an important personality. The fact was that on one occasion I was invited by C.B. Patel, the publisher of the Gujarati-language weekly newspaper *Asian Voice* and an important figure in Asian media, to a charity event in the House of Commons. This was sponsored by Keith to raise money for cyclone relief in Gujarat.

At this event, I committed to donating £1,000 to the cause. Keith phoned me a few weeks later and subsequently sent someone to collect the donation, asking for it in cash as it was easier to transfer to India that way. This was recorded in my firm's accounting book. I had also taken two small advertisements costing £250 in Keith's constituency calendar for two years. After Keith became a Labour minister, I had no contact with him at all until 1 February 2000, when I was invited by the British high commissioner in New Delhi to his residence to attend a reception in Keith's honour.

On 8 February, I put out my defence in a trenchant letter to Elizabeth Filkin, asserting that the newspaper allegations that I had given Keith 'thousands of pounds' were completely untrue. Neither Zaiwalla & Co. nor I had at any time made any payments personally to Keith or his office, nor did he approach either me or my firm to give him any. I went on to add that Milne was currently being investigated by the City of London Police for false accounting and theft, and that he had failed to honour the substantial monetary award in my favour made by the arbitrator. I was advised by the police that they would not continue the investigation as I had started a civil claim in an arbitration against Milne.

The problem I faced was that the allegations against me were based on what surfaced in the course of a parliamentary inquiry. Because reports to parliamentary committees are, quite properly, covered by parliamentary privilege they cannot be acted upon in court. Therefore, I had no legal remedy to bring defamation proceedings against the *Sunday Telegraph* or against the vengeful Milne. He really knew how to work the system.

Milne's deceptions led to a bleak period. I couldn't run the firm as there was no money available. I was forced to take loans, including £50,000 from a moneylender in Scotland who, when I couldn't initially pay it back, threatened me with all sorts of violence.

I was honest with all my clients and the bank. Although my professional reputation was intact, there were no funds available to run my firm. I had to downsize the firm in 2001 and was forced to make everybody redundant, paying them their redundancy in full.

The bank threatened to put a complete freeze on further lending. The rent on the flat in Pont Street was many months in arrears, but my landlady was incredibly understanding. I drove a Daimler, but this had been bought in better times. I still had just sufficient funds to pay the school fees and my son Varun's £925 airline ticket when he wanted to travel on his gap year. After that I had only £28 left in my account to spend.

By then I owed the bank and other debtors a lot of money, over £600,000. If it hadn't been for the helpfulness of a manager at NatWest's branch on Chancery Lane, I do not know what would have happened. He took me to meet his director at the bank's headquarter in the City. The director was very sympathetic, giving the firm an additional £70,000 overdraft facility, which lasted till the end of 2002. (Today the firm is once again in a healthy state and doesn't owe a penny.)

My dealings with Milne had almost ruined me. At one point my ex-wife called and told me to consider either an IVA or bankruptcy, but what kept me going was my faith in God. I prayed, I did not panic, and I took practical steps.

My offices at 33 Chancery Lane were on a long lease and were furnished in a very smart, corporate manner. The landlords made a claim of £1.4 million against me for premature termination of the lease. I took advice from Justin Fenwick QC and he said I was liable for this as damages.

I prayed at the Bahá'í shrine and asked for God's assistance. I then saw Satya Sai Baba, an Indian saint, in a dream. He opened the door of the room I was in, not at all happy. He touched me and said, 'I've got a lot of things to do, solve many problems, and now I've been asked to sort out your problem. Okay, I will sort it out,' and he went away. Some two weeks later, I got a letter from the landlords saying the claim against me on 33 Chancery Lane had been dropped. The miracle had happened.

A fresh start

I took a small, one-room office with another solicitor in 46 Chancery Lane and decided to rebuild my firm. This was a really stressful period. Opening the post was not easy because it contained demands for payment every day.

I was helped enormously during this period by my loyal friend Rashmi Thakar. I was introduced to her for the first time by Gulam Noon, who later became Lord Noon, at a dinner hosted by the billionaire Lakshmi Mittal at his Summer Palace residence in London. When everyone else was saying I was finished, Rashmi stood by me. I shall always remember her kindness.

For a time, I used my Pont Street flat to meet clients or in a hotel rather than meet them in my shared office. I went back to the drawing board. As I had done when I started, I went to India, Dubai, Singapore and got new clients. But now I stopped first-class air travel and went economy class instead. The chauffeur I had went back to India, and I drove my own car.

While I was trying to keep my business alive, the parliamentary select committee inquiry into the conduct of Keith Vaz continued. In February 2001, I gave evidence before the committee. In its final report, it found the allegations made by Milne were completely untrue. The report also acknowledged that my name had been put forward for a high honour.

After this, I finally started to emerge from the dark tunnel I had been in since my divorce. My professional reputation was still there. I was getting new clients. I was moving from darkness to sunshine. I met a wonderful Eastern European lady who became my girlfriend.

The Tchenguiz family

I met the billionaire Vincent Tchenguiz at a large event at Dorchester Hotel. The connection between us was instant and soon we became good friends.

A year after first meeting him, he telephoned me early one morning. He had a summary judgement made against him by Mrs Justice Gloster for some £3.4 million in respect of a claim made against him by some businessmen called the Rayden brothers.[52]

Vincent was disappointed with the judgement but had been advised by his solicitors, Osborne Clarke, that there was no prospect of appealing it, and so he asked me to take over the case from them. Further research indicated there was a serious possibility of fraud on the claimant's part. My firm's innovative approach saw the same judge, Gloster J., set aside her earlier summary judgement. I instructed Stephen Nathan QC as counsel, and he worked brilliantly.

52 Rayden v. Edwardo Ltd (In Members' Voluntary Liquidation) [2008] EWHC 2689 (Comm)

After that we started acting for Vincent, his brother Robert and sister Lisa.

One of the interesting cases that my firm handled for the Tchenguiz family concerned the legal issue of whether emails obtained unlawfully from a person's computer could be used as evidence in court proceedings. This issue arose in matrimonial proceedings between Lisa and her husband, Vivan Imerman. Imerman had a workspace in Robert's office. He allegedly downloaded Imerman's personal documents, which he wanted to pass on to Lisa to use in the matrimonial proceedings. Imerman applied to the court to injunct Robert from doing so and unusually joined me, Robert's solicitor, as a defendant. The Court of Appeal judgement in this case[53] has become historical in that the Court of Appeal held that the evidence obtained unlawfully from a person's computer cannot be used as evidence in an English court. I was personally joined in this litigation because, as the Tchenguiz family's solicitor, my firm was in possession of those documents.

Vincent was very pleased with my firm's services and he agreed to a reasonably good monthly retainer and gave space in his Park Lane office for my firm. I handled many cases for him, including against Erste Bank, and with Michael Brindle QC I helped Vincent to settle particulars of a multi-million-dollar claim against the Icelandic Kaupthing Bank. It was also on my advice that he commenced civil proceedings against the UK Serious Fraud Office (SFO) and was successful in recovering substantial damages.[54]

I found Vincent to be a rare individual with brilliant business instincts and a penchant for fun. He liked my out-of-the-box thinking. I had the pleasure of being invited by Vincent to spend the

---

53 Imerman v. Tchenguiz [2011] 2 WLR 592

54 Tchenguiz v. Director of the Serious Fraud Office [2017] EWHC 2644 (Comm)

Christmas holidays with his family at his home in Cape Town for two consecutive years. Robert and Lisa, along with the Tchenguiz parents, were also there. Our friendship could be seen by the fact that I was the only outsider with the family for the holidays. I enjoyed these holidays with the Tchenguizs and met many of their close acquaintances but was unable to join them for a third year, as I had already committed to spend time in Goa with other friends.

As his friend and solicitor, Vincent would expect me to meet him every evening to discuss strategy for his cases (which were many). Except for Sunday, Vincent and I would meet at 9 p.m. at the China Tang bar at the Dorchester or Annabel's nightclub. On Sunday evenings, I would meet Vincent at 5 p.m. at his office. This was also a good opportunity for me to meet his other business friends who would join him from time to time.

I stopped acting for Vincent when his in-house team insisted on appointing Stephenson Harwood, a larger law firm, alongside my firm to act in his claim against the SFO and the Icelandic Kaupthing Bank. Stephenson Harwood and I worked together for a short period, but before long I recognized that they did not want my firm to continue working on the case with them. I withdrew from the team to avoid escalating a stressful situation or straining relationships.

Vincent and I have remained good friends. With him and his family speaking highly of my firm to his friends, work started flowing in, and from then on, my life began to spiral up once again.

9

Iran and Russia: The New Frontiers

My involvement with Russia was a truly unexpected story and happened as a result of my work for Bank Mellat of Iran.

Bank Mellat is Iran's largest private bank and is 80 per cent owned by private investors, with the government holding the remaining 20 per cent.

In 2009 the UK's HM Treasury alleged under Schedule 7 to the 2008 Counter-Terrorism Act that the bank was financing Iran's nuclear-proliferation programme. As a result, it banned Mellat's activities in the UK, claiming that two of the bank's Iranian clients had direct links to the programme. The first was Novin Energy Company which, according to Treasury officials, looked after the financial interests of the Atomic Energy Organization of Iran. The other was Doostan International, an intermediary company linked to Iran's Aerospace Industries Organization.

Winning 'unwinnable' cases

Bank Mellat claimed that it had done everything it could to sever any links with companies designated by the United Nations to have links to Iran's nuclear programme. It said that as soon as Novin was designated under the UN Security Council resolution, the bank stopped its business relationship with it. HM Treasury counter-argued that even if Bank Mellat had not provided financial assistance to the two named entities, it could knowingly or unknowingly provide services which could facilitate Iran's nuclear programme.

A legal battle between the bank and the Treasury in the UK courts followed. Bank Mellat had instructed Stephenson Harwood, a well-known English solicitors' firm, to challenge its listing. The bank lost the case against the Treasury in the High Court and then again in the Court of Appeal. Disappointed with the result, Bank Mellat decided to change its solicitors and so instructed Zaiwalla & Co.[55]

My name was put forward to Bank Mellat by the former legal director of the National Iranian Oil Corporation (NIOC), for whom I had previously resolved successfully a very difficult arbitration case concerning an oil rig. This involved a claim against Naftkav, an associate company of NIOC, from FEMCO, a Russian company then connected with Rosneft (the Russian government-owned oil company). FEMCO had given Naftkav an oil rig in Iran called Shakalinskiya on time charter. We were instructed by Naftkav, who had a very large counter claim against the claimant. This dispute was caused to be settled amicably by my firm. Against the $11 million claim, Naftkav received $4 million from a third party as a settlement of their counter claim without a hearing. NIOC was very happy.

---

55 Bank Mellat v. HM Treasury Supreme Court [2013] Lloyd's Rep. F.C. 580

In March 2013 the Bank Mellat case was heard by the Supreme Court, the highest court in the UK. It could not have been more high profile. The Treasury had adduced secret evidence in the lower courts, which had not been disclosed to the bank, to make good its argument that the bank had links to Iran's nuclear programme. The Treasury argued in the Supreme Court that the court should go into secret session to consider the sensitive intelligence which it claimed proved the bank was participating in Iran's nuclear programme. This is known in legal circles as 'closed material procedure' or CMP, in which claimants are excluded from the hearing which takes place behind closed doors. Such procedures had begun in specialist immigration and security tribunals more than ten years ago, but this was the first time that the Supreme Court had been asked to hold a CMP.

I had come to the Supreme Court in good heart because shortly before, in January 2013, the General Court (EU) had ruled there was no evidence to show that Bank Mellat was involved in Iran's nuclear programme.

The European Union Council appealed the decision, but I felt a lot would depend on what Britain's highest court did. If it ruled in favour of my client, then the EU appeal would fail. As the Supreme Court hearings began, I spoke to reporters, making Bank Mellat's position very clear. *'Sanctions are an important way to enforce international law in a peaceful manner, but they must be subject to the rule of law and require evidence,'* I said. *'It is vital for public confidence in the law that justice is not only done but is seen to be done.'*

I may well have been the reason why Lord Neuberger, its president, said in the judgement that the Supreme Court occupies a particular place in the constitution *'where all judgements should be open and be available to be seen'.* Somewhat unusually, I had written a personal letter to him, with a copy to the other side. In it I reported that the chairman of Bank Mellat told me over a lunch meeting in Tehran that Britain was a beacon of justice and yet he was not told of the evidence against his bank, which he thought unfair. Lord Neuberger went on to say that without reading the secret judgement of Mr Justice Mitting in the High Court, 'We cannot be wholly confident of disposing of the bank's appeal justly without considering the closed judgement.'

But, said Neuberger, 'We are very dubious indeed whether this will turn out to be the case … We have reluctantly decided that we cannot consider the closed judgement without having a closed hearing, as otherwise the contents of the closed judgement would be revealed to the public, including Bank Mellat and its representatives. This is a decision which is reached with great reluctance by all members of the Court, indeed it is a majority decision. No judge can face with equanimity the prospect of a hearing, or any part of a hearing, which is not only in private, but involves one of the parties not being present or represented at the hearing and not even knowing what is said either at the hearing or in a judgement in so far as it discusses what was said or produced by way of evidence at the closed hearing. Nonetheless, as Parliament has decided that, in certain circumstances, such a procedure is necessary and permissible in a trial before a judge.'

It was perhaps no surprise that the justices found in favour of Bank Mellat and were very critical of the Treasury. In the first judgement, read out by Neuberger, the justices said: 'Having held a closed hearing, it turned out that there had been no point in the Supreme Court seeing the closed judgement [which related to the secret intelligence], because there was nothing in it which could have affected [our] reasoning in relation to the substantive appeal. A [closed hearing] should be resorted to only where it has been convincingly demonstrated to be genuinely necessary in the interests of justice.'

Lord Sumption, delivering the second related judgement, said, 'The bank is entitled to succeed [in its appeal] on the ground that it received no notice of the Treasury's intention to make the direction, and therefore had no opportunity to make representations. The duty to give advance notice and an opportunity to be heard to a person against whom a draconian statutory power is to be exercised is one of the oldest principles of what would now be called public law.'

Having dramatically turned around Bank Mellat's fortunes, my firm exultantly gave a statement to reporters: 'Today's ruling is a victory for the rule of law as much as it is for Bank Mellat. The judgement puts enormous confidence in the independence of the British judiciary and sets an example that even controversial disputes can be resolved by applying the principle of the rule of law in the British courts.'[56]

Soon after the ruling, I set out the steps for Bank Mellat to claim damages from the UK government. This was to restore the bank to the financial position it would have enjoyed had the business restrictions not been imposed in 2009.

In a letter to the then attorney general, Dominic Grieve QC MP, I wrote, *'The Supreme Court is the highest court of the UK and the British government is obliged to honour its decision, both in letter and spirit ... The Supreme Court decision showed the world that British justice is independent and now we need to make a collective show to the world that the British government acts in accordance with the principle of the rule of law, regardless of any political exigencies.'*

The bank was very profitable before the sanctions and it had been forced to close down its operations in Britain. This affected its business considerably. Grieve stated that '... it is sad that this money will have to come from the taxpayer, but the rule of law has

56 Bank Mellat v. HM Treasury Supreme Court [2013] Lloyd's Rep. F.C. 580

to be upheld. The Bank Mellat case clearly shows that even in the world of sanctions, the rule of law still applies in United Kingdom. Regardless of international politics, Europe says there must be a reason to curtail the rights of an entity or individual.'

My firm started preparing the claim with the help of BDO, the international accountants, calculating what proportion of the bank's losses could be claimed as damages. We outlined 14fourteen areas where Bank Mellat was seeking compensation, principally concerning its foreign-exchange business.[57] This amounted to $4 billion. The particulars of claim was settled by Michael Brindle QC with junior counsel Amy Rogers.

The claim stated, '[The Treasury] was obliged to exercise reasonable care and skill when considering the exercise of its powers under [the Counter-Terrorism Act 2008] in relation to the bank ... but negligently failed to do so.' We also claimed that the UK government lobbied other authorities to impose their own sanctions, which ultimately caused the loss of profitable business, customers and banking relationships and dealing services. Shortly before this book went to print the case settled for a confidential sum.

From Russia with law

It was while I was successfully fighting for Bank Mellat and in particular after our victory at the Supreme Court that I first got involved with Russia. In some ways it mirrored the Iranian case, with a company fighting sanctions imposed by the West. This started in Russia, when the European Council imposed sanctions on the country following its annexation of Crimea in March 2014. Crimea had been part of the Ukraine – within the old Soviet Union – since

57 'Britain settles sanctions dispute with Iran's Bank Mellat', London: *Reuters*, 18 June 2019

1954 on the direction of the then USSR leader, Nikita Khrushchev (who himself had roots in the Ukraine area). Following the breakup of the USSR, Crimea (as part of the Ukraine) was detached from Russia in the 1990s. However, there was still a strong feeling among some Crimeans that their real identity lay with Russia. And prior to the Russian takeover, Crimea's parliament had decided to secede from the Ukraine in a controversial vote whose legality was disputed by the Ukrainian government. This was subsequently given popular backing in a referendum, with a majority voting to join the Russian Federation.

Russian president Vladimir Putin maintained that the Crimean referendum followed all international law, but this was not how it was seen in the West. The Venice Commission, an advisory body of the European Council, declared that the referendum was illegal under both the Ukrainian and Crimean constitutions and that it violated international standards and norms. Western politicians, led by John Kerry, the then US secretary of state, stated that the referendum was conducted under the cover of assault rifles and thus the result was obtained through violence. In response, some western governments and international organizations imposed sanctions on Russian individuals and businesses. Having been twice to Crimea when it was part of the Ukraine, I found almost everyone I met to be pro-Russia, so I was not surprised by the referendum result.

I was invited to Moscow for a meeting with the oil company Rosneft to consider challenging the sanctions in the EU court. As I travelled to Russia I could not help thinking of how as a boy of eight, I had been at that public meeting in Bombay and listened to Khrushchev and Bulganin. But that Russia, the one which sent Sputnik into space, was gone. The Berlin Wall had come down. Communism was history.

Before I went to the meeting, the head of my firm's Russia–CIS department, Zoya Burbeza, advised me that if I wanted to impress the post-communist Russians, I had to look smart. So, I went to Harrods and bought a new suit and a new pair of shoes. I only realized when I got to Moscow that I had bought the wrong shoe size.

I arrived on a warm evening and checked in at the Kempinski Hotel overlooking the majestic Kremlin and Red Square. I was received by an individual who introduced himself as Sergei, who, as I understood it, was high up in the Russian government. He said Rosneft was very impressed by my work for Bank Mellat, and that whatever I wanted to see or do in Moscow, including visiting the parliament, he could arrange.

That evening he took me for an excellent dinner in a Georgian restaurant. It was after the meal that things got really interesting. It was still light and so he suggested we take a walk. I agreed and so we went to a very beautiful park. Once there, he asked me how much it had cost for Bank Mellat to succeed in the English Supreme Court.

At first, I thought he was talking about legal fees. Then I realized what he really meant – a bribe. When I told him I didn't have to pay anything, he refused to believe me. He kept saying, 'No, no, you must have paid. How much? We want to know how much you paid, because we want you to do the same for Russia.' He did not mean the Russian government directly, but the Russian-owned company Rosneft.

He kept coming back to money and in turn I kept thinking that as an English solicitor I must defend the British justice system. I told him that the British judges are independent and honest. I said that in my many years of practice before the English court, I had never come across any sign whatsoever of corruption amongst British judges. I don't think he believed me. But the next morning he took me to meet the big shots at Rosneft.

We met members of Rosneft's legal team in the boardroom of their Soviet-era, concrete building opposite the Kremlin. The security was tight, and I had to give them my passport and wait for clearance just to get in. At this meeting, the Russians continued their assessment of Zaiwalla & Co. I didn't know about Russian law but that didn't matter. The point was that they wanted my knowledge of European law.

Rosneft had a team of lawyers already, led by a London solicitor called Joe Hage. Zaiwalla & Co. was to join the team, and on my return to London I went with a colleague to meet Hage, who was very friendly. His firm had only been around for a couple of years at the time and seemed mostly to specialize in acting for the super-rich. For instance, Hage acted for the Sultan of Brunei's brother in his case against the Sultan. I decided to consult my favourite QC, Michael Brindle, who had also appeared in the Bank Mellat case. Brindle advised against my firm having such a shared arrangement with Hage, but I wanted to see whether we could make it work.

At our first meeting, Hage gave me the first draft of the claim he intended to file in the EU court. He made it clear that my firm's name wouldn't be on it; we were to work entirely behind the scenes, playing second fiddle to his firm. That was something I was not prepared to do, and I made it clear to the Russians. That meant I did not act for Rosneft in the sanctions case, and in any event, as I understand it, Hage's law firm was subsequently sacked by them.

However, all this did mean we were approved lawyers for Rosneft. Securing the retainer wasn't easy, and I realized that Soviet-style bureaucracy still existed as the tender had to be signed by about twenty people. Client confidentiality means I cannot reveal most of the work I did for Rosneft, but we started handling cases mainly relating to the theft of money from Russia.

I had been used to dealing with clients from China, Iran and India who had a culture of courtesy and politeness. When dealing with the Bank Mellat case, Michael Brindle and I seemed to be given a gift at every meeting, sometimes Iranian handicrafts or a box of nuts or even an expensive carpet. In Russia, the atmosphere was very different. Very business-like, with no gift-giving, not even any smiling. They do not mix business with pleasure (although there is nothing wrong with that).

Dealing with oligarchs

I became involved in a case involving Yukos, Russia's second-biggest oil company. This had been owned by Mikhail Khodorkovsky, once Russia's wealthiest man but arrested and charged with fraud in October 2003. In May 2005, he was found guilty and sentenced to nine years in prison. In December 2010, while he was still serving his sentence, Khodorkovsky and his business partner Platon Lebedev were found guilty of embezzlement and money laundering, and his prison sentence was extended to 2014. Putin finally pardoned Khodorkovsky, and after his release in December he went into exile in Switzerland.

Yukos itself was nationalized and its shareholders brought a claim against the government. At the Hague, the International Court of Arbitration made a $50 billion award against Russia. Following this, Russia consulted a number of major international law firms, all of whom told them that the award could not be challenged. My reputation was for doing difficult cases like this. So, once again, I was approached by Sergei. I heard him out and said I thought there were grounds for challenging the award as it rested on an energy treaty that had been signed by the Russian government but which in my view was not correctly passed into law at the time. This is because Russian law required such international treaties to be voted upon and approved by its parliament. This, I was told, had not happened.

Just over a year before, I had won a case in the English court on the grounds that an arbitration award was not binding because there was no arbitration agreement.[58] The $8 million award was made by the Grain and Feed Trade Association (GAFTA) against the Indian government company PEC Limited.

In GAFTA, arbitration lawyers are not allowed to represent the parties at the oral hearing. So the Indian government's trade representatives appeared themselves and lost. They obtained an English barrister's advice that the award could not be challenged. They then came to me. Here my knowledge of having acted for India came in useful. Indian rules stipulate that when a government company enters into a contract over a certain value, it has to be agreed and signed by two directors (that is, not the usual single director). This rule had not been followed and so I argued there was no contract, and therefore there could be no arbitration and certainly no award. Although PEC was hesitant initially it took my advice.

My legal friends, including Michael Brindle, were not convinced I was right. On a trip to Iran, he and I were visiting the Zoroastrian fire temple in Isfahan and he told me I didn't even have a small chance of winning the PEC case. Nonetheless, I brought in Soli Sorabjee, the former attorney general of India, as my expert on Indian law. The other side brought Harish Salve, a top Indian lawyer. Both Sorabjee and Salve gave evidence before Mr Justice Andrew Smith on Indian law and were cross-examined. Sorabjee's evidence was accepted. We won.

The Yukos case was different because the decision against Russia was in The Hague. Rosneft asked me to identify a lawyer who could be successful in the Dutch court. I selected a very reliable person, Professor van den Berg. I told him my argument that the energy treaty had not been approved by the Russian parliament, and that therefore the arbitration agreement was non-existent. My suggested

---

58 PEC Ltd v. Asia Golden Rice Co Ltd [2014] EWHC 1583 (Comm)

argument won the case, saving Russia a liability of $50 billion.[59] There has since been an appeal, but I am not involved in that.

The Yukos victory opened a lot of doors for Zaiwalla & Co. in Russia. The Russians could not believe that my argument had won the case, and even more that I gave them the ground to challenge the award without charging them anything. (I had actually spent a lot of time on the case, including travelling to Brussels with Zoya and Rosneft's representatives to meet the new Dutch lawyer. This was one of those occasions when in order to win goodwill, you don't charge a party for your time.) In 2016, soon after the Yukos success, the Russian ambassador to the UK hosted an impressive lunch in my honour at his official residence.

After that I was invited by the deputy prime minister of Russia as a guest of the Russian government for the Saint Petersburg Economic Forum. In 2017, I was again invited and met the Indian prime minister Narendra Modi, who was the special guest. In 2018, too, I was invited but could not attend as I was recovering from an ankle surgery.

In many ways my most interesting Russian client has been Dr Alexander Dobrovinsky, a top Russian lawyer based in Moscow and London and known for acting for oligarchs. He was sued in London by Sergei Polonsky, a hugely controversial Russian businessman, for $600 million over an alleged fraud. Dobrovinsky initially went to the large firm White & Case, who had incurred very large fees without closing the case. Then he came to me.

Fearing he would be charged in Russia with fraud and embezzlement of funds from some real estate projects, Polonsky had been living in Cambodia, which then had no extradition treaty

---

59 The Russian Federation v. Veteran Petroleum Limited, Yukos Universal Limited and Hulley Enterprises Limited [2016] (C/09/477160 / HA ZA 15-1, 15-2 and 15-112)

with Russia. In 2012, he was jailed in Cambodia for three months on assault charges. During his imprisonment, he had limited access to phones and email and so had entrusted Dobrovinsky to sell his property empire of developments in London, the US, France, Moscow and elsewhere.

It was then alleged that Dobrovinsky claimed he was selling the business to an offshore company owned by Roman Abramovich, the Chelsea Football Club owner. Soon after the deal was completed, the metals billionaire Oleg Deripaska, who had also expressed an interest in buying the properties, revealed that the buyer was actually Roman Trotsenko, to whom Polonsky claimed he specifically told his lawyer he did not want the business sold because he did not trust him.

The case was heard in the chancery division of the High Court in April 2016 in front of Gabriel Moss QC, who was sitting as a High Court judge. My firm had engaged George Bompas QC and Andrew de Mestre. Moss handed down his judgement on 27 May 2016, rejecting the allegations made against Dobrovinsky.[60]

My firm's delight at the victory was understandable. This had been a fiercely contested application by a claimant to stay the trial of claims against reputable legal professionals. The application included serious allegations of wrongdoing, none of which were found to have any merit. The decision demonstrated that English judges examine applications critically and will not accept evidence, even when coming from lawyers, which does not meet the requisite standards of reliability and credibility necessary to do justice between the parties. This dispassionate and critical approach reinforces London's reputation as a leading venue for the resolution of international disputes.

---

60 Polonskiy v. Alexander Dobrovinsky & Partners LLP [2016] EWHC 1114 (Ch)

Maybe one of the by-products of this status, however, is that the cost of going to law in London can be staggering. For example, in January 2018 my firm was instructed by a Ukrainian oligarch who was suing two other oligarchs and his fellow nationals in the English courts. The three had been partners some years previously. The defendant had challenged the jurisdiction of the English court and after the hearing of this application, the judge, having given his judgement granting the jurisdiction application to the defendants, gave a later date for parties to make submissions on cost and application for leave to appeal. The claimant oligarch was dissatisfied with his legal team and instructed us to make an application for leave to appeal. Our client was shocked to find out that for a one-and-a-half day jurisdiction application, one of the defendants claimed costs of £2.5 million. He had instructed a US law firm with an office in London. Their breakdown of costs showed they had twenty-three solicitors working on the case. This was completely disproportionate and unthinkable at the start of my professional career.

Hogan Lovells dumped

On 14 February 2018, *Lawyer Weekly*'s headline read 'Hogan Lovells dumped in £300m oligarch domicile battle', with the subtitle 'Zaiwalla & Co. has replaced Hogan Lovells in an ongoing spat between two Ukrainian oligarchs'.

The claimant, businessman Vadim Shulman, originally turned to Hogan Lovells solicitors in his bid to reclaim profits he says he never received from his partnership with Gennadiy Bogolyubov. The High Court had delivered a judgement against Shulman on the grounds that the English Court did not have jurisdiction.[61] We were instructed in place of Hogan Lovells to apply for leave to appeal

61 Shulman v. Kolomoisky [2018] EWHC 160 (Ch)

to the Court of Appeal. We did our best, but the Court of Appeal refused leave. It was indeed very satisfactory that Shulman had selected Zaiwalla & Co. and not another City of London large firm.

However, if these cases involved people with colourful lives, it was nothing compared to the one I was involved with which involved the Sicilian mafia.

10

The Mafia Client

In the mid-1990s, I received an international call from Montreal from a man identifying himself as Joseph Zappia.

'I have a judgement against me of the Canadian Supreme Court in respect of my very substantial claim against the Canadian government,' he said. 'I want to go to the International Court of Justice in The Hague to appeal this.'

He explained to me that his claim related to his company's involvement in the construction of the Olympic village for the 1976 Montreal Olympic Games. He said he had been advised by Sajjad Haidar, a chartered accountant in the United Arab Emirates (UAE), to seek my assistance, having been informed that I had a good reputation for taking on difficult cases and turning them around.

I told Zappia I needed to consider it. Two of my colleagues on the ICC International Court of Arbitration in Paris were also judges of the International Court of Justice (ICJ) in The Hague. One of them was Bola Ajibola, who after retirement went on to become the Nigerian high commissioner in London. Bola told me that my proposed client had no chance of getting the ICJ (which is also often referred to as the World Court) to accept jurisdiction. That was because the ICJ can only look at legal disputes between states. A private party cannot sue a state in the ICJ without the consent of the state, something no state would do. So, I told Zappia that I could not take his case on.

In 1998 he phoned me again – this time from Rome. He said he wanted to start a new case in the English court and that the English solicitors he had contacted would not take it on. It was against Clifford Chance and he wanted to sue them for deception.

The case intrigued me. It meant taking on Clifford Chance, one of the world's biggest law firms. Zappia was clearly keen to fight, but I didn't know much about him. I had never met him. He told me that he had the contract for the Montreal Olympic village and that he was the first to set up a foreign construction the company in the UAE, but that was all.

It was not until some years later in 2012, with the publication of Andre Cedilot and Andre Noel's book *Mafia Inc*,[62] that I was to find out his true story. This is that he was a mafia leader. The book revealed he was born Giuseppe Zappia to Calabrian parents in 1925 and migrated to Canada. There he sweet-talked Montreal's mayor, Jean Drapeau, providing assurances that he could build the Olympic village (which was to house the Games' 9,500 athletes, coaches and delegates) in no time and at a rock-bottom price. Drapeau, ignoring advice from municipal bureaucrats, awarded the contract to Zappia company's Les Terrasses Zarolega without a call for tender. In November 1974, with the Games less than two years away, work had still not begun, and the provincial government had to take over. The subsequent budget overruns were to ruin Quebec's finances for years.

---

62 Andre Cedilot and Andre Noel, *Mafia Inc.: The Long, Bloody Reign of Canada's Sicilian Clan*, Random House of Canada, 2011

Zappia fled Canada. A police investigation led to him being charged on twenty-six counts of fraud, extortion and payments of secret commissions to the detriment of the Olympic Games Organizing Committee and several contractors. An international warrant was issued for his arrest. He was finally caught in Switzerland in 1985 and spent two months in prison before an officer from Canada was dispatched to bring him back to Montreal. Two key witnesses died before his trial could enter its final phase. Zappia was acquitted in 1988, and then went to Abu Dhabi and returned to his construction business.

It was this that had led to the case against Clifford Chance. He had constructed the Abu Dhabi Chamber of Commerce building and other infrastructure projects in the capital and Sharjah. However, he fell out with the then crown prince of Abu Dhabi, who is now the ruler, alleging that he sacked him without paying. He then sued the Abu Dhabi government for some $1.2 billion. He had worked out an unusual deal with Clifford Chance's office in Dubai insofar as they would get a percentage of the claim. They then started proceedings for him in New York through an associate firm, in order to establish that the New York courts had jurisdiction to consider the issue of jurisdiction.

In the meantime, however, the crown prince allegedly gave Clifford Chance a handsome retainer contract so that the firm then announced – according to Zappia – that they were going to act for the other side. An indignant Zappia said they could not drop him, but Clifford Chance insisted that they could.

Zappia becomes a client

This was Zappia's story when he approached me. I went through the documents and found there was evidence of some wrongdoing on the part of Clifford Chance. I took the case on and started the claim.

With my advice Zappia sued in the English court for breach of retainer contract and breach of fiduciary duty to the client.[63] Clifford Chance applied to strike out the case on the grounds that this was an abuse of the process and that there was no case. Forty-eight hours before the hearing I received a defence from Clifford Chance signed by Michael Brindle (which is how I first met him), admitting breach of contract and breach of fiduciary duty to the client. So, Clifford Chance was admitting there was a claim. But the drama is what happened after we won. The real fight was about the amount of the damages claim.

Zappia came to my office regularly and we became close. He was very charming with the gift of the gab, old by this time but very active. To look at him, there was nothing special, just a medium-sized man although with a very strong voice. But what I learnt as I came to know him was that he was a great showman. He told me he had been an opera singer, and while I never heard him sing, he certainly always seemed to want to be on stage.

He believed that he would succeed in getting his much-exaggerated claim against Clifford Chance in full. However, I was also beginning to realize that Zappia was an erratic man as he sacked my firm three times and then brought me in again on the case. Immediately after we had won the Clifford Chance strike-out application, he thought my firm was too small, so he went to Peters and Peters. He was not satisfied with them and then after a year he came back to me. A few weeks later he sacked my firm again after a disagreement on strategy to be adopted for his case. But we were soon reinstructed.

The case to determine under what categories of damage he could claim went before Mr Justice Scott. Scott, like all British judges, was

---

63 Zappia Middle East Construction Co Ltd v. Clifford Chance [2001] 2 WLUK 491

honest. He sent a message to me saying, 'I acted for Clifford Chance in the past when I was at the Bar, do you have any objection?' My counsel, Justin Fenwick QC, said, 'No objection, he's a good judge.' But Zappia said, 'No, no, no.'

In response to this the court brought in a new judge, Blofeld, from the regions (who, I noted with interest, happened to be the brother of a county cricketer). Meanwhile, on the other side. Ross Williams was acting for the underwriters and they wanted to settle the matter. They paid a six-figure sum in court to close the matter, plus our costs. Zappia would not accept this offer. He wanted between £300 and £400 million. The judge, however, cut down the ambit of the claim to a much more modest figure. Zappia again rejected this. He said he wanted a minimum of £150 million. The other side was coming to a meeting with me to try and settle the matter, so I specially went to Rome to persuade Zappia to give my firm instructions to put forward a realistic figure of £30 million to start the settlement talks. I told Zappia, 'Look, asking for £150 million is just not on. English courts don't normally award these sorts of amounts. It's not going to happen. Give me authority to propose £30 million from our side to start serious negotiations going.'

He agreed. But just before the meeting the next morning he called me and said, 'No way. Go and appeal.' So, we went to the Court of Appeal. The other side applied for security for costs. Zappia was offended that Clifford Chance (as his previous solicitors) had asked him to provide security for costs. He said, 'They know my wealth.' He arranged for me to travel to Geneva for a meeting with him and his Swiss bankers to confirm his wealth to me. On the basis of the confirmation I had orally received, I made an affidavit in court on his behalf that he had sufficient wealth to meet any cost ordered against him by the court. Security for costs was ordered for £50,000.

A strange turn of events

It is what happened next that first demonstrated to me what an unusual client I had.

What I did not know – but learnt later – was that Clifford Chance had in the meantime been in contact with Zappia for a back-channel settlement negotiation. Some Italian lawyer had approached him and told him that he knew somebody high up in Clifford Chance who would help settle the claim. He did not alert me to this. My counsel, Justin Fenwick QC, was a director in the Bar's professional indemnity board, which is run by the underwriters. Justin rang me and said, 'I understand that there is a meeting this evening with Mr Zappia, the senior partner of Clifford Chance and the head of the professional indemnity underwriters' syndicate to settle the matter. Do you know anything about it?' I phoned up Zappia and asked, 'Is it true you're meeting them for settlement?' He said emphatically, 'No, of course not. I wouldn't do it without you.'

Zappia later told me that Clifford Chance had told him through his Italian contact that if he involved my firm and Fenwick there would be no chance of settlement. I cannot say if this was true. The message was to deal directly with Clifford Chance through the Italian lawyer. They also told him that there is no need to put up security for costs. This, they said, would be a waste of money. Clifford Chance, it seems, held out the prospect to Zappia of a large settlement. For Clifford Chance to have private meetings with my client without telling me was professionally wrong but this is what happened. He was confident of getting a settlement and, I understand, discussed figures with Clifford Chance directly through the Italian intermediary lawyer. He also sacked me for the third time, saying, 'I don't need you now.' He had not paid my bills, saying he would pay after the settlement. There was no settlement.

Then came the hearing to strike out Zappia's appeal for not putting in the security for costs. For some reason, Clifford Chance had applied to the Court of Appeal to strike out his claim for not complying with the court's order requiring Zappia to provide security for costs. Twenty-four hours before the hearing, Zappia turned up in my office with his wife Francoise. He said that they had applied for striking out and that the hearing was the following day. Would my firm act for him?

I told him I was unable to accept to be reinstructed at this late stage. A lot of time had passed from the time he sacked my firm for the third time. Zappia pleaded, 'I'm going to appear myself. Can you help me prepare the bundles?' I said, 'You have come at the last minute, you have not put up security, and you've had private meetings with Clifford Chance without telling me. Okay, I'll help you prepare the bundles and assist you without my firm filing an appearance. I will sit next to you to help you on a gratis basis.' But I made it clear that my firm would not appear.

The other side had paid a six-figure sum in court and I suggested he should consider accepting it. Zappia's answer was an emphatic no. Clifford Chance, through the law firm acting for them, had indicated to me earlier that they were prepared to increase the settlement figure to close this matter. Zappia was confident he could win and as we went into the courtroom, he seemed a man in control and in a buoyant mood. He said he would explain to the court what had happened. The case was to be heard by three judges. The moment he saw the judges take their seats his confidence drained away. He could barely speak and was hardly audible in court. The judges told me I could help him with what to say but not to address the court. Zappia was obviously nervous and by the end was a completely broken man. The whole claim was struck off. The evening after the hearing, at about 5.30 p.m., the senior partner at Clifford Chance phoned me up. 'Mr Zaiwalla, please tell your former client if he contacts you that all the negotiations are now off.'

Getting paid

Now for me the question was getting my firm's fees. Zappia had paid counsel fees for some previous work but a large amount remained unpaid. My firm was owed around £350,000. The unpaid counsel's fee was around £180,000. He just didn't pay. His wife Francoise, a French Canadian, a good woman, appeared trustworthy. She said, 'Don't worry, you'll be paid.' But then soon after the end of his claim in the English court she died. So, I had to sue Zappia for my fees. My outstanding invoice went before the costs judge for assessment. Zappia instructed a small London law firm for the assessment proceedings. I got a judgement against him for costs of around £290,000 plus costs of assessment and interest. To this day the judgement remains unpaid. My firm had to pay the counsel's fees from our own office account. Despite repeated reminders he did not clear the unpaid fees. After some time, I had to incur the cost of instructing lawyers to pursue enforcement. As I did this I discovered something about Zappia that quite shook me, as Cedilot and Noel set out in *Mafia Inc.*

On 11 February 2005, the Italian police arrested Zappia at his deluxe villa in Rome. He was charged with attempting to win the bridge construction contract between Sicily and Calabria (intended to be the world's longest suspension bridge) on behalf of Vito Rizzuto, also known as 'Montreal's Teflon Don'.

Rizzuto was alleged to be the leading boss of the Sicilian Mafia in Canada, heading the notorious Montreal-based Rizzuto crime family. The Direzione Investigativa Antimafia (DIA) announced it had issued four other arrest warrants. They first targeted Rizzuto, but he was already in prison in Laval, Quebec, awaiting the decision on his extradition to the United States. The other warrants targeted three other middlemen: Filippo Raineri, a manager of buildings in downtown Montreal; Hakim Hammoudi, a Paris resident accused of being a liaison between Zappia and Rizzuto; and Sivalingam Sivabavnandan, a Sri Lankan businessman living in London. At a press conference in Rome, Colonel Paolo La Forgia announced that the group had planned to launder billions of dollars. A few months earlier, the conspirators had participated in a preliminary bid on the bridge contract through Zappia International. This front company had submitted an expression of interest to Stretto di Messina SpA, the public company created to oversee the project. According to La Forgia, the group had already sunk some $6.4 million into the venture. Alfonso Pecoraro Scanio, president of Italy's Green Party, said, 'The anti-Mafia police investigation confirms what we have been saying for a long time: The Strait of Messina bridge is a magnet for the Mafia and organized crime.'

Mafia Inc's authors document how Zappia knew Silvio Berlusconi, the former Italian prime minister who was keen on the bridge project. Zappia had confirmed to a reporter from the *Montreal Gazette* that 'I know him' and when asked for how long, he replied with 'for some time'. The authors also report the DIA managed to intercept two brief conversations between Zappia and Rizzuto. In the first recording, Zappia says he is sure he will win the bridge contract. In the other, Rizzuto advised his agent in Rome to persuade their Arab partners to cough up further millions.

Next, Sivabavnandan, the Sri Lankan partner, was arrested in France, then extradited to Italy. He pleaded guilty to charges of Mafia associations and served half of a two-year term. Hammoudi, the Algerian-born associate who had once lived in Montreal, turned himself in to the Italian authorities and was given a two-year suspended sentence. Raineri remained in the city of his birth, Montreal. Zappia's trial became bogged down in legal wrangling. As for Vito Rizzuto, having to answer charges from the Italian authorities was the least of his worries. He had more immediate concerns; namely fighting his extradition to the United States.

In December 2013 Rizzuto died in Montreal. Zappia, I have learnt, has recently passed away. I never got my money. I had to pay out of my own pocket. I couldn't enforce the costs judgement in my favour because he was under house arrest. There was no question of my trying to get my fees, plus he was also a very old man by the end, at ninety-two.

Although Zappia's was the most chilling case I have ever handled, there are a number of cases where my overseas clients have taken me for a ride. Some of my Indian clients have often proved difficult. There was an Indian company that had a joint venture with a large Belgian corporation. I went to Antwerp to settle the issue of the Belgian partner giving up his share in the joint venture. The company received several million euros' benefit as a result of my work. My firm's fees had been agreed to in advance. Yet after the work was done, the owner of the Indian company didn't pay up. I issued proceedings against him, but he did not acknowledge my firm's service of legal proceedings and I had to obtain a default judgement from the English court, which would be difficult to enforce in the Indian courts.

In an odd way there were two good results from the Zappia case. The first was my professional interaction with opponent counsel Michael Brindle QC. I did the interlocutory applications in the Zappia case myself and Michael was my opponent counsel. Later, my firm instructed him, and we worked as a team on many of our cases, with major successes for our clients. As well as being one of the finest QCs I have known, Michael always displayed integrity and straightforwardness towards his opponents.

Secondly, since then, my firm has started taking security from clients before we begin work. This is part of an overall change in how we operate, which has involved the office being reorganized and the recruitment of additional staff, all part of a process which has seen the firm expand.

11

The Great and the Good

In the spring of 2004 I received an unexpected call. It was from Mrs Takla from the Office of Tibet in London. She wanted to meet. What she told me at my office was even more surprising. 'His Holiness the Dalai Lama would like a private meeting with you on his next visit,' she said. 'He wants to have a one-to-one chat with you about Tibet.'

I could hardly contain my astonishment. I felt they must know about my work with the Chinese government. Clearly, the Dalai Lama was well informed. Soon there was another call from Mrs Takla. 'His Holiness the Dalai Lama is coming to Glasgow. Would you be so good as to travel to meet him? He wants to discuss the China issue.'

Excited though I was, my instinctive lawyer's caution made me decide to talk to the Chinese ambassador first. After all, China was my firm's client. The Chinese ambassador in London at that point was Ma Zhengang. I did not ask him whether I could meet the Dalai Lama but decided that I should as a courtesy mention it, given the Chinese government's hostility towards him. A few days after I told the ambassador, he called me to his embassy. I asked him why they were in conflict with him, risking giving China a reputation as being an intolerant nation. I said the Dalai Lama is Tibetan but is not claiming independence, and that he should have his monasteries back and be able to live in Tibet.

The ambassador was prepared for our meeting. He showed me books written in Chinese in which he said the Dalai Lama had endorsed the claim that "half of China belonged to Tibet" China belonged to Tibet or Tibet belonged to China? Please confirm. He said that I should meet the Dalai Lama, but that I should find out whether this really was his view.

I travelled to Glasgow with Katie Arnander, a good friend who had expressed her keenness to meet the spiritual leader. He was addressing a public gathering of several thousand people there.

Mrs Takla was with me all the time and once the address was over she said we should go see him. I wanted to take Katie but was told that our meeting was confidential and I needed to meet him alone.

The Dalai Lama received me warmly, and tea was served. Over an hour-long meeting he told me that he had found out I was one of the few non-Chinese in Europe whom the Chinese government trusted. He asked if I could assist him in creating a second-channel dialogue with China regarding his return to Tibet.

Having been briefed by the Chinese, I was ready with questions. I told the Dalai Lama about my discussions with the Chinese ambassador and asked him about his views on Tibet's claims on Chinese territory. He replied, 'They are my people. I have to keep them happy.' I saw the political side of the Dalai Lama that day. He wanted to go back to Tibet and was clear he did not want it to be independent. His priority was to be with his people, to be at the monastery in Lhasa and to be with those who wanted to follow the Gelugpa sect of Tibetan Buddhism.

I was aware of China's revised policy towards religion. The Communist Party had earlier banned the practice of religion, but the policy was now that Chinese citizens could follow a religion provided they did not have a direct controlling link with a foreign country. For example, they could practice Christianity but the head of the church in China should be Chinese, not the Pope or the Archbishop of Canterbury. I told the Dalai Lama that, on this basis, China could possibly be persuaded to allow him to come back to Tibet as head of the Tibetan Buddhist temple. I said I would speak to the Chinese authorities about him. It was a positive meeting, and he presented me with a white shawl and his staff asked me to pose for a photograph with him, which I did. He walked me to the lift when I was leaving, and before he said goodbye he took my right hand, put it on his heart and said, 'I trust you.' A few days later the Office of Tibet in London sent me the photograph which was taken after my meeting.

On my return to London I contacted the Chinese ambassador. I suggested the second-channel dialogue and reminded him that China had been facing a lot of criticism and demonstrations all over the world regarding the Chinese occupation of Tibet and their attitude towards the Dalai Lama. I stressed that the Dalai Lama accepted that Tibet was part of China and he did not want to be its ruler as he had been when Tibet was independent. He simply wanted to be back in Tibet under Chinese rule and to be the leader of his community.

I could see that the ambassador was not at ease at my suggestion, but he came back and said that because of China's close friendship with me, we could start the dialogue. The ambassador organized a meeting for me with the commercial consular minister at the Chinese embassy office in Bayswater, after which he reported to the Central Committee of the Communist Party of China. When I asked the ambassador some weeks later about progress, he said that the Dalai Lama was sending his brother to Beijing for further discussions, so I should keep the second channel dormant for the time being. Nothing further happened after that and as I did not hear anything further from the ambassador I treated the matter as closed.

I was invited to go to China in 2013 when the new government took over. While in Beijing I made discreet inquiries, at a high level, if any progress had been made in this regard. The response was, 'After he dies, the problem will be over.' Clearly, the Chinese government was not interested.

I was not arrogant enough to think I could have helped provide a solution to the Tibet problem, but I had to try. I came away from my meeting with the Dalai Lama thinking that he was straightforward and honest, and he deserved my help. I saw a similarity in him to Mahatma Gandhi. Gandhi was not an orator. He was not an original thinker. He was not a writer. He had no new philosophy. Satyagraha is part of the ancient Indian culture. His ahimsa, or the principle of non-violence, was strengthened through his correspondence with the Russian philosopher Leo Tolstoy, who in turn was influenced by his contact with Bahá'u'lláh, founder of the Bahá'í Faith. Gandhi's greatest strength was his honesty, not least with himself. When the British viceroy asked him what he wanted, he said he wanted the British to leave as rulers and come back as partners. I found the same trait in the Dalai Lama.

In the course of our conversation, the Dalai Lama acknowledged that Tibet had made economic progress during Chinese rule and that this had benefitted his people. Today the majority in Tibet is Han Chinese, not Tibetans. India could learn from this in solving the Kashmir issue. Under Article 370 of the Indian constitution, citizens from outside Jammu and Kashmir could not settle there. But if more Indian businesses could establish themselves in the troubled state, it would bring in jobs and improve the economic situation of the Kashmir region. Economic upliftment usually, in the long run, lights the common thread of humanity, which exists latently in all human beings.

Benazir Bhutto

I had an interesting discussion on the Kashmir issue with a politician who could have helped solve it, Benazir Bhutto. My firm was instructed by her when Nawaz Sharif became the prime minister of Pakistan. I had first heard Benazir speak when she was Pakistan's PM and addressed the Confederation of British Industry in London. I was struck by how well she judged the audience and also by her subtle, feminine touch. It was some years later when we met in a more casual atmosphere, over a lunch hosted by Tony Baldry. By then she was no longer PM.

At the lunch at her sister's home in London, Benazir told me that she and Rajiv Gandhi, when they were the prime ministers of their countries, had made substantial progress towards finding a solution. She also admitted that for the Pakistan government, any solution on Kashmir could only happen if it was approved by the Pakistan military. She was positive about finding an answer if she ever became the PM again. She also told me clearly that, to her knowledge, the Kashmir insurgency was financed by 'Saudi Wahhabis'.

The years since I had first heard her speak had been turbulent for her. She had won power in the 1988 election after transforming her father Zulfikar's Pakistan People's Party (PPP) from a socialist to a liberal one. But she fell out with the military and conservative circles in her country; her attempts at reform failed; her administration was accused of corruption and nepotism; and she was dismissed in 1990. She returned to power in 1993, but again her attempts at reform led to trouble and her government was dogged by several controversies, including the assassination of her brother Murtaza, a failed 1995 coup and a bribery scandal involving her and her husband Asif Ali Zardari. In response, Pakistan's president again dismissed her government. The PPP lost the 1997 election and in 1998 she went into self-exile in Dubai, leading her party mainly through proxies.

Sometime after Tony Baldry's lunch, I was walking towards an Indian shop in Knightsbridge close to my Pont Street flat when I got a call on my mobile phone from Qadri Baba. I had been introduced to him in Dubai by Akram Shaikh, an old friend who lives there. I had been told that Baba, a Muslim holy man, had spiritual powers. Given my affinity for spirituality, I was keen to meet him, albeit as a friend and not as a guru.

My interest in Baba had been aroused when I read the fascinating *Autobiography of a Yogi* by Paramahansa Yogananda,[64] in which he describes his experience of meeting spiritual masters from various world religions. When I first met Baba, he produced from the air a yellow stone and gave it to me and asked me to make a ring of it and wear it to bring me good luck. I did have the ring made but wore it only for a day or two.

I was intrigued by his call because he had never phoned me before. What he then said was even more surprising. He said he wanted me to say hello to someone whom I already knew – and then passed the phone to Benazir. After we spoke she gave the phone back to Baba, who told me he had recommended to Benazir that I should be her lawyer. Moreover, he wanted me to come straight away to Dubai to take Benazir back with me to London. He said, 'Come tonight and take her tomorrow, it is urgent.' I told him I could not come that soon but that I would come the following day, and that was agreed. He gave me an email address to give my flight

---

64 Yogananda Paramahansa, *Autobiography of a Yogi*, New York: The Philosophical Library, 1946

details and said I would be picked up at Dubai airport and taken to Benazir's home.

I left the next day and arrived early morning in Dubai, where I was driven straight to Benazir's home in a car provided by ARY Jewellers of Dubai. When we arrived, I was greeted first by Abdul Rezak, the chairman of ARY Group, who explained to me that the Pakistan courts had convicted Benazir, handing down a prison sentence, and that it was important Benazir left Dubai safely and entered the UK. Abdul Rezak told me my task was to accompany her on a flight the same night to Heathrow.

Just before we left, Benazir was told there was a call for her from her husband, who was at that time in prison in Pakistan. Her face lit up and, although she went to another room to take the call, I could hear in her voice the pleasure she felt talking to her husband. She was obviously in love with her husband, contrary to the rumour at the time that their relationship had broken down.

The flight to London was memorable. Abdul Rezak had provided first-class tickets and at the Dubai airport we went through the VIP departure gate without any hurdles. The only other passenger in the first-class cabin was the Italian wife of Adnan Khashoggi, the Saudi arms dealer. Benazir knew Lamia, and she introduced me to her. I got to know the former PM very well during the flight. She spoke openly and it seemed that she liked and trusted me. I found her to be a tender soul. Like me, she was very much into spirituality and we discussed homoeopathic medicines, in which she appeared to have faith.

When we landed at Heathrow there was no VIP reception for Benazir. We had to stand in the immigration queue and as we did so Benazir said, 'Sarosh, for me whenever I have to pass through British immigration, I still get a pang in my stomach as I used to get when I had to travel to the UK as a student.' However, no sooner had we got through that it became clear she was no ordinary immigrant. A car whisked us to the BBC Studios for an interview, and I was very impressed by how she handled the journalist's questions.

My firm soon began acting for Benazir, with the formal instructions coming from Wajid Hassan, former Pakistani high commissioner to the UK, who was then living in London.

Hassan told me Benazir already had a legal team in Pakistan who had a firm in London that they used for their legal work in Britain. They were not happy at my firm being instructed as we had a history of acting for the Indian government, but he said Benazir had overruled their objection.

At that time, Pakistan's prime minister was Nawaz Sharif. He was opposed to Benazir, and she told me that Sharif and his party had concocted allegations of corruption against her. The Pakistan government had instructed Clifford Chance to seize Benazir and her family's assets in the United Kingdom, and Benazir feared she would be extradited. We stalled all attempts by Clifford Chance to do this.

In due course, Benazir and I become very close. She would speak to me with complete openness and trust, even on personal matters. She was concerned that I was a single man after my divorce and I had not remarried. I told her that I was not inclined to remarry. Benazir insisted that I meet women for marriage purposes, hosting a special lunch at her sister's London apartment for me to meet some, as she put it, 'nice Iranian girls'. Her mother was Iranian, and she knew that as a Parsi I had ancient connections with Iran. And so I had a wonderful lunch with five ladies, four prospective wives in their late thirties or early forties and Benazir. After the women left, Benazir asked me if I had made a choice. When I told her that I did not find any of them suitable, she said next time she would find me younger women. This was another human side of Benazir. She would always tease me about finding a girl for me to get married to and said a man like me should not remain single.

While Benazir may not have been able to act as matchmaker, she was the one client I always looked forward to meeting, with her smile and gentle teasing. During these years I had commissioned Angela Colman, the English artist, to travel to India and do some watercolours for me. I wanted a collection of original paintings of India through English eyes. I then published these as *India: Colours of the Continent*,[65] which I dedicated to my late father. This book was launched at my office by Sir Colin Campbell, the vice chancellor of Nottingham University. Benazir came for the launch.

Two years or so after my firm had started acting for Benazir, I was in China when I heard of yet another military coup in Pakistan. General Musharraf took over and Nawaz Sharif moved from the prime minister's residence to prison and was eventually exiled in Saudi Arabia. I returned to London to find the coup had cheered Benazir up. She told me over the telephone that now there was nothing for her to fear – we could close my firm's file on her case.

Not long after that I was in Dubai. Abdul Rezak invited me to his home to see Qadri Baba, who thanked me profusely for looking after Benazir during her stay in London. He then told me that Musharraf had approached Benazir to take over as PM from Nawaz Sharif, but Benazir had refused because, as a democrat, she would only do this if elected by the people. Qadri Baba told me that this was a mistake and predicted that she would never be PM again.

Qadri Baba would prove right in his prediction, although his claim that Benazir turned down Musharraf's offer cannot be substantiated. As made clear in Anatol Lieven's *Pakistan: A Hard Country*[66] – widely considered the best book on Pakistan – there was

---

65 Angela Colman, *India, Colours of a Continent: The Zaiwalla Collection*, London: Zaiwalla and Co., 1999

66 Anatol Lieven, *Pakistan: A Hard Country*, London: Penguin UK, 2012

an alliance between her and Musharraf eventually, but this came about in October 2007 and paved the way for her return to Pakistan.

Worried about the stability of the country, the US pushed Musharraf to meet Benazir and come to an arrangement that might strengthen his legitimacy. In this, they were supported by the UK government. In January 2007, Musharraf held his first meeting with Benazir at a hotel in Abu Dhabi. More talks followed in June. It was agreed that the Pakistani authorities would drop all charges of corruption against both her and her husband. It was also agreed that if Musharraf stepped down from his military position and was elected as a civilian president, then Benazir would be willing to serve under him as PM. Musharraf also agreed to lift the ban on individuals serving more than two terms as PM. Much of the work for this was done by Condoleezza Rice, US secretary of state, and Jack Straw, British foreign secretary. In October 2007, Musharraf was elected president by Pakistan's parliament. In keeping with the agreement between Benazir and Musharraf, PPP representatives abstained rather than vote against Musharraf's nomination. Musharraf signed an amnesty covering cases against Benazir, and everything was clear for her to return.

Before that, there was time for a visit to London and I was invited to a dinner in honour of Benazir, hosted at the Cavalry and Guards Club on Piccadilly by Lady Olga Maitland, a former junior defence minister in John Major's government and a good friend. Benazir was thrilled to learn that I was with a beautiful Eastern European woman and we talked not about politics but about my girlfriend. She wanted to know more about her, how did I find her, and there was much good-humoured conversation. What I could not have known was that this would be the last time I would see Benazir.

She returned to Pakistan in October 2007, which annoyed Musharraf as he had requested she only return after the 2008 election when it was expected she would become PM again.

Musharraf, who had himself survived several assassination attempts by Islamist militants, had warned Benazir that she too would be a target. So she requested that the US or the UK, who had helped her do the deal with Musharraf, take responsibility for her security. They refused, and her security detail was instead organized by Musharraf. On the afternoon of 27 December 2007, while in Rawalpindi, she was assassinated.

Musharraf blamed the Pakistani Taliban. However, in August 2017, ten years later, a Pakistani anti-terrorism court declared Musharraf a fugitive in Benazir's murder trial. The court dismissed charges against five alleged Taliban militants accused of being involved in the killing, while two police officers were found guilty of 'mishandling the crime scene', becoming the only people to be convicted in the case. For many in Pakistan, the verdict, the first to be issued in the decade since the assassination, offered no clarity into who actually orchestrated the killing.

It was a tragic example of how the politics of India and Pakistan could not be more different. India can proudly claim to be the world's largest democracy. Since it became free in 1947, every change in government has come through the ballot box. In Pakistan, there are military coups and no elected government has served its full term. Yet, one thing unites the two countries, and it is spirituality.

P.V. Narasimha Rao, Indian prime minister

I had met Benazir through a Muslim holy man and was to meet P.V. Narasimha Rao, the Indian prime minister, through a Hindu holy man. This was because of the Downing Street dinner in 1991 I had helped organize for influential Asians.

After that dinner, Chandraswami, known internationally as 'the godman of India', said he wanted to meet me. He was supposed to be the most well-connected man in India. He was introduced to me by Ketan Somaia (who was alleged to be the money bag for President Moi of Kenya and who is now in jail in London after being found guilty of a $19.5 million fraud). I met Chandraswami for the first time at a London hotel. He said if I arranged a meeting with John Major, in return he would take me for breakfast with Rao, who was then India's PM.

Rao was a devotee of Chandraswami. The story goes that Rao had met Chandraswami some years before and he had said, 'You are going to be the prime minister of India.' When Rao, who had been a health minister, was not given a seat to fight by Rajiv Gandhi in the 1991 election, he announced his retirement. He went to see Chandraswami and told him his prediction had been wrong. Chandraswami said, 'You stay back. You will be the prime minister.' Four days later Rajiv Gandhi was assassinated. A few days after that, Congress won the election and Rao was indeed made PM.

Chandraswami took me to Delhi the same week I first met him, at his own cost. We travelled first class and he put me up in a five-star hotel. I stayed for two days and he took me for breakfast with Rao in the prime minister's residence. When we went in through security, no questions were asked. Rao came to meet us dressed in traditional Indian attire. He always dressed like that except in England, where he wore Nehru jacket and trousers.

Rao could claim to be the most intellectual prime minister of India. He knew several languages and according to Natwar Singh, one of India's most high-ranked diplomats, 'Unlike Nehru, his knowledge of Sanskrit was profound. Nehru had a temper, Rao, a temperament. His roots were deep in the spiritual and religious soil of India. He did not need to "discover India".'[67,68]

---

67 K. Natwar Singh, 'How PV became PM', New Delhi: *Hindu*, 2 July 2012.

68 Jawaharlal Nehru, *The Discovery of India*, Meridian Books, 1947

I liked Rao. He was practical. He was soft-spoken, calm and with no ego. What I liked best about him was he was always to the point. As a lawyer himself we found much to talk about.

Rao told me that he had been briefed on my firm's success in the ISRO arbitration in London.[69] It was a huge case. A damaged Indian satellite did not take off. India had not paid McDonnell Douglas, so they were suing under the contract saying it was India's fault. It went into arbitration and at the hearing McDonnell Douglas dropped the claim and we won.

The brief stay in Delhi was long enough for me to realize the power of Chandraswami. That evening I went to his home, a palatial ashram. There was a swing in which he used to sit and cabinet ministers would sit there before him. Chandraswami used to say in Hindi, '*Aaj* cabinet *mein kya hua*?' (What took place in the cabinet today?) And the ministers would tell him about the day's meeting. He was a particularly powerful man when Rao was PM and ministers would tell me he was 'Mr Controller'.

The next time he was in London I fulfilled my side of the bargain. At the reception going into 10 Downing Street, we had to wait for some time. John Smith, the then Labour leader, was there and he asked me in a high, superior voice, 'What is this man doing here?' Chandraswami was dressed in dhoti and kurta in the usual Indian fashion. He had all sorts of rings and gold around him, and we had to make special arrangements as we went through security so he did not have to take them off. He was quite a personality. He took pictures of the occasion and published a photograph with John Major and me in his brochure.

While Chandraswami was never a client, Rao was. He brought in economic reforms that transformed India, moving from Nehru's socialist pattern of society to a freer market system. In the 1996

69 Union of India v. McDonnell Douglas Corp [1993] 2 Lloyd's Rep. 48

election he led Congress to defeat. He not only lost power but was soon having to defend himself against corruption charges. Lakhubhai Pathak, an Indian businessman known as the 'Pickle King' and living in England, alleged that Chandraswami and his secretary K.N. Aggarwal, also known as Mamaji, cheated him along with Rao out of $100,000. The amount was allegedly given for the promise of the Indian government giving him a contract for supplies of paper pulp in India, and Pathak alleged that he spent an additional $30,000 entertaining Chandraswami and his secretary.[70]

I had four meetings with Rao. The first was at his home in Delhi when he was the PM, and the others were in London at the Indian high commissioner's residence in Kensington. The London meetings were for legal consultations. The allegation was that Pathak had met Chandraswami and wanted confirmation (when Rao was prime minister) about the contract, and that Rao had said, 'Yes, that will be done.' Rao denied this. Rao wanted a United States senator to give evidence at his criminal trial as he was in his room at the time Rao was alleged to have given confirmation to Pathak. Rao consulted me on how he could get the senator's evidence by way of commission. In legal parlance, 'commission' is a method of obtaining evidence from an overseas witness through a local court process.

One of the interesting things Rao told me concerned a discussion about his election result with Geoffrey Howe, who was Margaret Thatcher's foreign secretary. Howe had asked him, 'Did you have an issue on which you lost the election?' He had responded with, 'No. The country was doing very well. It had turned the corner under my leadership. We had had an exchange crisis. I turned it around. I had no problems. I thought everybody would vote for me.' Geoffrey

70 'Chronology of Lakhubhai Pathak case', Delhi: Rediff, 22 December 2003

Howe had then told him, 'Never go into an election without an issue.' He told me this story more than once.

The Rao corruption case would pop up again for me, although in unexpected circumstances. Rao's 1996 defeat had seen Atal Bihari Vajpayee of the Bharatiya Janata Party become prime minister. In October 2002 I was given India's Constitution Day award for my outstanding contribution to international arbitration. I received the honour from Vajpayee at his office in the Lok Sabha. This was when the proceedings were going on against Rao in the Pathak case. When I said to Vajpayee that I hoped to see him in England, he said, 'Not as an accused, I hope!'

In 2004, Rao and Chandraswami were acquitted of the charges. Encouraged by this, Rao harboured hopes of becoming PM again when the country went to the polls in 2004. The Congress party won the election and soon after I received a message from Rao. He wanted urgently to meet me at his home in Delhi. He thought I was still close to Sonia Gandhi and he said, 'Tell your friend Sonia, allow me to be prime minister for six months.' He looked very old. Sonia instead chose Manmohan Singh, who had been Rao's finance minister and been in charge of the 1991 economic reforms.

Within months, in December 2004, Rao died. He was eighty-three. That last meeting with him showed me that politicians can never give up power or reconcile themselves to loss of office.

Ban Ki-moon

If holy men introduced me to prominent Indian and Pakistani officials, how I first came to meet Ban Ki-moon was due to where I was sitting on a flight.

I was going to Nairobi to attend the wedding of an Indian friend, Siddharth Chatterjee. Siddharth was an ex-army officer, a Bengali, a very prim and proper man. He used to come and stay with me in

London sometimes. While working for the UNICEF, he met Ban Ki-moon's daughter and they became engaged. At that time Ban was South Korea's foreign minister, and we were on the same Emirates flight to the wedding.

We got to know each other well during our stay in Nairobi and became friends. Among other things, we discussed how I could help him get elected as UN secretary general. His main opponent was a candidate from India: Shashi Tharoor. I told Ban I had previously acted for the Indian high commission, so if he wanted my help against Tharoor I would have to do it discreetly. In particular, he wanted my support to get Mongolia's vote, and as I was close to its government, I said I would try. I also said I could help secure Britain's. I wrote to Tony Blair and Cherie replied to me saying Britain would support Ban. I sent on a copy of Cherie's letter to him. The Indian government made the mistake of officially backing Tharoor, and on a visit to Delhi I pointed out that by doing this they had put up the backs of China and Pakistan.

Two or three months after he got elected, Ban invited me to New York for tea at his official residence, along with my then girlfriend. The guestbook revealed that the guest before us was Kofi Annan, the former UN secretary general. Ban thought my girlfriend was my daughter and his wife had to set him right on this. Over tea, he told us many stories and the most amusing one was when some British sailors were captured by the Iranians. Margaret Beckett, who was the British foreign secretary, phoned the Iranian foreign minister and demanded their release. The foreign minister replied, 'Madam, we are not part of your old colonies.'

Iraq and a hard place

The handover of Hong Kong and the issues over Tibet are not the only times I have attempted to use my skills to deliver harmony.

In the spring of 1999, I contacted Iraq's ambassador to the United Kingdom. I explored with him the possibility of acting for Iraqi clients in their London cases and travelling to Iraq for that purpose. Such foreign trips were not uncommon as my firm's client base has always been overseas.

I set out to build a professional relationship with the ambassador, giving him information on the kind of legal work my firm did in London for overseas clients. He said that he was aware of Zaiwalla & Co. and would be happy to arrange for me to travel to his country. In the autumn of the same year, the ambassador facilitated a visit for me to Baghdad.

I was excited by the idea of visiting Iraq, a country I had never before been to. My timing was unusual. Because of the allegation that Iraq possessed weapons of mass destruction, relations between the UK and Iraq were strained. By way of caution, I wrote to the British Foreign Office informing them of my planned visit, explaining that I was going to scout for business for my firm and for exports for the UK.

My plans changed at the last minute as an arbitration hearing for a Chinese client, CNPC, went beyond the fixed dates. However, the ambassador was kind enough to rearrange the trip of legal services from the spring of 2000.

Because the whole of Iraq was subject to a United Nations no-fly zone, there were no direct flights available to Baghdad. I had to travel to Amman, Jordan, from where the ambassador arranged for me to travel at my own expense by taxi to Baghdad. He assured me that the taxi driver was known to him and I would be safe. The drive through the desert took seventeen hours. The Iraqi government had booked me into Baghdad's best hotel, Al Rasheed, which was also the only one with anything approaching western standards.

The next morning the Iraqi team came to meet me and set out my programme. I was given a chauffeur-driven limousine and a government minder. Meetings were arranged with ministers and senior directors of Rasheed Bank and the Central Bank of Iraq, both of which had expressed an interest in using my firm's services. Rasheed Bank mentioned a case commenced by Citibank in the English court where they had been served with proceedings but had taken no steps. The Central Bank of Iraq also had a case which had been commenced against them by the Commercial Bank of Kuwait for two claims on a loan agreement totalling $1 billion. The trade and commerce minister whom I met was very positive, telling me that if Iraq was involved in any cases in London, my firm would be their first choice.

During my first stay in Iraq I also had an informal meeting with what was said to be a high-level government team. At this we discussed a possible legal challenge to the validity of the no-fly zone in The Hague. My initial response was that it was possible to issue proceedings against the UK, USA and other countries involved in the ICJ or, alternatively, against the UK in the English court with the USA included as a necessary party. Doubts were expressed by the Iraqis as to whether the ICJ would be fair. I assured them that the English judges would be completely independent.

Baghdad was an interesting city. I could see that life went on normally and was told that there was practically no crime. Although there was no democracy, people lived happily, and I found the bazaar busy. The only unusual thing was that because the Iraqi currency had substantially devalued, in exchange for my British pounds I was given local currency in a large plastic bag.

During my four-day stay in Baghdad, my hosts organized one and a half days of sightseeing, including to the historic ruins of Babylon, founded around 2300 BCE by the ancient Akkadian-speaking people and located along the River Euphrates about fifty miles south of the city. They also arranged at my request a visit to the Karbala mosque, one of the two holiest shrines for Shia Muslims.

There were contrasting experiences too: at one meal in a Chinese restaurant in Baghdad, the pianist sang Cliff Richard songs.

My return journey followed the same route, with the same seventeen-hour taxi drive back to Amman. A few days after I got to London, I saw the Iraqi ambassador, who said he had had good feedback from my visit and asked me to stay in contact with those whom I had met.

Some six months later, he called on me again. He said that the Iraqi government would like me to come back to Iraq for further discussions concerning the no-fly zone.

So I returned to Baghdad, and at the first meeting on this visit, my firm was instructed to act in the English litigation commenced against Rasheed Bank by Citibank.[71] This was when the Saddam Hussein regime was still in place, but we continued to act for the bank even after the US-led invasion of Iraq. The fees were ultimately paid by the British Foreign Office, albeit after a very long delay.

I was also informed that the Central Bank of Iraq had decided to instruct us in the proceedings commenced against them by Commercial Bank of Kuwait. At the meeting with the Iraqi government team, I was told they had decided to work with us to issue proceedings in the ICJ against both the USA and the UK. Likely costs were discussed, and I assured the Iraqis that my firm had the capacity to instruct the best English QCs to act for them in these proceedings and, if necessary, top-level European counsel too. The meeting ended on a positive note.

In due course, I sent to the Iraqi government, through the ambassador, my note on the prospect of commencing proceedings in the ICJ, along with the likely cost. Nothing further was heard for some time, but in early January 2002 the ambassador contacted me to say the Iraqi government urgently wanted a meeting.

---

71 Citibank NA v. Rafidian Bank [2003] EWHC 1950 (QB)

Again, I travelled back to Baghdad, this time flying via Damascus on an old Boeing 707. On this occasion, government officials were the only people I met. I had in the course of my earlier visits mentioned that my firm had worked with Tony Blair when he was at the Bar. After pleasantries, they asked me if I would communicate a message from the Government of Iraq personally to Blair. They explained that Iraq did not want war, but that western countries were refusing to speak with them. The message I was requested to communicate was that Iraq would be willing to start settlement negotiations on all issues of concern to the West directly with the UK, and with the USA through the UK. I was particularly asked to stress that Iraq would have an open mind about reaching a settlement which would avoid war, and that therefore all options were on the table for discussions.

When I asked how I would be able to tell the PM that I had their authority to convey the message, I was told that they would send a coded message to the Foreign Office confirming that I had the mandate. I was also informed that a meeting was taking place on 19–20 April 2002 between Iraq and the UN secretary general, at which Iraq would agree to the resumption of weapons inspection. I agreed to do my best to carry this message to Blair.

I returned to London on 15 February 2002 needing to find a way to see Tony Blair. The opportunity came when I learnt of the Labour Party's spring gala dinner. I managed to get an invitation through Patricia Scotland, a minister in the Foreign Office whom I knew well. Blair and his wife Cherie arrived before the guests sat down for dinner. As always, Blair received me warmly. I told him that I needed a private word, so we went to one side and I conveyed the message from the Iraqi government. I told him they knew war was imminent and that they had no chance of winning against the USA and the UK. They sought peace and were prepared to put everything on the table to settle matters.

Blair listened to me for around ten minutes, and I explained that the Foreign Office would know I had the authority to bear the message. Blair told me to write him a letter setting out what I had said, which I did on 9 April 2002. I got a formal response from 10 Downing Street on 23 April 2002, in which I was told, *'Mr Blair would like to thank you for your kind offer to act as a facilitator, however he regrets that he is unable to accept.'*

This is a source of huge personal regret. If a more positive approach had been taken, the second Gulf War is likely to have been avoided. A settlement could have been reached, with Saddam Hussein seeking asylum in a third country and the million lives said to be lost in the war saved.

Chris Eubank, world champion boxer

For all the great politicians I have met in my life, I rank meeting the boxer Chris Eubank almost on a par with meeting Benazir Bhutto or P.V. Narasimha Rao. I was in Dubai with my friend Akram Shaikh, who said the UAE housing minister Sheikh Rakadh Bin Salem Bin Rakadh would like to meet me. When I saw him, he said he wanted me to help him out with a concern he had with Chris Eubank, who was training his son to box.

Eubank, who was world middleweight and world super middleweight champion, had employed a French woman, Amanda Bros, a PR professional in London who handled publicity for film stars and celebrities. The problem for the Sheikh was she was Jewish, which for a man in his position could cause enormous problems. Eubank was put in touch with me and I met both him and Amanda Bros. After this I was able to reassure Sheikh Rakadh that she was a decent person and there was nothing to fear.

I liked Eubank too. In the boxing world he had a reputation for being a showman, but I found him a delightful chap. Soon

I was representing him. He had received a large advance from HarperCollins for his autobiography. But they wanted the advance back and threatened to issue proceedings against him. I met the publishers at their office near Hammersmith and we were able to settle the matter.

The result was Eubank and I became good friends. I went to his home in Hove, not far from my Littlehampton house, and he and his charming wife came over to see me too. Eubank was impressed that as a brown-skinned man, I had succeeded in starting my own firm in the City of London. He told me, 'You are like me. You did it.'

12

Changing Britain: Class, Not Race

On 14 April 2016, the *Financial Times* ran a long article on me. It was in the 'At Home' section, one of the supplements that come with the paper's weekend edition and one of its best reads. I had given the journalist and photographer access to where I started this book, my weekend retreat on the coast of West Sussex (although I also have an apartment in London, near the Houses of Parliament, which is my weekday home).

The writer, Alexander Gilmour, described in detail some of the highlights of my life, from trying to get Tony Blair to talk to Saddam Hussein to the many famous men and women I have acted for, some of whom I have mentioned here. I showed Gilmour around the house, the photo of my father I keep in my bedroom, a cricket bat signed by John Major and his cabinet in the 1990s, my daughter Freya and my son Varun's simple bedrooms from where you can see the English Channel, which laps the beach beyond my garden.

In the photo of me accompanying the piece, I look relaxed, sitting in an armchair in front of the fireplace, dressed casually in jacket and shirt. It catches me well, more than a decade on from the bad times I had experienced personally and financially. I felt I had regained control of my life, far removed from the years of my regrettable involvement with the Bachchans and the divorce from my wife, which triggered the challenges that followed.

It was my daughter Freya who christened the house Neptune, named after the Roman god of the sea. Every summer I host a gala party at Neptune and it is an occasion to entertain my guests who have become friends during my adventures around the world. I also have a small retreat facing the Mediterranean Sea in Villefranche Sur Mer in Cote D'Azur, South of France. In the summer of 2019, we had our firm's summer party at Kensington Palace Gardens.

The Oceanics case

My homes are a physical illustration of what I have achieved, an Indian qualified as a solicitor in England using his acquired skills and knowledge of India to good effect. The case that best illustrates this is one from the late 1990s concerning an English company called Oceanics. The story sounds like a script for a Bollywood movie.

Oceanics had a serious problem with its Indian subsidiary known by the same name based in Mumbai. While the Indian arm was a wholly owned subsidiary of the English firm, as far as Indian law was concerned, Oceanics India was legally owned by an Indian who had worked at Oceanics in the UK. In India this is called benami ownership. The word means 'without name' or 'no name'. Benami ownership started in order to get around the legal system's cumbersome restrictions on foreign ownership and it means the real beneficiary is not the one in whose name the property is purchased. In 1988 the Indian parliament passed the Benami Transactions

(Prohibition) Act, but the law has not proved very effective and has been updated twice, in 2011 and then again in 2016.

Oceanics India had assets including cash to the value of £3–4 million. Oceanics became aware of the problems of benami ownership when they discovered that their Indian employee had dishonestly claimed the Indian company as his own. Oceanics UK hired the leading Mumbai solicitors' firm Crawford Bailey but they could do nothing. If a benami company is set up in India, the real owner cannot bring an action in the Indian courts. This is where I came in.

Oceanics approached me and I then spoke with the Crawford Bailey partner. He maintained that there seemed to be nothing his firm could do, but if I could achieve a result, both he and Oceanics would be very pleased. I had to come up with a strategy. So, I spoke with Fali Nariman, a senior advocate in Delhi. After explaining the problem, I asked him if he would be able to give me a note of advice confirming that although the Benami Act prevented Oceanics UK from bringing proceedings in the Indian courts, the real beneficial owner of Oceanics India would still be Oceanics UK. He said yes and that if I drafted a short opinion for him, he would consider signing it. The next day I sent Itamar Rosen, a solicitor in our firm, to Delhi to see Fali Nariman. He made a few necessary corrections and then signed the note.

I then told a director of Oceanics UK to accompany me to Mumbai, where Rosen joined us. When I reached Mumbai, I contacted a Parsi gentleman, a Mr Contractor. He was a retired assistant commissioner of police in Mumbai who had set up his own security company. His office was shoddy and located in a dilapidated house in central Mumbai, but I was confident he could deliver what I wanted. I asked him to provide me five or six security personnel, all in khaki uniform and each carrying a stick. He put the squad together and the next morning we all took the hovercraft service from near the Taj Mahal Hotel to New Mumbai.

I was now more like a court enforcement officer.

On reaching Navi Mumbai, we rented four two-seater autorickshaws for the day and went to the local police station near Oceanics' office to meet the chief inspector there. He told me that I should go to the nearby police headquarters, meet the assistant police commissioner and get his approval for what I wanted to achieve. The Oceanics director, who had come from London, Rosen and I met the commissioner and explained the situation about the Indian employee falsely claiming ownership of Oceanics India. I showed him Fali Nariman's opinion and other evidence of remittances from Oceanics UK. He was impressed and agreed to one of his inspectors accompanying us on his police bike, a revolver strapped to his side. I told my team that the plan was to enter the Oceanics India office with the police officer and get the dishonest employee to clear out. If this sounds dramatic, it was, but I also insisted that we be gentle and courteous throughout.

What followed was the sort of scene that featured in Bollywood films, except now I, having acted as a lawyer for Bollywood stars, was in real life recreating the role they play in many of their movies.

We went in with our security guards with sticks in their hands and the police officer with the revolver at his side. He told the dishonest employee who had usurped the ownership of the company to vacate the offices immediately. The dishonest employee began shouting in protest but soon realized he had no option but to leave. Fortunately, the other workers there were familiar with the English company director and readily took instructions from him. He told them to get a locksmith to change the locks and got hold of all the confidential documents the dishonest employee had relating to the true ownership of the business. Those were the days of fax, and he immediately started transmitting the documents to Oceanics UK.

Happy as I was with this remarkable coup, I was also a little worried. I had been told by my client that the dishonest employee was a friend of a local politician who was a local goonda (a hired thug) and he could arrange through his politician friend for us all to be beaten up. The police officer who had accompanied us to secure our entry had done his task and left. I gave instructions not to panic and get on with the work. I asked Rosen to stay with the director and I stood guard at the entrance downstairs. As it turned out, there was no threat. After about five or six hours we felt safe and were in complete control of the Indian branch. Truth had prevailed. We then arranged a round-the-clock security watch at the office and informed the police headquarters that we were the real beneficial owners and if the dishonest employee wanted possession back, then he would have to apply to the Mumbai High Court. I was confident he could not succeed.

Despite the high drama, we obtained the possession for the English company by a strategy which was perfectly legal. It could not be challenged in an Indian court. In the end, Oceanics had to pay its dishonest employee some minor compensation, but it was a small price to pay for the victory we had achieved.

Bikini killer

Just before this book was being finalized, news came in that Rajendra (Raj) Sethia was found to be innocent after thirty-five years on bail in India. Raj was alleged to have defrauded Indian banks in London, and in the 1980s he set a new record as the UK's largest bankrupt, owing some £182 million.

This brought to mind an extraordinary experience. I had acted for Raj when he purchased Jokhi Tea Garden in India for millions of dollars. After Raj's bankruptcy, his brother Ranjit claimed that he was half owner of the tea garden, something which the trustee in the bankruptcy disputed. The English judge, Hoffmann J., ordered further evidence. The QC, William Blackburn (who later said that he would not have missed this experience for the world), and I went to Delhi to interview Raj and obtain his statement. He was at that time in Tihar Jail, India's maximum security prison. We got an order from the local magistrate's court and with this, Blackburn and I managed to get admission into the outer segment of the jail. But despite the order we were not allowed full access. An Indian journalist who happened to be there said his friend Charles could assist us. A window duly opened and this Charles appeared out of it. I gave him the order and ten minutes later the jail door opened, and Blackburn and I went in, escorted by Charles.

It was Charles who was in control at that prison, make no mistake. After securing our access he arranged tea and biscuits, and said he would like to speak to me before I left. He had heard from Raj that I was a noted lawyer and so he asked me for my card, which I gave to him. Later I learnt that he was Charles Sobhraj, the famous serial killer known as the 'Bikini Killer' and 'The Serpent'. Years later, after he was released from prison, he called me at my office and said that he was in France and wanted to discuss a business project with me. I politely declined.

Truth before the deities

I admit that this out-of-the-box approach to law is exceptional, and I have never again had to take such measures. But there have been many cases that presented complex problems to which I have found unusual solutions, where the interest of justice required it. At all times I stay within the law, but it does require some imagination.

For example, in the mid-80s, I was contacted by an Asian solicitor from Wembley who said that he had a dispute with a gentleman living in India and that they would both like to meet me to see if I could mediate and resolve their dispute. The Indian gentleman was the owner of a shop which sold quality saris imported from India.

At that time, there were legal restrictions on an Indian having a business overseas without the permission of the Reserve Bank of India. Such permissions were not easily given. So, the Indian businessman and the Asian solicitor came up with a plan to establish the business in the name of the Asian solicitor, for which he would get some remuneration. In other words, technically the legal owner would be the Asian solicitor, but the real owner was the Indian businessman.

However, they had now fallen out with each other in connection with an alleged value-added tax fraud. I agreed to be their mediator or facilitator gratis. On the appointed day they came along with all the books and documents. They both put forward their case. All the legal documents confusedly suggested that the Asian solicitor was the owner and had liability for the debt and also for the alleged VAT fraud. The Indian businessman said he had nothing to do with it and was just involved with supplying the saris. My instincts told me that there was something wrong and the solicitor was probably correct.

The Indian businessman was quite vocal, so I came up with a plan. I diverted the discussions in a friendly way to Indian culture and led it to Indian gods. Both of them were Hindus. In Hindu religion, each family has their own family deity whom they fear, respect and worship. So, for about ten minutes we discussed the power of various deities; it is believed there are thirty-three principal gods and hundreds of demigods in the Vedic pantheon. After I had ascertained from both individuals their deities, I came back to the dispute and said that I wanted each of them to keep in their mind their individual deities and then tell me the truth.

The Indian businessman became very perturbed and offended and said I should not have done this. He was perspiring and went berserk. He then said that he had to speak the truth because if he was to lie under the name of his deity, it would be an unbearable disaster for him and could also cause loss of his family and his business. He then admitted that he was responsible for the VAT fraud and the solicitor was only a front. The solicitor thanked me and they both went away.

The moral of this is that if both of them had gone to the English court, the Indian businessman would have lied through his teeth under oath. But he could not lie after I had asked him to speak the truth under an oath to his personal family deity. So, fitting the strategy to the individuals concerned in a flexible way can often lead to the best and most truthful result.

Doing it 'My Way'

Most lawyers today think of strategy as a way to ambush the opponent. I have never followed this approach. I have always been fair to my opponent, giving them the opportunity to deal with the questions of law contended by me for my client. My first principle is always to maintain a high standard of integrity, always acting with courtesy and politeness no matter how difficult the opponent is. Even if you make an error, if you follow this rule your mistake is likely to be excused.

My second principle is 'law is for justice and not justice for law'. Often one finds solicitors and barristers simply following the conventional view of the law without seeing how best the law could be worked to obtain justice.

In following these two principles, there is also an overriding requirement to show silent courage and pursue what you believe to be the correct interpretation of the law. This has never failed me, and I have almost invariably been successful against large international firms before the English and European Union courts.

Looking back, I recognized early that as an outsider in the City of London, I had to follow the approach described in a Heineken Beer advertisement some time ago: 'the parts other beers cannot reach'. That meant not striving for acceptability with my peers, and in particular the elite of the legal fraternity. The type of client work I had gave me an advantage, making me free to do things, as a Frank Sinatra song put it, 'My Way'. Not having to be clubbable gave me the freedom to formulate innovative legal submissions to obtain justice for my clients. It brought me some fame, too. In the late 1980s, whilst on a visit to Athens for a meeting with my Greek clients, I was invited for dinner by a senior English solicitor who had given up his maritime law practice in London and started his own shipping-related business in Greece. Over dinner he told me he had invited me because he was curious to meet someone he saw in London as 'the boy who said the emperor had no clothes'. He said he admired me for taking on the City and proving its maritime lawyers wrong.

This notoriety had its drawbacks too. It made me too much of my own man. But if I had wanted to be part of that elite group, then more often than not I would have to accept the popular view of the law. That is something I would not do.

Compounding interest

An example of this was the case of a vessel called *La Pintada,*[72] to which I have referred earlier. One of the Commonwealth's most popular judges, Lord Denning, had in a majority judgement in the Court of Appeal held that compound interest is payable when the debtor delays payment. Lord Justice Oliver had given a dissenting

72 La Pintada Compania Navigacion SA v. President of India (The 'La Pintada') (No.2) [1984] 1 Lloyd's Rep. 305

judgement. My client, the Government of India, usually paid balance of freight and demurrage late to ship owners, sometimes after more than a year. I took the view that Denning had got the law wrong and Oliver's approach was correct. The P&I clubs that represented the ship owners and also the English Bar firmly held the contrary view. My client in New Delhi told me that under the Denning judgement, the Indian government faced a liability of over $5 million. So, when the arbitrator's award against the government was challenged in court I added a new ground. I said that by automatically making a debtor liable for compound interest for late payment, the court was making the debtor an involuntary banker, which was wrong.

I knew that his point would make any judge think long and hard.

When the case went up to the House of Lords, we won unanimously before five judges. This was India's first victory in a commercial case before the House of Lords. If I had accepted the popular view of the law, this would never have happened.

Our success in the Lords had an interesting background. For the court hearing I needed to instruct a barrister, but all those I contacted advised me that the case was hopeless and that they would not be willing to appear for my client. But then a young Tony Blair approached me and said that he would like to work with my firm. He was from a labour law chambers, which to me meant he would have an open mind to my proposed grounds for challenging the award. So I went ahead and instructed him, something Tony was thrilled about because maritime law cases were considered a very privileged law practice. He said he wanted to work on this case with his senior, Derry Irvine QC, who was also a labour law specialist.

I had a two-hour case conference with them and both agreed that my view on the law was correct. I communicated this to my client, the ministry of shipping in Delhi, and received instructions to retain Derry and Tony as the Indian government's barrister team for the hearing before the court challenging the arbitration award.

Around 9 a.m. on the day of the hearing, I received a call from Tony saying they would like to meet me outside the court half an hour before it was due to start, and that Derry wanted me to bring a representative of the high commission in London with me. Mrs Charawalla from the high commission accompanied, and to my shock and surprise Derry told us the Indian government had zero chance of success in challenging the Bruce Harris award, and that he wanted instructions to drop the challenge. Derry also told Mrs Charawalla that if the hearing went ahead and he made the submissions I had instructed him to, the Indian government would get a bad name.

I disagreed and said the hearing must take place. It is a good thing that it did. Mr Justice Staughton, a brilliant judge, had read the submissions on law I had made in my affidavit and had obviously done his own research based on this. He asked some questions on the issues of law involved, which Derry was unable to answer. The other side's counsel was Martin Moore-Bick, who later became a Lord Justice of Appeal and now chairs the Grenfell Tower fire enquiry. Moore-Bick made his submissions, and the judge gave an extempore judgement in the Indian government's favour, remitting the award back to the arbitrator for reconsideration. This is reported at (1983) 1 Lloyds 39, in which the reader will see that Tony Blair was the counsel instructed by my firm for my client, president of India. President of India is a nomenclature which was in those years used when the Government of India was a claimant.

However, I was naturally concerned that neither Derry nor Tony seemed prepared for the court hearing and I therefore removed them from the case before our success in the Lords.

I have the ability to achieve successes for my clients based on legal propositions, which I personally formulate, that are sometimes considered outrageously incorrect but are still accepted by the court. I started this approach with a simple formula. Every day on the journey from my home to my office and back, I would read every judgement reported in the *Lloyd's Law Reports* and also the *Weekly Law Reports*. I enjoyed reading them and the insight they gave into not only maritime law but also other areas of law. When I would get a new case, I would meticulously read the client's file from top to bottom without rushing to any conclusions. This gave me a grasp of the facts. I would then take a view on where the justice lies and formulate the legal issues accordingly.

I will never allow a client to fabricate evidence and have had no hesitation in withdrawing from a case when I find this has happened. Very recently, a potential client from Iran sought to instruct my firm in a case where an oil rig was purchased by an Iranian company for some $80 million. The state-owned company paid for the rig, which was said to have been delivered to the buyer, but it never was. The head of the company, who had signed for delivery and authorized payment to the seller, had since fled the country. The seller had applied for and obtained an asset-freezing order from the English court. At the second meeting, it became clear that the person who wanted to be my client was involved in this fraud. Deciding to be tactful, I told him that my firm was very busy and so he should seek representation elsewhere. My experience tells me that such an approach in life brings protection from the Divine.

UK evolving into multiculturalism

The faith I have in the English legal system is genuine. I have great respect for the independence and fairness of the British judiciary and also the English Bar, which maintains a very high standard of integrity. Long may this remain. I am grateful that a society to which I came as an outsider now accepts me. I feel very much at home.

Some doubt whether Britain has solved its racial problems, but I am confident that it has evolved into a genuine multicultural society.

The society I grew up in in Mumbai was also multicultural, with different communities living side by side. But it was also a society that had often been invaded, and where large numbers of people had over the centuries come from distant lands and made it their home. While different communities co-existed, they did not intermarry; on the odd occasion where they did, inter-community tension was the invariable result. Integration in India has always stopped on the threshold of the bedroom.

When I arrived in Britain, immigration was a much-discussed issue. In those days it meant immigrants of colour from the Commonwealth. Many in Britain said we should be sent back. My early years in my new country made me all-too aware that I was set aside from the majority community by my skin colour. People from the Indian subcontinent were often called 'Paki', even though Pakistan was a country I had never been to. This was the experience of so many immigrants in Britain in the 1970s and 1980s.

Even by the mid-1990s, Asian solicitors were not held in a high regard by some in the UK and still faced racial prejudice. One English lady came to my office to discuss her late mother's estate, which included a collection of valuable antique porcelain. When I agreed to act for her, she said she would pay me a fee of £10,000, writing out a cheque as an advance on costs. After I asked for a copy of her mother's will, she told me quite sheepishly that the original will actually stipulated that the porcelain collection should go to her sister, but she believed her mother had been bullied into this. She then produced an unsigned will and told me she knew how to forge her mother's signature and proposed that we change the will and that I could attest to it. When I said this was illegal and I would have nothing to do with it, she said she was told by a friend that Asian solicitors did such things for a higher fee. Threatening to call the police, I gave her back her cheque and showed her the door.

My continuing connections with my homeland have above all been about my profession and less my feeling of belonging. I belong where I am, not where I came from. Earth is my country. I consider myself as a citizen of the Earth, national of Britain and native of India. That perhaps sets me apart from many others.

India will always remain in my heart. George Lamming, the Barbadian writer, has spoken of how while many of his generation lived in England, the Caribbean was their home. That is where they wanted to be buried. Similar sentiments have been expressed by the Irish historian Clair Wills, whose parents migrated to Britain from Ireland, who said that for many migrants, a 'future homecoming was limited to where their bones were buried'.[73]

I came to Britain first of all to study. Like many Indians of my generation, and like my father before me, I saw British education as superior to anything India could provide at that time. While I settled here, I then used the growing legal needs of my homeland in fields such as shipping to build up my practice. I was helped by the fact that there were good people in this country who were willing to help me, like the arbitrators Cedric Barclay, Clifford A.L. Clarke and many others at the Bar and in the judiciary.

It helped that as I was taking the first steps in the legal profession, Britain itself was going through vast changes in the economic and political sphere. The election of Thatcher in 1979 changed the thinking that the government should always play a central role in the economy. Then the Big Bang and the arrival of electronic trading magically transported the City of London from the nineteenth century to the threshold of the twenty-first almost overnight. In the

---

73 Clair Wills, *Lovers and Strangers: An Immigrant History of Postwar Britain,* London: Penguin UK, 2017

1980s few questioned a light touch on the regulatory reins, and it did not seem that anything could go wrong.

Thatcher's government changed things for the lawyers as well and I benefited from this. While in India the division between barristers and solicitors was abolished after Independence, this has not happened in Britain. But the last four decades have seen widespread changes, allowing solicitors more scope to have what is called rights of audience in many courts.

These changes were well-timed for me. The Legal Services Act came in when I had had my own firm for just over a decade, and I often used such rights of audience to present my out-of-the-box solutions to cases. But even before this legislation, it was made easier for solicitors to argue cases in courts. I was always ready to present legal arguments, even if the case I was making was not one the barrister I had briefed considered worthwhile. As a solicitor I often got the better of my own QC, as happened with the *Lips* case in the House of Lords in 1988.

While the legal barriers were coming down, I also felt that I benefited from the way the country changed since the 1970s. Margaret Thatcher, John Major, Tony Blair and their successors deserve credit for this. All three of them had an enlightened policy on diversity. Colour of the ability and heart were more important than the colour of skin, religion or flag. After forty years here, I feel the Britain I live in now is a totally different, and better, place.

It is not so much a racist society as a classist society. The UK has changed hugely in its attitude towards foreigners. Unlike the United States, which is a country of immigrants, the United Kingdom has been a country of natives. It exported people to faraway places, populating much of the world, but large-scale immigration is something new, chiefly a post-war phenomenon. I have found that in England insofar as immigrants were concerned, the attitude was that there were only two kinds, either the good, aristocratic class, or the low, coolie class. This is understandable because Britain ruled what are now Commonwealth countries for 300 years, and it would not have been easy for the indigenous community to accept as equals those whom they ruled before. But to their credit the majority of them have done so.

I have been successful in my profession and my rosy picture of modern Britain is not always supported by the evidence we have of how black, Asian and minority ethnic lawyers have fared here. The top level of the judiciary remains largely closed to them, although things are changing (and helped in part by my seeking to address the problems I faced with the Britannia P&I club many years ago now). Bear in mind too that if only around 7 per cent of judges are from ethnic minorities, only one in seven QCs and one in three partners of law firms are women. We are seeing progress but still have some way to go. I would like the English Bar and judiciary to maintain their high standards. So, I would not favour positive discrimination for appointments of judges. For this purpose, the sole criterion of merit should remain.

My point would be that unlike in the past, the powers that be are aware of the problems and are trying to do something about them. In March 2015, the Law Society launched its Ethnic Minority Lawyers Division, which provides a forum for black, Asian and minority ethnic lawyers. The guest speaker at the sold-out launch event was Baroness Warsi, the first-ever Muslim member of the British cabinet, sitting in it as chairman of the Conservative Party.

Back in 1990 the Society of Asian Lawyers (SAL) was formed, and it recently honoured me with a lifetime achievement award, presented by the head of Solicitors Regulation Authority. The SAL is now the UK's largest independent legal society, with nearly 3,000 legal and other professional members. It is made up of forward-thinking Asian legal professionals who want a voice for the Asian legal community, as well as a forum to discuss important relevant issues and developments. Its members encompass a cross section of the legal world and include partners in City firms, leading barristers and QCs, in-house counsel, high street practitioners, legal executives, trainees, pupils, students and everyone in between.

As entry into the legal profession gets more diverse, I hope it is just a matter of time before legal partnerships become more diverse too, some overdue colour in the pristine whiteness of so many firms.

That there is still a good distance to be travelled justifies my decision back in the 1970s to stride out on my own and not take up a job with a big firm. This would never have provided me the opportunities I have had, despite the ups and downs along the way. I hope my story shows how a person determined to succeed can break glass ceilings and fashion a world for themselves that is fulfilling. I am more convinced than ever that Britain provides opportunity to those who are willing to fight for it.

I admit a small part of my success has also been due to a little luck – meeting the right persons, at the right place, at the right time. But it is correctly said that luck favours the brave. It also requires showing of courage to take an out-of-the-box approach to law when necessary to obtain justice. And, of course, always maintaining one's integrity and a courteous behaviour. I also attribute this to the grace of God.

What cannot be answered is what my life might have been and whether such would have come my way had I not decided to leave my homeland and journey to the land of the former colonizers of India. While I am proud of how India has defied the odds and become the world's largest democracy, I am also aware that my native land is one where you require 'pull'. This is the word Indians use to denote a benefactor who helps you, a person with the right connections to smooth your path and ensure success.

In my chosen land, the one where I have opted to live, I had to be my own pathfinder. I knew nobody but still found that a person of ability can prosper and shine without any connections. The remaking of Britain since the war has not been without problems. Indeed, throughout the time I have been writing this book the issue of Brexit has been hanging over the UK. The issue has puzzled people across Europe and around the world, including India. I believe Brexit should not happen. But in the referendum of 2016, the British people voted for better or for worse to leave the European Union and their vote has to be respected.

However, the debate has unleashed worrying tensions for the future. Not least among these is whether Scotland might opt for independence and the people of Northern Ireland vote to join the Republic of Ireland. The long-term implications of that could be grave. Without Scotland in particular, there would be no Great Britain and what would emerge would be a 'little England'. This would also have international political consequences. The United Kingdom at present is one of the five permanent members of the Security Council of the United Nations, with the power of veto. The question which will undoubtedly arise is whether England (or maybe England and Wales) could continue as a permanent member if the UK dissolves.

Many countries would jump at the opportunity to claim permanent membership of the UN Security Council, including India and Brazil. India has already put forward its claim. So, the chance could arise in a not-too-distant future for India to be selected as the permanent member in place of the UK. The wheel of history can turn in curious ways.

Nonetheless, Britain it is a resilient country which will always find a way out of its problems, however insurmountable they may seem. It is a country which has changed, and I believe will continue to change for the better. I am pleased to be still playing my part in this.

Index

About the Author

SAROSH ZAIWALLA is an important figure on the London legal scene. Coming from a distinguished legal family in Mumbai, he arrived in London in the early 1970s to qualify as an English solicitor. Undeterred by the casual racism prevalent at that time, he went on to set up Zaiwalla & Co. Solicitors, the first ever English law firm to be established by an Indian national. With tenaciousness he developed a strong international commercial practice, with a reputation for taking on and winning contentious, 'unwinnable' cases.

His client list is a roll call of high-profile individuals and corporations, including the President of India, China National Petroleum Corporation, Bank Mellat and NIDC of Iran. At a personal level, he has engaged with world leaders, including prime ministers and politicians, the United Nations secretary general, and the Dalai Lama. In October 2002, Zaiwalla was recognized on India's Annual National Law Day by Prime Minister Atal Bihari Vajpayee for his contribution to the field of international arbitration law.